THE DECLINE OF THE WASP

PETER SCHRAG

A Touchstone Book
Published by Simon and Schuster

The publishers wish to thank the following for permission to reprint material in this book. Any inadvertent omission will be corrected in future printings if notification is sent to the publisher.

City Lights Books for the selection from *The White Negro* by Norman Mailer, copyright © 1957 by Dissent Publishing Associates.

Commentary for the excerpt from "Issues" by Norman Podhoretz, June, 1970.

Coward-McCann, Inc., for the selection from *A World of Our Own* by Peter Prescott, copyright © 1970 by Peter S. Prescott.

Delacorte Press for the selection from *Bomb Culture* by Jeff Nuttall, copyright © 1968 by Jeff Nuttall. Reprinted by permission of the publisher, Delacorte Press.

Dial Press for the selection from *The Fire Next Time* by James Baldwin, copyright © 1962, 1963 by James Baldwin. Reprinted by permission of the publisher, The Dial Press.

Harcourt Brace Jovanovich, Inc., for selections from *The American Establishment* by Richard Rovere, copyright © 1962 by Richard Rovere, and for *Decline of the New* by Irving Howe, copyright © 1970 by Irving Howe.

Houghton Mifflin Company for the selection from *Nixon Agonistes* by Gary Wills, copyright © 1970 by Gary Wills.

J. B. Lippincott Company for the excerpt from *Remember Me to God* by Myron S. Kaufmann. Copyright © 1957 by Myron S. Kaufmann. Reprinted by permission of J. B. Lippincott Company.

McGraw-Hill Book Company for the selection from *Soul on Ice* by Eldridge Cleaver, copyright © 1968 by Eldridge Cleaver. Used with permission of McGraw-Hill Book Company.

W. W. Norton & Company for the selection from *The Recovery of Confidence* by John W. Gardner, copyright © 1970 by John W. Gardner.

Pantheon Books, a Division of Random House, for the selection from *Hard Times* by Studs Terkel, copyright © 1970 by Studs Terkel.

Playboy for the selection from *The Playboy Philosophy* by Hugh Hefner.

Random House for the selection from *Portnoy's Complaint* by Philip Roth, copyright © 1969 by Philip Roth; for the selection from *Shadow and Act* by Ralph Ellison, copyright © 1964 by Ralph Ellison; and for the selection from *Against the American Grain* by Dwight MacDonald, copyright © 1962 by Dwight MacDonald.

World Publishing Company for the selection from *Miami and the Siege of Chicago* by Norman Mailer, copyright © 1968 by Norman Mailer.

Yale University Press for the selection from *The American Mind* by Henry Steele Commager, copyright © 1950.

FOR DIANE

CONTENTS

ACKNOWLEDGMENTS

Anyone who writes something called *The Decline of the WASP* is a volunteer for an instant inquisition. The title should satisfy most of the functions of an introduction—most introductions, after all, are too apologetic anyway—but it begs no end of questions about the state of the author's mind, his soul, his spirit, maybe even his body. Who is this guy anyway? Where did he come from? What's his *shtick?* Even a flattering jacket blurb can't establish authority in matters where, as any reasonable person should know, no authority is possible. Perhaps, had I been so inclined, I might have written an autobiographical book about a succession of cultural identities, about the languages I spoke, the accents in which I spoke them, and the style which they represented each at its own time: German, Luxembourger dialect, French, English with a Brooklyn accent, English with a flat New England accent, English as spoken in West Texas, WASP talk, Jew talk, jive talk.

The changes came rapidly. I was born a German Jew, moved to Luxembourg when I was four, to Belgium when I was eight, and to the United States when I was not quite ten. Each of those moves involved the assumption (in my head, if nowhere else) of a new national identity. Growing up in Queens in the forties, I regarded myself simply as a New York Jew; thereafter, going to Amherst College, I tried (with less success than I imagined at the time) to become a WASP, an attempt I did not give up until, years later, I began to suspect that there were, for me, other and better ways of being an American. (I also learned that while a journalist must, in some measure, always be an outsider, I had become an American chauvinist who carried in his head a conglomerate of cultural attitudes.) Each of these places and situations colored the books I read, the response to the people I met, and the view I had of what the history writers call "the national experience."

The Decline of the WASP owes its existence to a rereading —of books, of personal experience, and of American life in general. The debt is diffuse. Ten years of writing about American life cannot help but restore one's appreciation of the cultural complexity of the country. Each observation, each piece, each interview, moreover, is conditioned by the people one knows, the editors for whom one works, and the attitudes one carries on the trip. But within that general context there are also individuals that can be named: Midge Decter and Willie Morris, my editors at *Harper's*, who, even when they disagreed with the conclusions of their writers, encouraged them to express themselves freely, and who, because of that, ran the best general magazine in America; Colin Greer of Hunter College, who fed me material and suggestions and kept moving the ideas along; Jim Cass and Norman Cousins of *Saturday Review*, tolerant men and good editors; and, most of all, Diane Divoky Schrag, who should not be embarrassed (even as a liberated woman) if I say that this book is as much hers as mine.

P. S.

THE
DECLINE
OF THE
WASP

1

THE LAST ROUNDUP

I

He was our man. The all-purpose, real-life, bigger-than-life, wide-screen three-dimensional stereophonic composite amalgamated now-and-forever certified American. Our man. Who built the country and held it together, who was what every immigrant was supposed to be and every healthy boy to idolize, who spoke plain, fought fair, worked hard and feared God, and whose every thought, in the judgment of a supposedly sober historian, "was permeated with optimism, with the sense of a spacious universe, and with confidence in the infinite possibilities of human development." Part Leatherstocking, part Teddy Roosevelt, part John Wayne, with a little Ben Franklin thrown in for good measure—frontiersman, cowboy, soldier, entrepreneur—plus a lot of other things besides, a real-life nephew of you-know-who, red white and blue, free white and twenty-one, who didn't fire until he saw the whites of their eyes, damned the torpedoes, met the enemy (and it wasn't us), couldn't tell a lie, and regretted that he had but one life to give for his country.

Our man. His country. From the beginning America was a place to be discovered; it was a little imperfect, maybe—

needed some reform, some shaping up—but it didn't need to be reinvented. It was all given, like a genetic code, waiting to unfold. The Fathers had provided, and if that wasn't enough one could always call on Providence, which favored us above all others. We all wanted to learn the style, the proper accent, agreed on its validity (or kept our mouth shut), and while our interpretations and our heroes varied, they were all cut from the same stock. Whether we were small-town boys or the children of urban immigrants, we shared an eagerness to become apprentices in the great open democracy, were ready to join up, wanting only to be accepted according to the terms that history and tradition had already established. It never occurred to us to think otherwise.

What held that world together wasn't merely fond belief in some standardized Parson Weems–Poor Richard–William Holmes McGuffey version of textbook Americanism, a catalogue of Accepted Values and Favored Maxims—although they were certainly part of it—but also particular institutions and people that we identified with our vision of the country. Our man. Not some sheeny-chink-dago-wop, not some yellowbellied Jap Polack hunky, not some long-dicked nigger, not some drunken mick, not some guy with sauerkraut and Limburger cheese on his breath, but an American. White Anglo-Saxon Protestant. A WASP. From cradle to grave, from literature to politics, from the meetings of Rotarians to the reflections of statesmen, the WASP idiom permeated so much of everything that we hardly noticed it.

This is the argument: History made the WASP; then the WASP made history; and now history has apparently abandoned him, has tossed him aside, and has left his fellow travelers without focus, without durable heroes and without a common ethic. From history's pet to history's fool, he was, for three centuries, the heir of all that we regarded as most admirable, most hopeful and most civilized in the West. Out of the particular version of the Renaissance that created the Elizabethan adventurer—entrepreneur, explorer, investor, conqueror of nature—and out of the particular version of the Reformation that created the Puritan, this country forged an ethic, an image and a style which not only defined what we were as individuals or a nation, but came to represent (in our minds, and often in those of Europeans) the ultimate in Western possibilities. European writers, and sometimes our own, have been prophesying the end of those possibilities for over a century, but the pervasive sense that it was really happening—the nagging unremitting belief that something has gone fundamentally wrong—is relatively new for most Americans. We have had no end of analyses and theories of what that wrong is— the failure of capitalism, the collapse of the middle class, the excesses of technology, the rapidity of change—and we shall surely have more. Yet for this country all of these factors are also involved in something else, and that is the enervation of the central, integrating ethic of American life, and the decline of the mythic personality we came to regard as the embodiment of the American.

Our mission was the mission of the West: we not only chose ourselves, we were also chosen by others. We were the great conquerors of nature, the exploiters of the forest, and the hosts of opportunity. We were the people who really believed—not only in our philosophical speculations, but in our gut—that every day in every way we would become better and better, that history was progress, and that tomorrow would inevitably be an improvement on today. We were the heirs of Florentine bankers, of London merchants, of Manchester industrialists, of the downtrodden and the poor, of Levellers and Roundheads, of incipient democrats and land-starved farmers, of mechanics and tinkerers; we were the children of the age of reason, the age of steam, the age of progress. We would make the desert bloom, would build great cities where there had once been wilderness, and would, at the same time, guarantee every participant a share of the benefits. There would be no class structure in America just as there had never been, on this side of the Atlantic, a feudal age. No special titles, no noblemen, no peasants, no underclass, no king, no queen, no rituals, no establishment. There were Cassandras in our midst prophesying collapse or decay—Thoreau and Emerson and Henry Adams—but most of us paid little attention to them; they were drawing-room affectations, or material for courses in literature, and not for practical men. The country, we believed, could be turned to profit forever: moral profit, social profit, economic profit. There was a fortune in every forest, a million in every ore deposit, a real-estate killing at every harbor. And we, the Americans, were the people who would do it. We would celebrate only ourselves, would sing nothing but the praises of the common man.

We did not, of course, shed all our European baggage at the water's edge. We were selective shedders. Although we regarded ourselves as new men, people who had escaped the impersonal forces of history, who could control our destiny, and who had left the restraints of the Old World behind, we brought with us (along with things like smallpox) particular attitudes and ideas that made us suitable conquerors of nature and the world's outstanding competitors. We were the special men of the West; we did not, like the Spaniards, come to seek the golden city of Eldorado, had no conquistadorial fantasies, were not going to be part of a temporary expedition. We had come for a new style of life, and not simply to find riches which would help support the old.

We therefore assumed a special burden. As individuals we

abandoned the security (real or imagined) of familiar lives, places and associations. As a nation we opted for a new and special version of history, discarded the safety of established structures and conventions, and banked, almost unconsciously, on the belief that growth and profit would remain an endless process. Until World War II we were indefatigable in our efforts to make it work, to open new opportunities, to provide homesteads, to build schools, to curb monopolists, but it rarely occurred to most of us that the conquest of nature could become physically excessive and psychologically inadequate. We did not consider the idea that at some moment we would require a source of personal and national identity based on something other than personal enterprise, something beyond the "conquest of nature," a new ethic for social action and new means of creating consensus and culture. Europe might fail—or had failed already—but in America the recurring dreams of centuries could be realized: This was the new garden, the American was the new Adam; the new Jerusalem was at hand. We were the last children of the Renaissance.

America carried the hope of the West, and the WASP was the prototypical American. As a consequence the successes and failures of certain qualities in Western civilization were magnified among Americans generally and WASPs in particular. When the task of "civilization" was to clear forests, exploit resources, build factories, create corporations and found colleges,—when the job was to "tame nature"—we were the most successful people of all. When fields and forests and air and water appeared to be the unlimited and casual riches of nature, we were the most adept at converting them into something useful. When "opportunity" was defined as the essential element in the pursuit of happiness, we were the happiest people in all creation. When the dream of a brotherhood of man required not merely equality of condition but identity in style and attitude, we were the most equal nation of all. When identity was founded on assumptions of Western preeminence, all Europeans could (we thought) be Americanized and all Americans could be assured that their Americanism was all that mattered, and that it was more than adequate in establishing a man's sense of himself and in placing him in the cosmos.

But when all of these special Western attitudes began to fade and change, when we began to discover that in taming nature we might destroy it and ourselves along with it, when the preeminence of the West began to look doubtful, when technology and its products no longer were regarded as unmitigated blessings, when Western confidence began to totter at Dachau and Hiroshima, the forces that magnified and enlarged the American reduced him, first, to a normal human scale and now threaten to make him feel as if he were a little less than a person. He had the most to gain, and now he seems to have the most to lose. The European, who also shares the declining fortunes of capitalism and technology, and who also suffered the impositions of new worlds and new demands (in Asia, in Africa, in the Middle East) had never expected as much, had never placed all his bets on infinite progress and perfectibility. He did not believe in integration and only rarely in equality. He had lost wars, suffered invasions, survived revolutions and therefore understood tragedy and defeat, all the things that the American had junked on the way across. For our man—still an innocent—history had been a big euphoric trip, and the trip is over. The decline of the WASP is probably the central factor in America's agonies with itself and the world outside. The WASP was our man, and the WASP ethic and culture were the essential elements of our Americanism. We are losing them, and are therefore losing ourselves.

If one thinks about these things at all, they become overwhelming. How much of our identity is founded on the history of America-as-WASP, and how much is the myopia of WASP historians? Maybe Henry Commager *invented* America, or George Bancroft, or Charles Beard, or Frederick Jackson Turner, or Admiral Morison. Whatever its "scientific" base, history is, after all, an effort to explain the present; it is written in the present, and if the present is taken as essentially healthy and positive, then the historian will be more concerned with the ancestry of the winners than with the progenitors of the defeated or the invisible. Maybe, underneath all—along with the discovery (or the social decision) that there were black inventors and slave poets and Jewish writers, even in the nineteenth century—we will discover a whole tradition of non-WASP culture that cannot be patronized with hindsight and sentimentality. Which is to say that spirituals and gospel singing, Southern cooking, and whatever was genuinely aristocratic in American life may have *depended* on the black imagination, and not merely on the results of exploited black brawn; and that ethnic pluralism—Irish, Jewish, Italian—produced substantial underground currents of thought and belief which were obscured by the arrogant dominion of WASPs. But who is to know? American radicalism in the years after 1890 was heavily infused with Jews and Italians—Emma Goldman and Alexander Berkman and Arturo Giovanitti—but that, too, was relegated by historians to the category of minor aberrations and almost forgotten. For 150 years the politicians, the writers, the poets, the social theorists, the men who articulated and analyzed American ideas, who governed our institutions, who embodied what we seemed to be, or hoped to be—nearly all of them were WASP. Hawthorne and Melville, Twain and Howells, Veblen and Beard, Holmes and Story, Adams (John, Brooks, Henry) and Lodge, James and Dewey, Lester Frank Ward and John Fiske, Bryan and Wilson, Henry George and Edward Bellamy and nearly every other major American statesman, writer and scholar before (and perhaps including) John F. Kennedy. Of all the major figures discussed by Commager in *The American Mind*, not one is a Jew, a Catholic or a Negro. The American mind was the WASP mind.

And America was a WASP preserve. In the process of settling the country and developing its institutions, in the writing of history and the celebration of tradition, the very word "American" became a norm that was culturally, ideologically and physically WASP. "We welcome the German or the Irishman who becomes an American. We have no use for the German or the Irishman who remains such," said Theodore Roosevelt.

We have no room for any people who do not act and vote simply as Americans, and as nothing else. An immense number [of immigrants] have become completely Americanized, and these stand on exactly the same plane as the descendants of any Puritan, Cavalier, or Knickerbocker among us, and do their full and honorable share of the nation's work. But where immigrants, or the sons of immigrants, do not heartily and in good faith throw in their lot with us, but cling to the speech, the customs, the ways of life, and the habits of thought of the Old World which they have left, they thereby do harm both to themselves and us. . . . If [the immigrant] tries to retain his old language, in a few generations it becomes a barbarous jargon; if he retains his old customs and ways of life, in a few generations he becomes an uncouth boor. . . . It is urgently necessary to check and regulate our immigration by much more drastic laws than now exist; and this should be done both to keep out laborers who tend to depress the labor market, and to keep out races which do not readily assimilate with our own, and unworthy individuals of all races—not only criminals, idiots and paupers, but anarchists of the Most and O'Donovan Rossa types. . . . We freely extend the hand of welcome and of good fellowship to every man, no matter what his creed and birthplace, who comes here honestly intent on becoming a good United States citizen like the rest of us; but we have a right, and it is our duty, to demand that he shall indeed become so, and shall not confuse the issues with which we are struggling by introducing among us Old-World quarrels and prejudices.

The ethnic provincialism went beyond racism, beyond Roosevelt's belief that the temperate zones were naturally reserved for "the higher races," and that any democracy that admitted—for example—a lot of "Chinamen" was trifling with the destruction of civilization: the WASPiness here is as much in the tone as in the ideas, in the supreme confidence of *us* as against *them*, the tone of the sanitary club whose members look out on the grimy hordes trooping in and out of Ellis Island or (more lately) the houses of Harvard and the colleges of Yale. They never thought of themselves as anything but Americans, nor did it occur to anyone else to label them as anything special until, about twenty-five years ago, their confidence began to decline and they started to lose their cultural initiative and preeminence. There were, it goes without saying, regional distinctions—Texans, Yankees, sons of the middle border—but whatever was simply "American" tended to be WASP, if not ethnically, then in style. There was, indeed, no "other"—was, that is, no domestic base of social commentary, no voice except their voice for the discussion of "American" problems. The ethnics had their place and their loyalties, but insofar as that place was *American* it was defined by WASPs. We could distinguish Jews, Irishmen, Italians, Catholics, Poles, Negroes, Indians, Mexican Americans, Japanese Americans, but not WASPs. When WASPs were alienated it was because, as in the case of Henry Adams, the country had moved away from them—because there were too many uncouth boors—not because they regarded themselves as alien in heritage, tradition or belief. The complaints tended

to be proprietary, and the turf, finally, was as big as all creation; it was, in our most grandiose moments, the hope of all
mankind: The WASP complained that the old place was going down because the tenants weren't keeping it up properly.
He was the inheritor of the earth, the fittest of the fit. All
others required fitting—in public schools, settlement houses
and classes in Americanism—and when the WASP began to
interest himself in social science he concerned himself primarily with "minorities," poor people and ethnic misfits. No one
studied the Rockefellers, the Carnegies or the Mellons, but the
sociologists had a field day with the immigrants. The WASP
was the landlord of our culture, and his values, with rare exceptions, were those that defined it: hard work, perseverance,
self-reliance, puritanism, the missionary spirit, and the abstract
rule of law.

The WASP style extended to almost everything: to the
way people spoke, how they thought, what they believed in
and what they should look like. "Americans" ate, slept,
worked and dreamed WASP. In *The American*, Henry James
called our man (what else?) Christopher Newman:

A powerful specimen of an American. But he was not only a fine
American; he was, in the first place, physically, a fine man. He appeared to possess that kind of health and strength which, when found
in perfection, are the most impressive—the physical capital which the
owner does nothing to "keep up." If he was a muscular Christian, it
was quite without knowing it. If it was necessary to walk to a remote
spot, he walked, but he had never known himself to "exercise." He
had no theory with regard to cold bathing or the use of Indian clubs;
he was neither an oarsman, a rifleman, nor a fencer—he had never
had time for these amusements—and he was quite unaware that the
saddle is recommended for certain forms of indigestion. . . . His
usual attitude and carriage were of a rather relaxed and lounging kind,
but when, under a special inspiration, he straightened himself, he
looked like a grenadier on parade. He never smoked. He had been

assured—such things are said—that cigars were excellent for the health, and he was quite capable of believing it; but he knew as little about tobacco as about homeopathy. He had a very well formed head, with a shapely, symmetrical balance of the frontal and the occipital development, and a good deal of straight, rather brown hair. His complexion was brown, and his nose had a bold, well marked arch. His eye was of a clear, cold gray, and save for a rather abundant mustache he was clean shaved. He had the flat jaw and sinewy neck which are frequent in the American type; but the traces of national origin are a matter of expression even more than of feature, and it was in this respect that our friend's countenance was supremely eloquent. . . . It had that typical vagueness which is not vacuity, that blankness which is not simplicity, that look of being committed to nothing in particular, of standing in an attitude of general hospitality to the chances of life, of being very much at one's own disposal, so characteristic of so many American faces. It was our friend's eye that chiefly told his story; an eye in which innocence and experience were singularly blended. It was full of contradictory suggestions, and though it was by no means the glowing orb of a hero of romance, you could find in it almost anything you looked for. Frigid and yet friendly, frank yet cautious, shrewd yet credulous, positive yet skeptical, confident yet shy, extremely intelligent and extremely good-humored, there was something vaguely defiant in its concessions, and something profoundly reassuring in its reserve.

A Marlboro man who doesn't smoke? The heir of Daniel Boone and Davy Crockett, Honest Abe and General Lee, the builder, tinkerer, woodsman, cowboy, athlete. The muscular Christian (without knowing it); the Lone Ranger, Jack Armstrong, Captain Midnight, frank yet cautious, shrewd yet credulous, positive yet skeptical, confident yet shy. Physically a fine man, well-formed head, shapely balance of the frontal and occipital development, flat jaw, sinewy neck. The qualities of his character and country were fused and confused in a mixture of "history," mythology and fact which makes the separate elements indistinguishable. The mythic qualities of the frontier (later ascribed to the common school) transformed the newcomers from the East and the Old World into new men; it cleansed them, and gave them, as Turner wrote, "that coarseness and strength combined with acuteness and inquisitiveness; that practical inventive turn of mind, quick to find expedients; that masterful grasp of material things, lacking in the artistic but powerful to effect great ends; that restless, nervous energy; that dominant individualism . . . and withal that buoyancy and exuberance which comes with freedom." As society on "the eastern border grew to resemble the Old World in its social forms and its industry, ever, as it began to lose faith in the ideal of democracy, [the frontier] opened new provinces, and dowered new democracies in her most distant domains." Christopher Newman, made again and again: powerful to effect great ends, acute, restless, buoyant, free. How many Americans actually acquired those characteristics—how much was wishful thinking—isn't crucial. De Tocqueville was fascinated and Dickens horrified; yet undoubtedly the country produced a laconic toughness, a kind of national cool which made conquest feasible without hysteria and chaos, and without formal class lines and rigid social structures. What was more significant, however, was the pervasive fantasy of "Americanism" which grew from the Newman image, a fantasy of equality and homogeneity that was certified by Fourth of July orators, politicians, writers of dime novels, and the historians of later years. In reading about these things now, it is stunning how much of what was "American" or simply human was left out: the lives of slaves and mill hands, the industrial hovels of Lowell and Holyoke and Chicopee, the never-ending awareness of poverty, disease and death, and of separation and destruction which inevitably hound marginal men, even in the most benevolent of nations. Tocqueville was aware of these things, and so were the reformers of the nineteenth century, but they rarely impressed

24

themselves on the national conscience or the historical memory. With certain exceptions in our romantic literature—Ahab, for example—WASPiness minimized the emotional, although it was often romantic; its rhetoric denied inequality, although inequities of race were consistently observed in practice; and it recognized the factors of struggle and survival primarily through its Darwinian praise of the winners.

Wherever men and women met in typical gatherings—camp meetings, militia drill, Grange picnics, political conventions, church sociables, Chautauqua assemblies—they met on a basis of equality [Commager wrote]. Leadership fluctuated and was dictated by the situation itself rather than by antecedent social position. Education mirrored society, and the public school was the great leveler. The playing field, which was equally important, had its own standards. Like the frontier it placed a premium on ingenuity and physical prowess, and like the frontier and the school, it was leveling.

Commager, in that particular passage, was writing about the nineteenth century, when the public school was hardly universal, and when it leveled almost nothing except, occasionally, the skulls of its students. The fact that every town had its squire (banker, mill owner, lawyer) and that everyone knew who he was and treated him accordingly, or that New England millworkers lived in filth and earned $2.50 for a seventy-hour week, or that every city had its Irish wards, and later its little Italy and its Jewish ghetto, and that their citizens rarely crossed neighborhood lines except to fight or jockey for power, or that background, ethnic and economic, was and is manifestly the great determinant of success in school—these things vanish in that ride toward the sunset. Does Commager, then, falsify? Is he ignorant? Does he propagate mythology? Most likely he is simply doing what most American historians have done, which is to equate WASP with American (or, worse, with "people"). Those who treated each other equally at those meetings did so because their differences were negligible; there were no Orthodox Jews or Catholic priests or Negroes at those Grange picnics and Chautauqua assemblies; there weren't any Irish mill hands or Chinese laborers; perhaps there was an Indian on display, or a blackface minstrel, or an actor playing a drunken Irishman or an effeminate Frenchman, but if they reinforced anything it was the special, unique, blessed quality of being *American* and free. In that freedom there was equality. We hold these truths to be self-evident: All WASPs are created equal, more or less.

The vision of the American as WASP, and vice versa, gave particular place to childhood (meaning, generally, boys) and to growing up. If there was any place or any time when Christopher Newman could enjoy the advantages of his particular Americanism, it was as a boy. In a country that valued, however ambivalently, its innocence, even men could be boys, and often managed it. But boys could be boys without reservation. Which is to say that they could live the American vision more emphatically than anyone else. Commager, writing about the recollections of Mark Twain, Thomas Bailey Aldrich and William Dean Howells:

The setting was everywhere rural or small town, and almost all the families lived in respectable poverty. . . . the code of the boy's town was everywhere the same, and it was one which mirrored faithfully enough the code of the adult world. Every boy was mischievous but few were vicious: the bully, the thief, the liar, the sneak were ostracized more effectively than among grownups. Everybody had his own high sense of honor and enforced it. He was brave, stood up for himself, fought for his rights and fought fairly, learned to take a dare and a risk, scorned a coward, a tattletale, a sissy, and a skulker. He was gregarious, played in gangs, was loyal to his playmates, and rarely cherished enmities. He was chivalrous toward women, respectful to grownups, indifferent toward girls until adolescence, and then

26

romantic about them. He was thoughtless rather than unkind, collected pets indiscriminately, and unfailingly was attached to some dog. He had a lively imagination which found expression chiefly in games; lived in a world inhabited by Indians, cowboys, pirates and smugglers; and learned much from the town ne'er-do-wells who told him tall tales but rarely corrupted him. . . . He was fair in his dealings with others, a good loser in games, would not take too sharp an advantage, and scorned every form of meanness. He was simple and democratic, knew few distinctions of class or color, resented snobbery or affectation, made friends readily with the poor and the shiftless, and was uncomfortable in the presence of wealth.

Our boy. It is hard to find a better description of how the official American wanted his kids to grow up, or how he liked to think of his own childhood. The selective memory, part Boy Scout manual, part English boarding school, part fiction. Did those kids ever wake up with screaming nightmares, put drunken fathers to bed, watch their parents brutalize each other, masturbate under the covers, get a neighboring girl pregnant, burn down the schoolhouse, heave rocks at the village idiot, taunt the weak and the stupid, or hate niggers? Where did the robber barons learn to cheat and swindle or the members of Congress to accept bribes? The question of accuracy here is not as important as the idealized description, which reduces the boys in question to people whose greatest virtue was honor and whose most notable vice was to be "mischievous." There seemed to be no passions, no lusts, no grief, no enduring hatred, just that cool, sexless kid who loved his dog. The kid was white—what else was there in the small town but untaxables like niggers and Indians, or misfits like papists?—and he learned early enough that the safety of interracial friendship owed its existence to the hermetic racial barriers which accompanied adolescence. Where could Huck and Jim be friends except in childhood or in the insularity of a raft on the Mississippi? The dream of anything beyond always flowered at the edge of territories which had just closed. Being an Indian, or black, was all right for kids, for play, or—obviously—for Indians and blacks, or for reverie, but it wasn't for Americans.

Growing up to be an American was enshrined in WASP terms. You got off the raft at the water's edge, and there the material had the familiarity of a Grant Wood painting or a print by Currier and Ives: the small town, the homely virtues, the suspicion of unequivocal expressions of feeling (except perhaps in matters of honor, meaning in war), the commitment to thrift, hard work and what Alger called "pluck," the elevation of abstract principle over personal loyalty, except among outlaws (and, of course, among "politicians"), the belief in the system and its ability to respond. The schools were organized on those premises, and to a great extent still are. They offered "nondenominational" prayers and Bible readings, always Protestant, patronized deviant kids and deviant ethnic groups and enforced codes of dress and behavior that weren't so much middle-class as WASP, and which could be turned to the task of embarrassing recent immigrants (and others) whose accents were strange, or whose food was peculiar, or whose manners were too personally expressive and (therefore) threatening for toleration in the classroom. In later years, the schools celebrated "good government" and moral and physical cleanliness, virtues which were promulgated to teach manners to the uncouth boors just off the boat, and to control political precincts which were in danger of falling into the hands of Irish politicians. (And, more recently, into the hands of blacks.) As always, the winners wrote the history of the war. The WASPs and those sons of immigrants—usually Jewish—who used the system to get ahead touted its virtues: all those doctors who were the sons of immigrant peddlers, all those lawyers whose fathers worked in sweatshops to put

Abie through CCNY, or maybe, would you believe it, even Harvard. A whole chorus of professors, Oscar Handlin and Lawrence Cremin and Robert Havighurst, celebrating immigrant mobility through the common school and hardly aware of the Irish, the Italians, the Poles, the Negroes, the Lithuanians, the Indians, who remained in their precincts and ghettoes and reservations and barely moved at all. When the system worked, it worked only on WASP terms; you changed your name and junked your accent and named your children Lynn and Shelley and Morris, and you didn't mind their growing contempt for your ethnicity. But often it didn't work at all, and the casualties, who disappeared from public reckoning (there were, after all, no words for "dropout" before World War II), collected in places called South Boston, Charlestown, Harlem, Daly City, Cicero and South Side Chicago. In the late 1960s we began to call them the forgotten Americans, which was the nicest thing about them that anyone had ever said.

II

At the heart of it all was the ethic of success and mobility, our own brand of Puritanism which fused the Protestant virtues in justification of what we called enterprise. "The end," said John Cotton, "is to improve our lives to do more service to the Lord, the comfort and increase of the body of Christ whereof we are members, that ourselves and posterity may be the better preserved from the common corruptions of this evil world, to serve the Lord and work out our salvation under the power and purity of His holy ordinance." And since we were the Lord's chosen people, having been lifted up to "heaven as to advantages and privileges," it was hard to see how, in the long run, things that were in the private interest were not also in the interest of the Lord and the nation. All of that, of course, is old news; it has been discussed thousands of times. But there is something else: After we flagellated ourselves in the service of the Protestant ethic, later reinforced by the strictures of social Darwinism, we castigated ourselves for having served it, splitting the process into separate stages. The first was making it; the second was cleaning up. John D. Rockefeller clobbered his competitors to build Standard Oil; Nelson and David "serve" the public. Henry Clay Frick collected blast furnaces and Bessemer converters; then he collected art. Andrew Carnegie created U. S. Steel; then he created libraries, foundations, and the International Endowment for Peace.

The cleanup was as important as the creation, partly because it assuaged critics and decorated its vulgarity, and partly because it helped select out the ethnically unfit. Necessarily a man must get his hands dirty to make a pile; that was part of American democracy. You carved empires, built cities, and felled forests with your own brawn and your own guile. You even sent your rich sons into the plant to dirty them up and therefore qualify them as certified managers. But then how could anyone tell you from those dirty foreigners who were streaming off the boat? How were you different from some boisterous Indian who found oil on the reservation, from a Jew who had grown rich in the department store, or from some black operator who had parlayed his Georgia funeral parlor into a fortune? If money alone made men equal, as the historians suggested, then how could you keep Jews out of the eating clubs and spades out of the fraternity? And how could you keep a lot of upstarts from competing? Clean up, sanitize, talk manners, talk background, talk new money as against old money, promote business ethics and "good government," deplore ward politics, clean up. Teaching manners in the schools, wrote Charles W. Eliot in 1914, was an important part of the struggle against "objectionable social groups," among them the new immigrants.

"The average Jewish guy isn't 'to the manner born,' so to speak [says the social-climbing Jewish hero of Myron Kaufmann's novel *Remember Me to God*]. He hasn't had it taught in the cradle and had the benefit of good schools all his life. Probably his parents never had a chance to go to college, and probably his grandparents were immigrants from Eastern Europe. It's going to take a lot of hard discouraging work to unlearn all these foreign mannerisms and New York mannerisms of yours and set up some new brain patterns so you'll have some polish. . . . I want you to keep an eye on Bill Hodge. You learn what a gentleman is by watching one. And study the guys from Groton and St. Mark's. Their facial expression. How they modulate their voice. It's always clean and distinct and pleasing to the ear. An American should be proud of his language and handle it with respect, because it's the language of Shakespeare."

If the Jews knew it, so did the WASPs, and if the Jews or the Irish eventually learned to open some doors there might always be others beyond.

Inevitably, "Americans" were better at making money than at using it. They had confidence in their ability to build empires, even if the empire was nothing more than a string of groceries or a small railroad or a local bank. That required verve and hustle and something for which they had no word, *chutzpah*. But collecting art presumably required taste, and even sending your kid to college demanded, at least of him, a minimum preparation and a modicum of intelligence. So they cheated in the name of "character"; they imposed quotas in their colleges, gutted the requirements, created special prep schools or converted old ones, glorified the gentleman's C, hired professionals to select their art and conduct their charities, and married off their children to the remnants of European nobility. In fostering the creation of public schools (to which they refused to send their children) they created machinery not only for the development of reliable factory workers, but also for social selection according to WASP standards. After the frontier was closed and the large corporations were established, the school inherited their mythic association with making it, with upward mobility and economic opportunity. In practice, however, the school system was a selective mechanism which chose people in and out according to background, and which justified those selections on "educational" grounds. They were, in short, the engines of latter-day social Darwinism in America. The classroom too was a jungle in which the fittest survived. Those who failed were regarded as victims of their own inability and shiftlessness. The school taught people that their failure was personal, not systemic, and therefore justified. WASPs created the schools, not as leveling devices, but as institutions which would serve the distinctions—ethnic and economic—from which they could profit and in which they obviously believed. They were, as Horace Mann observed, a social safety valve; they did not, as he thought, keep people from being poor, but taught them that their poverty was deserved. In supporting those schools and in encouraging other "good works," the made-it WASP could not only cleanse his own conscience, he could also cleanse the manners, morals and bodies of those who were less fortunate.

Despite all that, the Protestant ethic created more confidence in becoming than in whatever was to follow. It was rural, individualistic (in rhetoric if not in practice) and demanded considerable self-denial. It did not say much about situations of abundance, or about life in large cities, nor did it assume anything other than WASP standards: American Indians found it altogether incomprehensible, and so, later, did the rebellious children of WASPs themselves. The qualities and manners associated with corporate enterprise were not necessarily—or even, perhaps, occasionally—appropriate to the conduct of a good society, no matter how generous the philanthropy or how ambitious the efforts in sanitation. Although WASP rhetoric insisted that anyone can make it, the winners must have learned in the last fifty years, even if they didn't know it in 1900 or 1920, that the virtues to which they attributed their own success were not necessarily applicable or even possible in other cultures—that the American version of "development," meaning capitalism, was not necessarily fit for export to India or Latin America, and possibly no longer even appropriate in the ghettoes of Watts or Harlem. Perhaps, in fact, they only pretended to believe it. For the last hundred years "Americans" themselves have had doubts about who could and who could not make it on our terms. Immigration policy after 1924 suggested, quite obviously, that WASPs were more fit for the competitive struggle, or more acceptable as competitors, than Italians, Slavs and Greeks. Jews who played the same game as "Americans" were ostracized as cheats and hustlers even after they cleaned themselves up with art and philanthropy. The proper gentleman's clubs (which had accepted the few Jews—German Jews—who applied in the first decades of the nineteenth century) were closed, and the corporations were declared off limits. In any case, the ethic of making it, which we proclaimed to the entire world, was justifiable only in WASP terms: in Boston they hung out shingles that no Irish need apply, and in California they beat up the Orientals who were willing to work for less than "Americans." Yankee shrewdness, which was honored, was nothing more, or less, than Jewish deviousness, which wasn't. Making it, in short, did not merely grow out of the Puritan tradition; it required, in some form, the maintenance of that tradition for use as a means of curbing sheeny shysters, Irish pols and Italian hoods who applied the ethic according to their own standards and according to whatever conditions WASP exclusiveness imposed. In the 1930s Michael Gold once attacked Thornton Wilder's version of Christianity as "that newly fashionable literary religion that centers around Jesus Christ the First British Gentleman." It was used not only for the necessarily dirty work of capitalizing corporations, building organizations and exploiting land and labor, but also for the subsequent processes of sanitation. Making it, in WASP terms, was the trick of the deferred social conscience which could be sent into exile while you dealt with immigrant labor and frontier Indians, and which could then be summoned back —once the money was made—and used to teach your subjects manners. As a promise, it was extended to all Americans—a man with spirit, ambition and perseverance could make it— but it was extended with a wink to those who were smart enough to know and "American" enough to understand. Ultimately the WASP ethic was itself commercialized; it was packaged and sold to the greenhorns off the boat and the rubes off the farm: plastic surgeons for nose jobs, hair straighteners, "beauty consultants," orthodontists, Horatio Alger novels, Dale Carnegie courses, and all the rest. The sons of the chosen people were flattered when they were told that they didn't look Jewish, and uncounted millions of black men and women tortured themselves with lye and other concoctions to get the kinks out of their hair and the negritude out of their skin. Transformation and assimilation were sold on the open market; you learned that "success" began by redoing yourself. Nobody ever called anybody a dirty WASP.

III

The image permeated everything: serious books and comic books, magazines and movies, education and sports. America-as-WASP, the WASP as the American preeminent. Long after the First World War, when American innocence was supposed to have come to an end and the frontier was closed, when the great gluts of ethnic immigrants were allegedly melting into the nation as equals, and when their politicians had started to take over the cities and often the states, WASPs still wrote the novels and reviewed them, edited the magazines, ran the colleges, defined the ideals, and acted as the nation's critics and conscience: Hemingway, Eliot, Frost, MacLeish, Anderson, Lewis, Steinbeck, Wilder, Wolfe, Benét, Sherwood, Edmund Wilson, Van Wyck Brooks, Fitzgerald (who was more Princeton WASP than Irish), Faulkner, Parrington, Agee; *The Saturday Evening Post* under George Horace Lorimer (with covers by Norman Rockwell); *The National Geographic*, which made bare teats acceptable in a mainstream magazine by photographing them only on black women; *The Atlantic* under Edward Weeks; *Harper's* under Frederick Lewis Allen and his predecessors; *Reader's Digest* under everybody, then, now and forever. There were, of course, exceptions: Untermeyer and Lippmann and Nathanael West, Eugene O'Neill and James T. Farrell. And yet the tradition and style, the tone and heroes were WASP. It was Dick Diver in *Tender Is the Night* neglecting his work and thereby destroying his brilliant career, and Robert Jordan, tough, stoic, behind his futile machine gun at that Spanish bridge; it was the small town in the Midwest, which, however sharp the satire, was sufficiently large and American to be worth attention; it was the American farmers of the West fighting the trusts and railroads and their sinister agent, S. Berman (Sam? Sol? Simon?); it was the New England of Frost and the Altamont of Thomas Wolfe and the California of Steinbeck. It permeated the English department of nearly every college in the country, all of them run by WASPs who idolized Swift and Pope, Dryden and Samuel Johnson and that greatest contemporary culture hero of them all, T. S. Eliot. If the conservatism of the Southern agrarians was a little scruffy, a bit unkempt, if the new criticism was a little too slick, the Anglo-Catholicism of Eliot was absolutely right—civilized, mannered, and rooted in two thousand years of Western tradition. Eliot was a mind, a spirit, and, above all, a gentleman. "I began to feel uneasy about my work," wrote Louis Kampf about his graduate education a decade ago, "when it dawned on me . . . that I was taking a friend of Lord Bolingbroke's (a Tory) as my model. Neither Swift nor Pope would have received me in his home. Kampf, the Jewish socialist from Washington Heights, sitting in his Chinese garden swapping epigrams with Dr. Arbuthnot!"

For more than a century we fussed with something called the American language, and always in the same terms. There were, after all, Jewish novelists and Negro poets, but their works were often so identified and thereby sent off to a literary Ellis Island or a plantation all their own. At the turn of the century Howells had patronized Paul Laurence Dunbar, who was probably the first professional black writer in America. Dunbar wrote formal verse (which he liked but no one wanted) and Negro dialect verse sentimentalizing the Old South, which he sold. Those poems, Howells said in an introduction, represent "divinations and reports of what passes in the hearts and minds of a lowly people whose poetry had hitherto been inarticulately expressed in music, but now finds, for the first time in our tongue, literary interpretation of a very artistic completeness." Our tongue. In the succeeding generation very little changed. Langston Hughes was a Negro, not an American, poet, and Henry Roth was a Jewish writer. Edna St. Vincent Millay and Robert Frost were Americans.

The mainstream, mythic, all-purpose American led a charmed life. Long after Twain and Melville understood that the territories were closed, after Billy Budd was hung in the name of law and order, and after Huck Finn lit out for places that were no longer there, the style and character persisted—even thrived—through the pop cult of the twenties and thirties and forties. The heirs of Leatherstocking and the heroes of Horatio Alger came back in the form of Dink Stover and Frank Merriwell, of Tom Mix and the Rover Boys, and of an endless succession of pulp-novel and comic-book characters who had blond hair, blue eyes and what was inevitably called "an open countenance." As often as not the bad guys were swarthy or foreign, Chinese dragon ladies and Italian hoods, and displayed exotic forms of underhandedness against the fair-fighting, straight-shooting hero.

But the apotheosis was electronic. Hollywood. Radio. Television. Although—or perhaps because—the movies (and later the networks) were dominated by Jewish producers and saturated with ethnic performers, they celebrated the only acceptable real American around and gave him a new lease on the national life. The all-American boy of the thirties, forties and fifties was manufactured by Jews. Louis B. Mayer took second-generation-Polish calendar models and turned them into WASPs, and the American became a packaged product. The ethnics changed their names—Doris Kappelhoff became Doris Day, Bernie Schwartz turned into Tony Curtis, Margarita

Carmen Cansino became Rita Hayworth, and Dino Crocetti became Dean Martin—and played out the myth of the mainstream. (Jim Ameche was the first Jack Armstrong on the radio; Don played Alexander Graham Bell). Those ethnic types who remained sufficiently original for identification were almost inevitably second-class citizens: the blundering Irish sidekick, the Filipino valet, the Jewish comic. If your name was Marx you had to be funny or you'd be dead in Akron. The Hyman Kaplans were lovable jerks, immigrant Sambos and Uncle Maxes; Rochester said "Yassuh, Mr. Benny," and rolled his eyes, and the Abies, Mikes and Pats were played for laughs.

The genuine American was John Wayne, Gary Cooper, Clark Gable and Gregory Peck, a mythic man who transcended particular films or plots or situations. "The secret of the power of Hollywood gods and goddesses," wrote Parker Tyler in a brilliant book called *Magic and Myth of the Movies*, "is that they seem to do everything anyone else does except that when they die—in movies—they die over and over; when they love they love over and over. Even as the gods do, they undergo continual metamorphoses, never losing their identities, being Rita Hayworth or Glenn Ford no matter what their movie aliases." Hollywood did not merely package the American dream, nor did it just offer, as Tyler says, "an enlarged personnel of the realistically anthropomorphic deities of ancient Greece"; it also perpetuated and resurrected—indeed, turned into flesh—the WASP hero and the WASP ideal. For the first time, with film, we could all see the perfect American, the national type, could vote on his qualifications at the box office, and could watch him come back, time and again, in a new mask and new costume, to live and fight another day. At the very moment of the *Götterdämmerung*, when everyone knew that the frontier was closed, and when people like Turner began to wonder what would replace it in re-creating his Newman-American, Hollywood reopened it, brought Leatherstocking back, began to teach those who had not learned what the American was, and led the rest of us in rituals of celebration. Where the schools and the farm and the shop failed, the movies came to the rescue.

The process was hardly subtle. It taught the great audience that the real American rarely expressed emotion, and that while he might be glamorous and even "romantic" his capacity for any genuine human relationship, which included real sex—not just screwing—was limited. Strong feelings untempered by cool led to trouble, and were usually associated with weak characters, with villains, comics or women. "The robbers who are shot," Pauline Kael observed in 1954,

the Nazis who are knifed—they are cowards or fanatics who don't deserve to live. Fear, on the one hand, and on the other devotion to a "misguided" cause to the disregard of personal safety are evidence of subhumanity. The villains are usually more expressive than the heroes because their inhumanity is expressed precisely by the display of extreme human emotions. (Gregory Peck, who is always a hero, is rarely called on to register any emotion whatever. The devil can be expressive, but the hero is a stick of wood.)

In the Hollywood efforts that followed World War II, even the occasional ethnic heroes—and God knows there weren't many—required sanitation and became WASPs. Pauline Kael again, in a review of the film based on Bernstein's musical *West Side Story*:

The Puerto Ricans are not Puerto Ricans and the only difference between these two gangs of what I am tempted to call ballerinas is that one group has faces and hair darkened, and the other group has gone wild for glittering yellow hair dye; and their stale exuberance, though magnified by the camera to epic proportions, suggests no social tensions more world shaking than the desperation of young dancers to get ahead—even at the risk of physical injury. . . . Maria, the sweet virgin fresh from Puerto Rico, is the most machine-tooled of Hollywood ingenues—clever little Natalie Wood . . . Natalie Wood is the newly-constructed love-goddess—so perfectly banal she destroys all thoughts of love . . .

I had a sense of foreboding when I saw that Friar Lawrence had become a kindly old Jewish pharmacist called "Doc," but I was hardly prepared for his ultimate wisdom—"You kids make this world lousy! When will you stop?" . . . These message movies dealing with Negro and white, or with Puerto Rican and white, like to get a little extra increment of virtue—unearned—by tossing in a sweet, kindly, harmless old Jew full of prophetic cant. (Presumably, Jews should not be discriminated against because they are so philosophic and impotent.) The film makers wouldn't dream of having a young, pushing, aggressive Jew in the film—just as they don't dare to differentiate or characterize the racial backgrounds of the white gang.

That impotence, comic or "lovable," which was common to most of the ethnic characters who weren't villains was required by the hero's own dubious virility. For though he was, in the end, faster on the draw, more noble in battle and tougher than all the rest, his qualifications as a lover left a great deal to be desired. (Teddy Roosevelt, in real life, was a superb model: off to the West for the outdoor life, up San Juan Hill, and then back to the lecture circuit with endless references to "the undersized man of letters [who] in his delicate effeminate sensitiveness finds that he cannot play a man's part among men.") Partly, of course, he was a victim of Puritan mores and the priggish conventions of vestigial Comstockery: Law and order, coupled with Puritan morals in matters of sex, were required to control the ruffians of the frontier, and not merely to serve the Lord. But the American was also trapped, ever and again, by the problems of sanitation. Cooper (James Fenimore) struggled with the problem in his novels, and never resolved it, and so Cooper (Gary) had to live forever after in ambivalence. How could Leatherstocking be a man of the woods (or whoever), a frontiersman, cowboy, soldier, how could he be adept at the primitive arts of survival, and yet be civilized enough to be worthy of the higher things? You couldn't just drag the girl off to a frontier cabin without turning the story into a joke or a social calamity, so you had to clean up—maybe even turn, in the last reel, into a refined young man who had ventured West in the guise of a cowpoke. (TR again.) More important, however, was the fact that if purity (and innocence) were the requirements of a good American character, experience as a lover was pretty hard to come by. Virility, therefore, always had to be demonstrated not only by Good Works (catching the rustlers or the spies) but also by a body and a voice that were unmistakably masculine. (Small men—Jimmy Cagney, for example—were acceptable provided they were sufficiently hyperactive to allay suspicions of effeminacy. Otherwise it had to be mitigated through sadism and elevator shoes. Alan Ladd stood on a box to make love to his heroines.) And since emotion was taboo, how the devil could one make love anyhow? The WASP hero was perpetually trying to prove that he had balls, especially in competition against ethnics and outlanders. Humphrey Bogart against Peter Lorre? Sidney Greenstreet maybe? Claude Rains? During the more innocent days of the faith, Cagney, in a sailor suit, snatched the girl from a whole barroom full of ethnic misfits—Chinese, Jews, Russians—and, in a musical extravaganza of bands and flying flags (*Footlight Parade*), marched her onto his ship. Since the girl appeared to be Oriental, she was clearly unfit for marriage, but superbly qualified for seduction and possession. At the conclusion of the film, the scene of marching sailors dissolves into a huge American flag which fills the screen, and against which the producers superimposed a picture of Franklin D. Roosevelt, who was, in those years of depression, the father of us all.

If Hollywood tended—either by accident or, perhaps unconsciously, by design—to caricature the wooden WASP and the ethnic freak, the producers of radio dramas and comedies found stereotypes a near-necessity. It was difficult to establish heroes and villains (or anything else) without obvious voice cues recognizable to the audience (many of whom were kids anyway); thus radio, using old materials, quickly became as stylized as the most precious, formal schools of art; Amos 'n' Andy, Rochester, Tonto, Kato, the Dragon Lady, the Barracuda, Mrs. Nussbaum, Senator Claghorn, plus a whole string of stupid Irish police sergeants, Italian gangsters, Oriental (or Spanish) master criminals, grunting Indians and comic Jews, all instantly recognizable by accent, cadence and quality of voice. The distinctions, of course, were not merely ethnic; sometimes they were regional, and often they relied, just as they had in the dime novels, on a "gruff voice" or a "pleasing manner of speech," which is to say, on distinctions of class. Even if the movies, radio and pulp literature paid lip service to the honest, hard-working poor (especially during the depression), they insisted on proper class distinctions in the choice of language, grammar and voice.

LONE RANGER: Tonto, I'm going to try a saddle on him.
TONTO: Uhh, no horse like that take saddle.
LONE RANGER: There never was a horse like that! Just look at him!
TONTO: Him shine in the sun—like silver.

MIKE: Sakes alive, Mr. Keen, it's another dead body. And saints preserve us, Boss, it don't have no head.
KEEN: Yes, Mike, this dead body has been murdered.
MIKE: You don't mean it, Mr. Keen!

WASH: Mist' Tom . . .

TOM MIX: Wash!

WASH: You figure we got a chance, Mist' Tom?

TOM MIX: I don't know, pardner. I figure death's got a running iron on us at last.

The all-American radio heroes, from the Lone Ranger to Jack Armstrong, were for many reasons more sexless than their movie counterparts. Emotion was out, and sex wasn't for kids anyhow. The Shadow, who learned how to cloud men's minds in the Orient (dig?), may have had a little thing going with Margo Lane (not to be confused with Lois Lane, friend of Clark Kent, alias Superman), just as Perry Mason would, in later years of television, become a little cozy with Della Street. But for the most part, love and its problems were relegated to the soap operas, where the Americanism was either institutional, honoring the family and the small town, or nonexistent, leaving the mythic American unencumbered, either by family or by feeling, to press the fight.

Meanwhile, however, something else was going on. Through the twenties and thirties, and especially in the depression, the theme of sanitation, of cleanliness, became increasingly significant. It had, in some measure, always been there, not only as a standard middle-class artifact, but also as a token of Americanism, of acceptance, which could be turned on foreigners, immigrants and various members of ethnic minorities. Thomas Jefferson was persuaded that Negroes smelled peculiar, and any number of later Americans were certain that black bodies secreted some sort of fluid which produced a distinctive negroid odor. (They were, of course, also certain that black genitals were larger, and their libidos supercharged.) During the heyday of "scientific" racism, when people like Madison Grant measured heads and bodies to prove the "superiority" of northern Europeans, some Americans came to believe that genetic virtues were directly proportional to the ethnic composition of the country. Anglo-Saxons, in other words, were several times as good as Mediterranean types. In the past forty years, under conditions of increasing ethnic "tolerance," *clean* became a central feature of the WASP model—partly puritanical, partly class-conscious, but also ethnic. Cleanliness was next to godliness. Italians had large pores, and their breath smelled of garlic; Jews sweated a lot; Irishmen reeked of whiskey. Americans were clean-cut, smelled sweet, and spoke plain. Parker Tyler, in his analysis of the film *The Grapes of Wrath*:

The immediate emphasis on the economic problems of the Okie family, the Joads, is directed toward housing, especially sanitation. First they find anchorage in the Hooverville camps . . . and there their miseries are almost too much to allow one to remain in the theater. But finally they reach a clean, modern, sanitation-blessed camp sponsored by the Department of Agriculture. Meanwhile a curious parallel has obtained; as the overloaded truck with the Joads and all they possess draws nearer and nearer to California, halcyon land of the movies, everything, including the photography and the plot, becomes neater, cleaner, and more shapely. Therefore the esthetic symbols of plot and technique reflect the modern sanitation which it is an important ambition of Ma Joad's to achieve, for sanitation is the symbol of clean and proper living in the material sense.

The depression, in its traumatic impact on national life, forced the "American" to turn from individual to collective values, from initiative to collaboration, and from ideals of strength and daring to the cult of efficiency and control. The depression, however tenuously, delivered the message of the Industrial Revolution and began to force a confrontation with the limitations that most Europeans had long understood. We had come to the end of the historical conditions that seemed to

44

make the WASP the preeminent citizen of the West: there was no more open land, no territory to be developed, no chance to go somewhere else and start again, no magic in individual enterprise and simple institutions. We were catching up with Europe. Perhaps tomorrow would not be inevitably better than today. Perhaps we could not remake the world. And yet, with the help of Hollywood, with New Deal rhetoric, with the use of the refurbished folklore of frontier collaboration, the hegemony of the WASP was preserved a few more years. Just beneath the surface there was enough xenophobia and anti-Semitism, enough racism and nativism, to make it necessary to represent social reform in absolutely "American" terms. The tenants of the culture were still dependents, and the proper people, we believed, could still make the country run and still deserved to be in charge. The trouble with the country was not in the ideal of enterprise but in its corruption, in the "malefactors of great wealth," and the solution rested in a little more centralized control, in a little insurance and social security, and in something called "the public interest" which was entrusted, by and large, to the same people who had been running the country since the beginning. The WASP could do no wrong. While New Deal pragmatists tinkered with the economic system, most Americans simply felt guilty, and internalized the terrors of poverty, personal failure and impotence. In some places the local barons of industry paid the clergy to keep the lid on, to remind their distressed parishioners that it was not the system but the individual who was responsible. Poverty was an indication that a man was un-Christian. Studs Terkel quotes Virginia Foster Durr:

Among the things that horrified me were the preachers—the fundamentalists. They would tell the people they suffered because of their sins. And the people believed it. God was punishing them. Their children were starving because of their sins. . . . The Depression affected people in two different ways. The great majority reacted by thinking money is the most important thing in the world. Get yours. And get it for your children. Nothing else matters. Not having that stark terror come at you again . . .

But if it was imperative to have money, it was just as important to *appear* to have it; the fantasy took a leap: from open land to cozy cottages, from boisterous initiative to cautious management. One tried to fake a state of grace and ended by believing the pretense. In the cosmology of James Fenimore Cooper, the depression meant that Natty Bumppo had finally run out of territories and had to clean himself up—wash, get a shave, and learn to speak proper. The entire meaning of a socialized world (for Americans, who were not supposed to talk about "class") was past achievement: if you had to cooperate, had to pass economic regulations or welfare laws, it meant not the beginning of enterprise (making it) but the end (clean up). If there was economic or social complexity, then in some measure the country was *made*. It was no longer a land for pioneers but one for consumers, bureaucrats and people who could live with their neighbors and whose attitudes and manners were therefore inoffensive. And so while the proletarian rhetoric of the depression lionized the common man and emphasized the nobility of people forced to peddle apples and stand in soup kitchens, it honored even more the vision of clean clothes, sturdy homes and clean, if not plush, surroundings. What we celebrated was not merely the ingenuity or the heroism of enterprise—although there was plenty of that—but even more the rewards of having made it and the people who had. (Ronald Coleman, Cary Grant, Walter Pidgeon; the Cockney as British gentleman.) We began to dream of the things which, as events turned out, we tried to realize after World War II. We were (remember) going to "settle down in Dallas in a little plastic palace." Put another way, the

WASP of the thirties (and a lot of other people) began to dream not only about being Leatherstocking or John Wayne, but also about the WASP-to-be of the fifties. The depression, which taught us to suspect that the old individualism might be inadequate, did not force the rejection of old heroes as much as it demanded new settings, costumes, and roles. Our modes of expression remained as anal as they had ever been, we threw pies and worshiped flush toilets, but now we also learned the word "security," which meant, among other things, escape not merely from poverty and unemployment but also from the dirty people—not fully Americans, if at all—with whom such economic problems were associated. The Irish might be poor, or the Negroes, but being poor was—finally—un-American and unclean.

IV

Given the WASP ideal, World War II was the Moment Supreme. It was the last great ritual, the last time that we believed—really believed—in the possibilities of the America that we learned about from the textbook. There have been moments since when we attempted—as in the New Frontier and the rhetoric of the Great Society—to re-create the mood, to find a moral equivalent for that war, but those attempts failed. World War I had been a party to hang the Kaiser; World War II was the last great cause, the last unequivocal act of self-celebration.

In part, it was a great relief, not merely from unemployment, foreclosures and scarcity, but from the accumulated frustrations of an industrial society which left few opportunities either to demonstrate our increasingly uncertain virility or, for many of us, to establish a legitimate claim to one hundred percent Americanism. It was a chance for everybody to join up, and if, in our inability to distinguish one Jap from another, we removed all the Japs from the Pacific Coast, we also managed to turn up the rhetoric of the melting pot to something approaching white heat. Suddenly it became possible for immigrants barely off the boat to receive their naturalization papers—all you had to do was join the Army—and for people whose seven-syllable names had been fodder for the radio comics to hear their fellow ethnics mentioned in the doomsday voices of Lowell Thomas and Gabriel Heatter. The roll call of the brave, dead or alive, was stuck on plaques outside the post office and read, to the sound of a muted trumpet, in the closing scene of a thousand films of war: Abrams, Bartalucci, Bell, Capoletti, Fuller, Hollingsworth, Kluscewicz, Maguire, Murphy, Rappoport, Richardson, Smith, Sullivan, Waszelewski, Ziegler. Whatever our differences—Protestant, Catholic, Jew, Texas or Brooklyn—we weren't Nazis or Japs. The clichés flew around the wardroom and the barracks, and little clusters of men gathered, in the lull of battle, to talk of home: the small town in Iowa, the girls of New York, the wide open spaces, the wife, the kids, the high-school sweetheart. They were going to let us have our pluralism and make us one nation at the same time, saying there really wasn't much difference between Christians and Jews, because we all believed in God, or reciting eulogies over William Bendix or Richard Conte or even some nameless black actor who had played steward or mess boy on a battleship. The movies and the radio dramas of those years taught us one thing: that the ethnics and the freaks—the gabby guys, the jokers, the wild men—were expendable, that, indeed, their death was often imperative, since it was the only way that they (or the producer, who had less faith in them than the script pretended) could irrevocably demonstrate their Americanism. If that boy was too Italian, he might be a little suspect; but a good leg wound would Americanize him. Sometimes the situation demanded impotence (that black mess boy—how could he prove his manhood within the outfit?), but even when it did not it was still necessary for the hero to make it through the picture and to lead the platoon back to safety. If Bendix got it, that was all right, but what if the Japs should get John Wayne or Randolph Scott? Out of the question, because they symbolized the perseverance and courage that would ultimately lead to victory. They represented America. In the very act, therefore, of celebrating our democracy—all those names—we reaffirmed the legitimacy of the ultimate WASP, tall, straight, and cool.

Nonetheless, the war did a great deal, even for those of us who were too young to fight but who would have gone at the drop of a hat. It put Jews on the map of American rhetoric, even if it failed to get them into the corporation or the country club, and it drove overt anti-Semitism and overt anti-Catholicism into the darker corners of American life. John F. Kennedy won the 1960 election on *PT-109*. More important, the war wooed us into a common Americanism, something that no other force and no institution, short of a genuinely open society, could have accomplished. *We* could be one of them, we could be Capoletti or Waszelewski, and could become, we thought, no less than Hollingsworth or Smith. It taught us style—made us want to learn—because now the Hollywood types and the heroes of pop literature, the clichés of the textbook, the daily news reports and the propaganda from OWI were all the same. The colonels and the generals, at least those we were allowed to see in the newsreels or in the papers, really did sound like all-American boys, cool, tough, polite, WASPish, and the few who did not—like Patton, for example—were condemned. Whom did you want in charge of that platoon or in command of that squadron, a hotheaded Italian, a lovable Jew or one of those tough unemotional types? The war became the big game—us against them—and the metaphors of football flew in abundance: "You're the captain, you call the play." "Are you going to play on this team or do you want a transfer?" "This is where we separate the men from the boys." "Thank you, sir, you've been a great coach." In the cosmology of sports, the dirty warrior can always be the clean-cut boy underneath, could, that is to say, preserve his amateur status. You played hard, then you showered and dressed and went home, which is, of course, what American wars were always supposed to be. (No terms, no negotiated peace; you play to win, then get out.) The war, moreover, provided a setting wherein the "American" as frontiersman and the "American" as team player could be the same man, each role carrying the possibility of the other: In every squadron there was one crazy bastard who chased a Jap Zero after he was ordered to turn back, and either got himself killed (because, of course, it was a Nip trap) or caught hell from the C.O., reformed and became a hero. You knew that every true American could hack it alone if he had to, but that, this war being what it was, you had to work with the team.

The metaphor of the team was loaded not only with the things the WASPs (and others) were later to become, but with the possibilities of social and ethnic integration. Things, of course, were always supposed to have been open, but every smart kid soon learned better. Now suddenly there was, or seemed to be, a new invitation. The WASPs were still in charge, but we all started to work our tails off to look, act and become like them. We were all patriots then, and we knew just how a patriot behaved.

Because it was the last moment when nearly all Americans (all white Americans) shared, at least rhetorically, a common vision, it became frozen, a kind of monument to the old WASP ideal. It is not simply that the economics of Hollywood and television keep bringing back the old films, or that we made films about World War II during the Korean War, but that there simply is no acceptable vision of patriotism, or of a single, firmly unified nation from any later moment. In the summer of 1970, when Bob Hope and Billy Graham synthesized Honor America Day, they managed no more than to bring out the fossils of 1945, much in the way a paunchy, balding athlete shows off his trophies: Red Skelton and Dinah Shore, Dorothy Lamour and Jack Benny, Hope and Kate Smith (who sang—what else?—"God Bless America"). Since the whole affair was billed as "nonpolitical," it required the invocation of an America that had momentarily managed to forget or deny its social and ethnic inequities. The entertainers of World War II could play against the illusion of cultural togetherness: Hope and his peers traveled around the world to entertain the boys; by playing gutless pretenders, they exorcised the fears of combat and death. But to make that comedy plausible, one had to accept the validity of the combat: fear in a doubtful cause or a war of questionable justice can't be laughed away, which is to say that without political unanimity the comedy of fear is impossible. (Hopeless?) The year 1945 was the last time we were together, the last time we had genuine confidence in the integrative, Americanizing qualities of the old WASP ideal. "American freedom," said Graham on July 4, 1970, "is rooted in a book, and that book is the Bible." It would have gone great in 1945.

V

The legacy of war was corporate, not individualistic, even though there remained great pockets—especially in what was sentimentally called the heartland—devoted to an older style. Technology was the real winner, not the free independent American, and confidence the loser. We had, without knowing it, rejoined the West, had lost our exemptions, our special favors, our immunity from complexity, mortality, compromise and sin. Since the WASP had been the special beneficiary of American conditions and beliefs, he now became the special victim of their decline. He too was a refugee of history, and for him, as for all refugees, caution rather than ebullience seemed to be the price of survival. Henry Adams had anticipated the change after the Chicago World's Fair in 1893 when he talked of the "mechanical consolidation of force which ruthlessly stamped out the life of the class into which Adams was born, but created monopolies capable of controlling the new energies that America adored." But what was apparent to him did not become apparent to most Americans until 1946, even though the spirit had been upon them since the thirties. We thought that we had sent Leatherstocking off to Fort Dix in 1941, and maybe we did, but when he was mustered out after Hiroshima he bore a striking resemblance to a corporate manager. If Capoletti and Waszelewski wanted to become old-style WASPs, if they had learned to be John Wayne, that was perfectly all right, but now there really wasn't much of a place for them in corporate management, which required a different sort of man. We did not worship the Bomb, but we had, without doubt, begun to love the processes and organizations that put it together and delivered it. Einstein was patronized—that lovable absent-minded professor who couldn't add up his grocery bill—but the Manhattan Project was revered. And what it, and General Motors and Martin and Boeing, could produce for war they and others, with a little government help, could also produce for peace. What was good for General Motors was good for the country.

The word was "Keep cool." The central figure became the org man, and the governing principle was caution. The returning GIs, who had learned never to volunteer, became the fathers of what was later to be known as "privatism," which meant playing the system, not bucking it, and never sticking out your butt for any cause. The manners and ethic of making it were replaced by the assumptions of having made it, and the focus shifted from production to consumption, from savings to credit, and from what David Riesman called the inner-directed man to the other-directed man. People who didn't have a dime lived like millionaires, because, well, it was un-American to be poor. The big thing was to be, as Willy Loman said, "well liked," and the favorable image became institutionalized. Corporations cleaned themselves up with public relations, air conditioning and plush carpets, hired "educated" managers in gray flannel suits, bought paintings and talked about "social responsibility." Enlightened self-interest. The higher recesses, not only in the corporations and the banks but in foundations, universities, the State Department and the general establishment, remained as WASP as ever, but it was the clean, new WASP, not that rambunctious, hard-driving pioneer who had started it. Whatever romantic streak that old American had in him had to go. Guys like that were out of date, maybe even a little dangerous, and so we gave the new men personality tests to establish their acceptability, and interviewed their wives to make certain they wouldn't contaminate the country club and the company picnic. Dale Carnegie went in for Andrew.

The era of sanitation: off to the suburbs where politics were "clean," where the schools were shiny and where the ethnic mix was homogeneous. Mow that lawn, clean that yard, get a little nervous and join the PTA. At the core of it was a heap of sentimentality, born not only of depression dreams but of an older mystique about clean land and dirty cities. People who were later to engage in nostalgic rituals about the proletarian days of the thirties, when there was a real cause, bought themselves ranch wagons, FHA mortgages, ticky-tacky homes and, along with them, a piece of the country, sixty feet wide and one hundred twenty feet deep. It was the big shortcut—no dirt between here and that dream, no foreigners, no spades, no poor people. If we couldn't make the whole country into a WASP nirvana where no one talked funny or got too pushy or wore peculiar clothes, we could segregate efficiently enough to enable the dreamers to live unmolested and even to think of themselves in their new neighborhoods as "pioneers." The children of the ethnic immigrants joined the crowd, adopted the proper style and manners and often became indistinguishable. "The war," wrote Andrew Hacker, "saw the end not only of ethnic humor but of many of the characteristics which once gave credence to the jokes. People who in 1941 were regarded as Kikes or Micks or Wops had by 1946 become simply Americans. That half decade did a work of assimilation that would otherwise have taken at least two generations." The price of joining up was often fearful: you checked your yarmulke, your garlic and your rosary at the door, learned not to assert yourself, and tried to drown in the euphoria of tolerance and nondiscrimination. The melting pot, as Will Herberg pointed out in the fifties, was nothing of the kind; it was a cover for a process in which "all ingredients

have been transformed to an idealized 'Anglo-Saxon' model."
But even then it often failed: after they had "moved" economically—up the great American ladder of opportunity—they
ended in suburbs that were almost as segregated, socially and
ethnically, as the neighborhoods they had left. On Long Island there are three Rockville Centres, one Protestant, one
Catholic, one Jewish; Scituate, south of Boston, is full of Irishmen, and Fort Lee, New Jersey, is Italian; Bronxville, Winnetka and Wellesley are as WASP as ever, and New Rochelle,
like Great Neck, is bar mitzvah country. When the Penn Central commuter train gets to Bronxville you know who is going
to get off and who will stay on to Tuckahoe and Crestwood.
"Men may change their clothes, their politics, their wives,
their religions, their philosophies, to a greater or lesser extent,"
wrote Horace Kallen years ago. "They cannot change their
grandfathers." While we talked about the marvels of acculturation, the primary social groups—family, church, club,
even occupation and union—often remained distinct. Neutrality was Anglo-Saxon. The establishment, moreover, from the
Council on Foreign Relations and the Ford Foundation to the
corporations and the banks, remained almost totally WASP
both in style and in personnel. No room for screamers, but
how we love the Blessings of Western Civilization. The occasional Jew or Irishman who sat on the board of directors not
only discovered that he lacked influence (and that the whole
outfit was composed more of committeemen than of tycoons)
but that he had already resigned his affiliation with his old
group: he wasn't any longer one of *our crowd*, but he wasn't
one of *them* either.

The ironies of that kind of assimilation reached wondrous
levels. For a decade after the end of the war we marveled at
ourselves, partly in admiration, partly in self-contempt: *The
Organization Man; The Man in the Gray Flannel Suit; The*

Crack in the Picture Window; Executive Suite; Marjorie Morningstar, who became, near as I can tell, the Jewish Mrs. Robinson. People sat in split-level houses with two-car garages writing attacks on the shabbiness of suburban life; plush preachers peddled the panaceas of positive thinking; while a thousand shrinks, at thirty dollars an hour, taught people the marvels of psychological efficiency, which meant repression. As the colleges opened up, thousands of Jewish kids (plus a small but growing number of Italians, Poles and Greeks) trooped off to the Ivy League and pretended they were WASPs. Tolerance itself, at first grudging, and then more re-laxed, was the most powerful invitation to transform: if they didn't notice you were Jewish, or behaved as if it didn't mat-ter, the least you could do was to act as if it didn't matter to you either. Moreover, you took steps to clean yourself up, to change your speech, to stop talking the language of the streets. In Astoria or Brooklyn, if you disagreed with someone you said "Bullshit." At Amherst or Harvard, or even at Michigan, you began your demurrer with "Yes, but." People learned to extol the virtues of impartial selection and "objective stand-ards," to cram for tests, even though the standards were set by WASPs whose understanding of "Western civilization," than which there was nothing greater, rarely included much that wasn't either Anglo-Saxon or French, and nothing at all that was black or Spanish or Jewish. The alternative was to be judged on "personality" by a guy in a blue blazer and white bucks, and that, we all knew, was worse. But what people, in college and out, learned best was the marvels of organization life and, with them, that greatest of WASP copouts: "I know they're not taking Jews [or Negroes], but I'm going to join and then work to reform the place from the inside."

In the democratic mythology of the fifties—the age of Eisenhower, Norman Vincent Peale and Madison Avenue—

ethnic tolerance, "objective criteria" and something called "the demands of a technological society" got all mixed up together. Machines and organizations were supposed to be color blind; good engineers or computer programmers were in demand regardless of background; objective tests were machine-scored; fair employment practices were not only required by law but imposed by the inexorable demands of the machine. And yet, somehow, it remained a WASP machine.

The new ethic of the postwar organization was clearly articulated in Herman Wouk's best-selling novel *The Caine Mutiny* (1951). But the book, which drew raves from most of the critics, was more than a defense of the organization; it also suggested the ethnic assumptions on which the machine had to operate. Wouk's spokesman in the novel, Barney Greenwald, is a Jewish lawyer and Navy pilot who is called on to defend the ship's mutineers in a court martial, a task he can accomplish only by demonstrating that Captain Queeg—Old Yellow-stain—from whom the mutineers had wrested command, really might have been crazy and was on the way to destroying the *Caine* as it steamed through a typhoon. Wouk obviously regarded the Navy as a symbol of the nation; its mixture of "new Poles and Italians and Jews, as well as the older stock" was going to "make the greatest Navy the world has ever seen." Here was the melting pot come back to life in an organization with certain special characteristics. At the end of the novel, after Greenwald has successfully destroyed Queeg on the witness stand, he turns, half drunk, on the officers he has defended and dresses them down. The Jew tells off the WASPs; he makes a point of his Jewishness. He only took on this task, he says, because the prime defendant, Lieutenant Maryk, was an innocent who had been implicated in the mutiny by a gutless intellectual named Keefer, and he realized that it was really Keefer who should have been on trial. As for

Queeg and the other career officers of the Navy . . . they were the men who had been protecting the country from the Nazis while softer people were still sleeping in their beds: "Old Yellowstain . . . was standing guard on this fat, dumb, happy country of ours . . . When all hell broke loose and the Germans started running out of soap and figured, well, it's time to come over and melt down old Mrs. Greenwald— who's gonna stop them? . . . Who was keeping Mama out of the soap dish? Captain Queeg."

Despite the acquittal, says Greenwald, getting drunker, Maryk's ambitions for a Navy career are ruined; he was the man who relieved Queeg, and was therefore the leader of the mutiny, the *Caine* episode will stain his record, and he will have to go back to the fishing business in California where he came from. No chance for the sanitary life in the organization now, only the prospects of a honky handling fish.

Has Barney Greenwald become Theodore Roosevelt, berating gutless intellectuals on behalf of a strong Navy and the robust life? Was the Navy a model not only of the organization, but also for the nation's opportunities to assimilate? Partly both. But this was also an opportunity for a Jew to tell off WASPs, to charge them with the only indictment that would stick: that they would have to learn the new style, that they were, in other words, not good enough WASPs. They tricked Maryk out of his opportunities in the organization, and they nearly allowed Hitler to make soap out of his mother. No mention that Queeg's Navy, and even the Navy of 1951, was segregated and anti-Semitic (or that Wouk's own mess boys say "Yassuh" while all others answer "Aye aye"); if the system was open and intelligent and equitable, what would have kept Maryk, who was a good officer, from his career, or allowed Queeg, paranoid as he was, to retain command? Barney Greenwald was pleading for the privileges of his second-class citizenship; he was not insisting on his individuality or his Jewishness within the system. Only Hitler and the Nazis seemed to make that significant; at any rate, it was, by his own confession, more important to them than to him. All Barney wanted for himself was the safety and prerogatives of asylum; all he wanted of *them* was the organizational loyalty and discipline that would provide it. And while he was pretending to chew them out, he was telling them how important they were, how much he needed them. He was kissing their ass.

But he, the voice of the novel, is not merely that of a costume Jew, even though Wouk is Jewish. Greenwald was necessary because, presumably, he had a special commitment to this war, because only his mother was a candidate for the soap dish. The goys, we are told, had an immunity that Barney and, perhaps for other reasons, Maryk did not share. To have made Greenwald into a WASP would have risked some unwanted yuks in the back row of the best-seller list; a WASP saying all that (even without the soap and the mother) would have sounded like a pompous ass or, worse, like a Nazi. Barney is plausible only because he is impotent. Still, he is obviously supposed to be talking like—or for—someone else, not merely the standard org man but the new-model "American" who will lead us all under the banners of cleanliness, conformity and security. He is, in other words, a hired mouthpiece announcing the new ethic, talking not for the Jews, and certainly not for individual freedom, but for what a Jewish novelist (or a Jewish intellectual trying to make it in their world) *imagines* they would like him to say. The hyphenate's plea to the WASP is to maintain the system, to abandon his individualism as destructive, and to permit corporate standards, however imperfect, to operate. In getting ahead within those standards he will gladly give up his ethnic identity; that has meaning only to Nazis.

What was left, after all that, was the man of caution. One of the major attributes of the old idiom was its self-confidence in its own Americanism. In following the ethic of the small town, in trying to make it, the old WASP was operating in a system designed by his people, operated by his people, and responsive to his people. He wasn't trying to stand on someone else's ground or beat someone else's game. But what are the possibilities in a nation that is urban (or suburban), in which the majority has (presumably) already made it, and where size and technology are rendering much of the system impersonal and unresponsive? It is no longer possible for anyone to control the country (or the world) as we once believed we could. When Truman fired MacArthur and we negotiated an armistice at Panmunjom, America made an "un-American" settlement—conditional peace; the concern was not victory but to keep some crazy bastard from pushing the button. Moreover, with the exception of the balanced ticket—in politics or employment—we have no urban ethic. Men whose fathers knew that they controlled their destiny, that history was somehow manageable on their terms, and that the nation was their special possession—was run, that is, by their kind—were forced to negotiate, compromise and seek tentative solutions. "This took courage, this took prudence, this took stoutheartedness," thinks Arthur Winner, Jr., the super-WASP hero of James Gould Cozzens' turgid Eisenhower-era novel *By Love Possessed*, one of the great successes, critically and financially, of the late fifties. Winner has just covered up, to his and Cozzens' satisfaction, some $200,000 worth of legerdemain perpetrated by one of his partners. (The partner, we learn at the same time, has known all along that Winner was having an affair with the partner's wife. Neither will say anything about the other's transgression, and they will remain friends.)

He travailed, he was heavy laden. The weight was terrible; yet there was no way to put it off. And so, not knowing how far it would have to be carried, not knowing how long, burdened so, he must daily, hourly affect to be unburdened. . . . Patient, Julius said: *In this life we cannot have everything for ourselves we might like to have.* . . . Yes; life which has so unfairly served so many others, at last unfairly serves me. . . . Have I, or have I not, been shown a dozen times those forms of defeat which are the kinds of victory obtainable in life? Givings-up—my good opinion of myself; must I waive that? Compromises —the least little bit of crook? Assents to the second best, to the practical, the possible? . . . Victory is not in reaching certainties or solving mysteries; victory is making do with uncertainties, in supporting mysteries. Yes, Arthur Winner thought, I must be reasonable.

The new WASP was the reasonable man, so enervated that becoming an accessory to embezzlement seemed like mortal sin and required discussion in Biblical cadences. *"In this life we cannot have everything for ourselves we might like to have."* The last stand of the Puritan. Only a man or a class of men who believed that they had been the proprietors of fate could move from a little juggling of the company books to that sort of banality without repressed laughter, either on their own part or on the part of the reviewers who, in that age of caution and compromise, ate it up.

The great attempt of the sixties to reproduce the romance of the age of discovery—the space program—turned into a national worship service for the machine. From Lindbergh (or Columbus) to NASA, from Jack Armstrong to Neil Armstrong, from the man who was still a conqueror trusting his own bets and his own skills, and therefore an underdog (no dry runs, no simulators, no mission control) to the org man, programmed and computerized to the last $24-billion step and the last televised statement, betting his life on the devotion and competence of anonymous technicians: courageous, yes, underdog never. The prudent hero. A symbol of modern man, to be sure (what if the trains stop or the electricity fails?), but also a sign of the decline of the great WASP virtues: self-reliance, initiative, irreverence. Lindbergh was free enterprise; Apollo was the work of a crowd. No ape could have flown the *Spirit of St. Louis* from New York to Paris. But we could have sent an ape to the moon. Or a robot. When it was all over, we couldn't tell one astronaut from another (excepting maybe John Glenn), or even remember who went on what trip. They all sounded like Captain Holbrook in United 491 telling you that you were now flying over Lake Erie (or was that Captain Edwards in Eastern 257 over Wilmington?): Armstrong, Aldrin, Cooper, Conrad, Borman, Lovell, Grissom, Shepard . . . Where were Capoletti and Waszelewski? Where was Barney Greenwald? Was it possible to conceive of NASA sending a Negro, a Jew or a woman? Muhammad Ali, maybe? Joe Namath? Norman Mailer (who wanted to go)? Can one conceive of an astronaut who does not fit absolutely congruously into the background, like Muzak in a supermarket or Spiro Agnew at a picnic of Legionnaires? Can one conceive of an astronaut's wife living in a Jewish section of the Bronx, or expressing opinions critical of the Vietnam War, or not taking the children to church on Sunday—or taking them some other day—or having a career of her own? Clearly space travel was not possible technologically except as a collective enterprise. But that is precisely the point. There was no longer a role for the "American" hero. Heroes are supposed to defy great odds alone, and now we were supposed to be all together.

The new WASP: stiff upper lip, tight neck tendons, and a mushrooming ulcer, going through life pretending, with Arthur Winner, that he was unburdened. Courage, prudence. The style became pervasive. John McPhee, in his 1969 book *Levels of the Game*, describes a tennis match between the Negro Arthur Ashe (then the highest-ranking American player) and second-ranked Clark Graebner, the WASP son of a suburban Cleveland dentist. Graebner speaks:

I've never been a flashy stylist like Arthur. I'm a fundamentalist. Arthur is a bachelor. I am married and a conservative. I'm interested in business, in the market, in children's clothes. It affects the way you play the game. He's not a steady player. He's a wristy slapper. Sometimes he doesn't even know where the ball is going . . . I've never seen Arthur really discipline himself. He plays the game with the lackadaisical, haphazard mannerisms of a liberal. He's an underprivileged type who worked his way up. . . . There is something about him that is swashbuckling, loose. He plays the way he thinks. My style is playmaking—consistent percentage tennis—and his style is shot-making.

Ashe speaks:

There is not much variety in Clark's game. It is steady, accurate, and conservative. He makes few errors. He plays stiff, compact, Republican tennis.

The issue here is not racial—it isn't some deferred-gratification white man with a tight ass playing against a happy-go-lucky nigger. Ashe, clearly, had to grub a lot harder than Graebner to break into the big time or to become a player at all. If he now manages his game with aristocratic flair, and not with a bourgeois lack of grace, if he is a swashbuckling type, it is not only because he doesn't have all that security to protect, but because taking chances was once the American style. Ashe, in not playing percentages, has as much in common with the old-ethic WASP as with what Graebner calls "a liberal." Graebner, so distant psychologically from the nineteenth century world of making it, could never be expected to recognize the frontiersman or the wildcatter in black skin. But probably he wouldn't recognize him in a white skin either.

Arthur Winner's real crime was not in committing adultery or in being an accomplice after the fact in embezzlement. It was loss of confidence, which, given the mystique of his class, was selling your birthright for a little security. What had been expansive became conservative and restrictive, enterprise turned to management, ebullience to caution. There were, of course, a lot of Jews, Irishmen and Italians who had joined up—who believed, at one pole of their social ambivalence, that they had become fully "American"—and were trying to live, act and talk like WASPs. And yet, at another pole, the newly-made-it sons of immigrants still have their doubts; they still behave, even as Vice-President of the United States, as if someone else were running the country. No one had ever made them think they were in charge, that the country was their special possession, or that they are the preeminent Americans, and they still don't believe it. Whatever convictions they had about special responsibilities for the control of destiny did not stem so much from background and heritage as from the styles of the people they tried to resemble. They had not been born to manage history. For WASPs, who had owned the country, or thought they had, the loss had to be greater. There was more to feel insecure about, more reason to play percentages. They seemed to become men who were hanging on, living off their cultural capital but rarely willing or able to create more. One can almost define their contemporary domains by locating the people and institutions that are chronically on the defensive: university presidents and trustees; the large foundations; the corporations; the State Department. They grew great as initiators and entrepreneurs. They invented the country and its values, shaped the institutions and organizations, and tried to teach the newcomers—lest they become uncouth boors—how to join and behave. But when technology, depression and the uncertainties of the postwar world frightened and confused them, they drew the institutions around themselves, moved to the suburbs, and talked prudence. "The normal American of the 'pure-blooded' majority," Mencken once said, "goes to rest every night with an uneasy feeling that there is a burglar under the bed, and he gets up every morning with a sickening feeling that his underwear has been stolen."

2

THE RISE OF
THE UNCOUTH BOOR

I

It happens gradually, but you notice suddenly. A new crowd, new faces, new styles, a new sound: un-WASP, non-WASP, anti-WASP. The center has begun to disappear, and the action originates at the periphery. Jews and Negroes, Catholics and immigrants: Mailer and Roth, Malamud and Bellow; Ellison and Baldwin; Harold Cruse and John A. Williams; Edward Teller and Henry Kissinger; Hans Morgenthau and Wernher von Braun; Ralph Nader and Cesar Chavez; Bruno Bettelheim and Erik Erikson; John Rock and Jonas Salk; Daniel Berrigan and Philip Berrigan; Paul Goodman and Herbert Marcuse; Abbie Hoffman and Julius Hoffman; Eldridge Cleaver and Malcolm X and Martin Luther King. The 1969 Pulitzer Prize for nonfiction was divided between a Jew from Brooklyn (Mailer) and a French immigrant (René Dubos) and the prize for fiction awarded to an American Indian (Scott Momaday). The targets of the big taunt of the late sixties were Mrs. Robinson, the uptight suburban housewife of *The Graduate* and the Simon and Garfunkel song, and the Middle American square who played golf every weekend, voted Republican and regarded his children as the carriers of his unfulfilled corporate ambitions. Goodbye, Mrs. Robinson; goodbye, Arthur Winner, Jr.; goodbye, *Saturday Evening Post*. *Reader's Digest* is still there, and *Foreign Affairs* and *Playboy*, all WASPy as ever, but *Time*, Henry Luce's baby, is edited by a Jewish refugee from Hitler, and the most respectable postwar journals of social thought and criticism, *Commentary*, *The New York Review* and *The New American Review*, are edited not by the Howells, the Allens and the Canbys, but by Podhoretz, Silvers, Epstein and Solotaroff; *Ramparts*, which revitalized the political muckraking invented by Lincoln Steffens, Ray Stannard Baker and Ida Tarbell, was launched as a Catholic magazine; William F. Buckley, a Catholic, is undoubtedly the most vocal right-winger in America, and *The National Catholic Reporter* has become the liveliest religious-political weekly in the country. But beyond people, or even readership, beyond the fact that publishing and editing and writing have become disproportionately the provinces of what used to be called minorities, is the simple fact that the style, ideas, traumas, perplexities and passions of American culture tend increasingly to reflect non-WASP backgrounds and interests, and that the unifying capabilities of the WASP idiom have plunged into precipitous decline. The new writers, the film makers, the musicians don't want to join up, and neither, apparently, do the younger members of their audience. The cultural issues of the late 1960s were not only ethnic or pluralistic, but also disintegrative—alienation, doing your own thing, dropping out, Italian is beautiful, the white Negro—and almost any sort of material was (and is) acceptable to the new audiences of the young as long as it is distinguishable from the WASP mainstream: the life of the black ghetto, rock music, long hair and pot, Hindu gurus and Zen philosophers,

Cuban guerrillas and Catholic radicals, black hustlers and Jewish anarchists. The chief villainy is to be uptight, and who, finally, was most uptight of all? The 1960s had been the decade of gaps—missile gaps, generation gaps, credibility gaps—when we became, in many respects, a nation of outsiders, a country in which the mainstream, however mythic, lost its compelling attraction. When the New Frontier and the Great Society failed, not only as programs but as rituals, so, at least for the moment, and perhaps forever, did the possibility of "assimilation" and traditional, World War II–vintage Americanism.

In a generation all the vectors changed, defenders became critics, the confident became the disenchanted, and the upstarts talked like traditionalists. If there were any camps of cultural contention, they consisted of the declining old establishment of politics, the arts and general culture; the new men of position, second- or third-generation people from the Bronx or Roxbury who had tried (with varying degrees of success) to trade their ethnicity for the manners and emoluments of privilege; and the uncouth boors—blacks, students, Chicanos and culture freaks of varying descriptions—who were, to say the least, reluctant about the terms on which they were supposed to make it and often unwilling to join at all. As the old WASPs began to lose confidence, the new men—politicians like Agnew and professors like Sidney Hook and Irving Kristol and Nathan Glazer—became the defenders of tradition; they talked about history and discipline and the established order of things, attacking both the WASP establishment (for selling out) and the unshaven slobs with their guitars, their drugs and their gutter language (for their refusal to buy). Where once John D. Rockefeller announced that it was God who had given him his money, the Spiros and the

Irvings regarded their own success as a vindication of the system—imagine, me a *professor!* —with hardly a thought about the price they paid or about the thousands of other ethnics who did not become professors or Vice-President or anything else. Nor did they seem to understand that, in an impersonal, technological age which had outrun the WASP ethic, they, like the old establishment, were peripheral people in a land which seemed to lack a cultural focus, where the center had been abandoned, and where nothing employing the old ethic of Americanism seemed to be capable of controlling the self-actuating power of large institutions. It may well be that the old establishment understands far better than the *arriviste* defenders of stability how ineffective elites are in a culture where size and complexity and the destruction of resources make the old American ethic not only irrelevant but dangerous, and where even the history which they wrote and promoted no longer seems applicable. At any rate, the prime defenders of tradition—the people who now profess Eliot and Pound and the importance of standards and due process and electoral politics and good manners—are, as often as not, new men, first-generation ethnic intellectuals who have moved into the universities or politics or cultural journalism in the last generation. They now seem to be holding the trenches which have been abandoned by the WASP elite; they, more than anyone, are battling against the upstart boors in the universities, are fighting the freaks, and seem to be most threatened by a counterculture directed at the positions they have so recently captured. And they are the ones who still act as if they believed that those positions are worth holding, as if the degrees, the tenure, the editorships and the grants for which they fought so hard still represented power and prestige and influence.

Some of what happened was to be expected—or, rather, could have been expected under the conventional scenario of assimilation. The immigrants, it could be said, had fifty years to learn English and do whatever it takes to write books or make movies. Almost half a century ago Mencken took the Anglo-Saxon into the arena and declared that his day was over:

Of the Americans who have come into notice during the past fifty years as poets, as novelists, as critics, as painters, as sculptors and in the minor arts, less than half bear Anglo-Saxon names, and in this minority there are few of Anglo-Saxon blood. So in the sciences. So in the higher reaches of engineering and technology. So in philosophy and its branches. So even in industry and agriculture. . . .

The descendants of the later immigrants tend generally to move upward; the descendants of the first settlers, I believe, tend plainly to move downward, mentally, spiritually, even physically. Civilization is at its lowest mark in the United States precisely in those areas where the Anglo-Saxon still presumes to rule. He runs the whole South— and in the whole South there are not as many first-rate men as in many a single city of the mongrel North.

Mencken was more accurate as a prophet than as an analyst. The assessment was premature. What was recognized as "American" in 1924 tended to be WASP. The doors were still locked, except perhaps in the "lower" art forms like film and pop music. And even there there might be problems: In writing *Porgy and Bess*, someone has said, George Gershwin, a Jew, disguised himself as a WASP to produce a "Negro" folk opera. Partly facetious, partly accurate. Could a Jew—as a Jew—have written anything folksy about blacks without looking like a vaudeville comedian reciting the story of Br'er Rabbit in Yiddish? Perhaps he was no less qualified than anyone else, but whose version of the Negro spirit (or whatever one wants to call it) could he accept? In that scene there were only white and black men, and who were the white men?

And yet, at another level, Mencken may have been right. Perhaps there had always been more theft and plunder than even the thieves knew and the historians suspected. What was original in American music, for example, had always come from exploited people—from mountaineers or blacks. It was black men, moreover, who had taught their white employers the few aristocratic graces they knew: headwaiters who decided who was important enough to sit where at dinner, maids and butlers who knew how to prepare the special dishes, the canapés, the bread and the ices, and who passed the art from one employer (or owner) to the next. Perhaps if we start looking we will find a whole stock of neglected literature and art, not merely black but Indian, Mexican-American, Chinese —songs and stories, trampled rituals and forgotten craft. We are just now breaking through the locked doors of our ethnic chauvinism to learn what's behind, are just beginning to discover in the feats of which we were once so proud as a nation heavy tinges of racism and genocide—empires built up, as Mencken said, "by swindling and butchering unarmed savages, and after that by robbing weak and friendless nations" without exposing "the folks at home to any serious danger of reprisal." Every black musician of the twenties and thirties knew that white performers were not only using his material but removing its vitality and *jazz*, its shit and humor and reproach, in the process. Tin Pan Alley thrived on stolen goods.

But the cultural outburst that followed World War II (or that we have since discovered) is more attributable to enervation than to assimilation. The juice simply went out of the old style. Loss of confidence compounded by loss of place. A double displacement. The old WASP culture had been rooted in regions, each of them sufficiently distinct for "character," yet each also acceptably American: Salem and Boston and Concord; Zenith and Winesburg and Main Street; Yoknapatawpha County; the Mississippi; Texas; California. The sense of place produced people with special accents, fashions and biases—personalities that they carried around like parasols and walking sticks; it produced cultures and values from which people could deviate; and it produced the sort of security that permitted them to be eccentric and crazy. It created vitality. For more than a century the stock characters of American humor, and later of serious literature, were variations of regional types—the Yankee and the ringtailed screamer of the frontier, or WASP versions (to which the subjects acceded) of stock Negroes, Irishmen and Jews. Hester Prynne, Captain Ahab, Huck Finn, Horace Benbow, Temple Drake. Now much of that material is gone. The black ghetto and the migrant camp are still there, and so is the memory, if not the fact of Irish Boston, of Brooklyn, of rural Mississippi and small-town Texas. You can still meet Southerners who carry their origins with them like a Faulknerian security blanket; or small-town products of the Middle West not certain whether they stepped out of a Norman Rockwell painting or fled from the life of George Babbitt. But even those sensibilities are fading. Most of the places that fostered a secure dual citizenship—American and regional—are gone, and so is the *sense* of place. What is there in a bedroom suburb? What is the inner sense of Bronxville or Winnetka or Howard Johnson's?

Three things were lost simultaneously: the security and vitality of a distinctive place: the WASP's unquestioning belief in himself as the preeminent American; and the conviction that Americans had a special destiny, a mission to reform the world or, at the very least, to keep its evils from contaminating them. If anyone proclaims these things now it is more

likely to be a Jewish sociologist at Columbia or an Irish politician from South Boston than a member of the old WASP
elite. The black revolt of the sixties—followed, or accompanied, by outbursts from other sectors—struck against a declining cultural self-confidence that was almost crippling. White
men—and Western civilization—we learned, represented only
a fraction of the globe, and if Latin Americans were still prone
to palace coups and banana revolutions, and if Africans were
no more immune to mutual genocide than Europeans, it was
still necessary to treat the new nations with respect and to pretend, even against long-cherished habit and conviction, that
the Third World had a vital culture all its own. Given the
existence of that Third World, given Castro and Che and
Frantz Fanon, and given the history of civil rights in America
since World War II, it is hardly surprising that there should
be a black demand for African studies, black history and
"open" admission to colleges and universities. What is significant, if not surprising, is the willingness of the great defenders
of Western culture—from Harvard and the Ford Foundation
through P.S. 10 and the local church—to accede, and to admit
that the old standards (color blind, objective and thoroughly
established in academic practice) are inadequate, and to doubt
the principle of "Western," white superiority. Even though
the concessions are often more rhetorical than real, even
though the barons of Runnymede get more time than the
kings of the Nile, the case is being defended with little assurance and with considerable doubt about "relevance." Core
curricula are going down the drain, not only in the name of
flexibility and individual choice, but through the inability of
academic departments to feel confident about the culture and
presumptions from which they grew. Suddenly it becomes
fashionable, if not common, for white teachers of English and

for Jewish critics of fiction to declare themselves incompetent to discuss black literature. Catherine Stimpson, a teacher at Barnard:

> The best questions for white readers to ask themselves about black literature are those of fact. They must call a moratorium on their normative judgments. Biases, like rodents on the ropes between ship and pier, run up and down their statements about value. They should also end all but the most tentative kind of descriptive criticism. . . . The white reader who assumes that he can usefully say whether a black writer is "good" or "bad" is likely to be enough out of touch with present realities to make his analysis of that writer suspect.
>
> American speech fails to describe our racial agony. Not only is speech untrustworthy because people and institutions have misused it in the past, but its grammatical structure is inadequate. We lack, for example, a pronoun to portray our false collectivity, a *we* to summarize a phony *we-ness*. No vocabulary exists to describe black literature.
>
> Nor do we possess a body of theory, one which is neither adventitious nor malign, that might give order to its contradictions and subtleties and flux. The neglected black critics provided only the beginnings. Black artists are now carrying on with the job. Only blacks can create such a theory.

The issue is not right or wrong but that people trained in literature and criticism, people who were supposed to know that aesthetic standards were applicable to any work, are giving up in the name of cultural pluralism; if they still continue to practice their trade at the old stand, many of them do so with a wary eye cast for signs of revolt and behind an incessant flow of memos and speeches asking for more choice, diversity and "relevance."

Simultaneously, the media help to create and sustain self-conscious new minorities: students, for example, and women, and blue-collar workers. What kids or black people do in one town is now immediately communicated to others. Normalcy doesn't make good television, but happenings do, and so performance in front of the cameras becomes a form of civic action within a "community" that could not have existed before electronics. The media have an obvious tendency to homogenize isolated pockets of minority culture; the synthetic country music broadcast from Nashville and Cincinnati, for example, tends to depreciate the art of the banjo and the dulcimer in the hollows of Appalachia, and the flat Midwestern accents of the network announcers gradually have their impact on the cadences of Alabama and Maine. But there is also an opposite tendency to unify and nationalize, to link Watts with Harlem, Columbia with Berkeley, and the East Village with Hashbury. And so, while "Americans" become increasingly standardized, certain minorities grow more visible, prompting Spiro Agnew to lust for the blood of the networks: too many freaks, too many protests, too much long hair, and not enough plain folks. Who are those TV guys anyway, the Washington–New York Axis? (In Minneapolis, a right-wing priest named Daniel Lyons slips the secret to a meeting of American Legionnaires: They're mostly Jews.) TV is undoubtedly directed at the Middle American audience, and it remains one of the great outposts of the WASP "mainstream," but it often finds its material in minorities and, in so doing, helps—despite all distortions and villification—to nurture them. It is almost as if the screen emits two simultaneous signals, one official and one culturally subliminal. Everyone sees the same thing, but not everyone gets the same message: the underground is cheering for the villain. When William Kunstler, the lawyer for the Chicago Seven and other bad people, appears on David Susskind's talk show, Kunstler wins with the kids, Susskind wins with the squares; and when Abbie Hoffman, the Yippie chieftain, tells a stuffy moderator on an educational network to shut up, old-style liberals are horrified, but the performance scores points for the cultural revolution. The very style that is supposed to repulse stout burghers is transmitted to those who want to learn. There is no telling how much TV teaches; but often it teaches precisely the things that it is said to be officially against.

The vacuum left by the old arbiters of the single standard—Establishment intellectuals, literary critics, English professors, museum directors and all the rest—has produced a sort of cultural prison break. And not only among ethnics, blacks or Indians, or among kids, but among a lot of others, including WASPs of all descriptions, who behave as if they have been waiting for this freedom all their lives. That a lot of the resulting activity is bad (and who, these days, can get away with saying that?) and that a lot will be transitory is hardly surprising. In a decade hundreds of thousands of "creative" people have proclaimed themselves artists and poets, a million amateurs have entered the culture biz, and God knows how many gurus, cultists, swamis and T-group trainers hung out their shingles. Look at any issue of the *Village Voice* or the *Berkeley Barb* and you feel as if you're in a carnival where the straightest people are rock musicians. No one can expect most of them to be good, or even to be serious. The wildcatters are working new territory, and a lot are going to go bust. But for the moment they're thriving: the Stones and the Beatles, the groups and the groupies, Polish Power and black studies, liberation schools and free universities, Norman Mailer's ego and Alexander Portnoy's mother, *The Graduate* and *Alice's Restaurant* and *Easy Rider*, the Woodstock Nation and the friends of the Panthers, rebellious nuns and protesting priests, *Rat* and *Screw* and a few hundred other underground papers, mixed-media shows and the Living Theater, bookstores of the occult, tarot cards and freaks and hipsters, miniskirts and maxicoats, beads and joss sticks, the *Politics of Experience* and the *I Ching*—all coexisting (barely, uneasily) with Lyndon Johnson's cornpone, Nixon's kitsch, Norman Vincent Peale's sermons, *I Love Lucy*, *Reader's Digest* and Apollo XII. If the 1960s produced the beginning of any sort of renaissance, its characteristic instruments are the hand-held movie camera, the electric guitar and the mimeograph machine, and if its efforts survive in nothing else, they will undoubtedly be remembered by the greatest outpouring of poster art in all history: peace doves and protest proclamations, the face of John Lennon, the bodies of John and Yoko, the pregnant Girl Scout over the motto "Be Prepared," the pregnant black woman over the slogan "Nixon's the One," and the copulating rhinoceroses with the injunction "Make Love Not War."

Until recently, when encounter groups, public therapy and other psychic ceremonies became fashionable, reason had been more or less successfully keeping passion in the locked closets of the official culture. And WASPs were the most reasonable people of all. There were—and are—obvious advantages in that; the Bomb, if nothing else, made cool reason an imperative against annihilation. Most people, moreover, are likely to prefer dispassionate men for airplane pilots, surgeons and judges. We have probably survived the last twenty-five years precisely because we kept hot men from taking charge. But their style didn't do much for cultural enrichment. Now everything that a graying nervous civilization kept jammed in those closets is coming out, whether it deserves to or not: sex in all forms, feelings, emotions, self-revelation, and forms of religion and ritual long condemned as superstition. "Honesty" replaces stoicism, and "love," however understood, overwhelms "work." It may well be that the kids are mining McLuhan's nonlinear culture, that print and cool reason (and old WASP idioms) will go under together. What is certain is that the old media—books, newspapers, magazines—no longer monopolize cultural articulation, and that people who work the new territories have moved a long way from the old mainstream.

WASPs, as WASPs, have been crippled by their own sanity, by their passion against the unreasonable. Too level-headed. Having confused their particular social order with the Immutability of Things (and with their own welfare), they have defaulted on their birthright of cussedness and irreverence. WASPs are willing to be "sick"—meaning that they can have their neuroses and their "reason" too—but never crazy. People who are crazy are almost invariably something else. Craziness—real craziness and its various marginal forms of unrestrained self-assertion—is the province of blacks and freaks and hippies. We no longer even have our Everett Dirksens, our John L. Lewises or our Sewell Averys. Which is why even WASP crimes these days are usually dull (price fixing, antitrust capers, tax fraud) and why we are so fascinated by Jimmy Hoffa, Roy Cohn, the Black Panthers, and the Mafia—would have to invent the Mafia were we ever to suspect (as has Daniel Bell among others) that it doesn't really exist. The Italian-American Civil Rights League is pursuing a futile course in trying to eradicate the words Mafia and Cosa Nostra from the newspapers and the documents of the Justice Department. We need the Mafia because WASPs are boring the country to death. The heirs of Jesse James and Clyde Barrow operate by a different style, their names are Colombo, Luchesi and Boiardo, but we cannot do without them.

II

In the beginning was the word. And the word was the Bomb. It became like a myth of creation, an apocalyptic distortion of a Promethean legend. Whatever moral assurance existed in the first years of the war about the justice of the Cause, whatever the certainties of killing Nazi racists and Jap murderers, they began, for many people, to evaporate in that flash at Hiroshima. It was not merely that the Bomb was used or might be used for genocide and global annihilation, but that it came for some people to symbolize all other technological horrors, economic and racial exploitation, the systematic engineering of death, and, finally, even the concentration camps of the totalitarian state. Even if it did not create alienation and disaffection, it gave them meaning, gave them a symbol and a language that most people could understand. The concentration camps had already shattered the racial confidence of "the West," but we, the English-speaking peoples (remember?), were, by virtue of higher ideals and institutions, above such Teutonic acts. With the Bomb we joined the world. It reduced us to a common mortality, made subjects of citizens, and placed us under the guidance of Dr. Strangelove. Within a decade after our "victory" we were taking advice from Teutonic rocket engineers, beetle-browed Hungarians and Central European tank thinkers adept at realpolitik and wise in the ways of Metternich. If the WASP establishment was father and master, the new generation of critics and students could now observe him, like a profligate in a Gothic novel, consorting behind the house with greasy foreigners and upstart Jews who talked about the balance of terror, second-strike capabilities, and megadeaths. All that bragging, all that talk about how he could lick anybody, all that posturing, and there he was, like any village bum, making deals with the speculators and the agents of the railroad. Moreover, he hadn't beaten the Japs fair and square, had, instead, roasted them to death indiscriminately, men, women and children, had violated their very genes, and now threatened, in his blundering stupidity, to poison the whole earth. Sometimes he thumped his chest in Puritan self-righteousness, talked about massive retaliation, about how he could knock the shit out of everybody if provoked, but the old confidence was gone. When it didn't sound absolutely insane it was pitiful. It was hard to believe any more that he was all that wise and strong, and a lot easier to believe that he had been something of a phony from the start. The old man had been found out, once and for all, and, like all such findings-out, this one slowly made it plain that it was time for the rest of us—kids and blacks, immigrants and colonial subjects of all sorts—to begin the process, however painful, of growing up and taking over.

The people who had passed puberty at the time of the bomb [wrote Jeff Nuttall in *Bomb Culture*] found that they were incapable of conceiving of life *without* a future. Their patterns of habit had formed— the steady job, the pension, the mortgage, the insurance policy, personal savings, support and respect for the protection of the law, all the paraphernalia of constructive, secure family life. They had learned their game and it was the only game they knew. To acknowledge the truth of their predicament would be to abandon the whole pattern of their lives. They would therefore have to pretend, much as they had pretended about ecstasy not being there, and they proceeded to pretend as cheerfully as ever. In any case, to look the danger in the eye might wreck the chances of that ultimate total security their deepest selves had contrived, death by H-bomb.

The people who had not yet reached puberty at the time of the bomb were incapable of conceiving of life *with* a future. They might not have had any direct preoccupation with the bomb. This depended largely on their sophistication. But they never knew a sense of future. The hipster was there. Charlie Parker's records began to be distributed. The hipster became increasingly present in popular music, and young people moved in his direction. They pretended too, but they did not enter the pretense at all cheerfully. In fact they entered the pretense reluctantly, in pain and confusion, in hostility which they increasingly showed. Dad was a liar. He lied about the war and he lied about sex. He lied about the bomb and he lied about the future. . . . The so-called "generation gap" started then and has been increasing ever since.

The war purged the guilt of the depression; people who had blamed themselves for the economic failures of the system, who had prayed for new chances, a new start, seemed miraculously to have been saved and cleansed by the catharsis of combat—often the combat of others—and by the collective technology it produced. For the kids there was no such tribal memory, no economic terror, no catharsis, no miracle. Time began with technology; it began with plastics; it began with the Bomb. They did discover (some of them) that the adults were liars (some of them), that the noble professions of World War II were shattered by the horror of Hiroshima and Nagasaki and the likelihood of more to come, just as the older professions of that "higher" Western civilization had been fouled by Dachau and Auschwitz. "The fact of the Third Reich alone," said James Baldwin, "makes obsolete forever any question of Christian superiority, except in technological terms." The British lost their Empire and we all lost our confidence. In Great Britain, which is what Nuttall was primarily writing about, it was probably true that most of those who were capable of confronting the postwar disillusionment and emptiness were young people. In Alan Bennett's play *Forty Years On*, which was a major success in London in the late sixties, the final theme revolves around "the lie carved in stone."

81

Once we had a romantic and old-fashioned conception of honour, of patriotism, chivalry and duty. But it was a duty which didn't have much to do with justice, with social justice anyway. And in default of that justice and in pursuit of it, that was how the great words came to be cancelled out. The crowd has found the door into the secret garden. Now they will tear up the flowers by the roots, strip the borders and strew them with paper and broken bottles.

History was a lie, and it would be necessary either to trample on the great words or to try to write new ones. (There was something hugely ironic about the early-morning encounter between Richard Nixon and student protesters at the Lincoln Memorial in the week after the invasion of Cambodia in the spring of 1970: lost and confused men, rummaging in the attic of tradition, looking for something useful, and hardly recognizing each other in their efforts. What was Lincoln thinking?) America, in this case perhaps more fortunate than England, had resources other than its youth—or at least we imagined we had. In the years after the war, a lot of people learned, if they didn't know already, that there was a lie carved in stone; by virtue of their status as social and ethnic outsiders—as imperfect Americans—they were able to plead not guilty to the charges of hypocrisy and brutality. (Which is not to say that black people, or Indians or Chicanos, were innocent of violence or incapable of perpetrating it; but they could plead innocent to the crimes of the nation.) As long as the official virtues, however hollow and unpracticed, were legitimized through the energy and vitality of those who professed them—as long, that is, as people believed that you could make it under the conditions of American life and remain personally *alive*—there was hope, but when the vitality ran out, the repressed energy of those who had never been allowed access to the secret garden (except as gardeners) had to assert itself. Norman Mailer in *The White Negro* (1957) hypothe-

sized the response to this "bleak scene" into the emergence of
the hipster,

the man who knows that if our collective condition is to live with
instant death by atomic war, relatively quick death by the State as
l'univers concentrationnaire, or with a slow death by conformity with
every creative and rebellious instinct stifled . . . if the fate of twentieth century man is to live with death from adolescence to premature
senescence, why then the only life-giving answer is to accept the terms
of death, to live with death as immediate danger, to divorce oneself
from society, to exist without roots, to set out on that uncharted journey into the rebellious imperatives of the self.

The source of Hip, Mailer wrote, is the Negro,

for he has been living on the margin between totalitarianism and
democracy for two centuries. . . . The bohemian and the juvenile
delinquent came face to face with the Negro, and the hipster was a
fact in American life. If marijuana was the wedding ring, the child
was the language of Hip, for its argot gave expression to abstract states
of feeling which all could share, at least all who were Hip. And in this
wedding of the white and the black it was the Negro who brought the
cultural dowry.

Any Negro who wishes to live must live with danger from his first
day, and no experience can ever be casual to him, no Negro can
saunter down a street with any real certainty that violence will not
visit him on his walk. The cameos of security for the average white:
mother and the home, a job and the family, are not even a mockery
to millions of Negroes; they are impossible. The Negro has the simplest
of alternatives: live a life of constant humility or ever-threatening
danger. In such a pass where paranoia is as vital to survival as blood,
the Negro had stayed alive and begun to grow by following the need
of his body where he could. Knowing in the cells of his existence that
life was war, nothing but war, the Negro (all exceptions admitted)
could rarely afford the sophisticated inhibitions of civilization, and so
he kept for his survival the art of the primitive, he lived in the enormous present, he subsisted for his Saturday night kicks, relinquishing
the pleasures of the mind for the more obligatory pleasures of the

body, and in his music he gave voice to the character and quality of his existence, to his rage and the infinite variations of joy, lust, languor, growl, cramp, pinch, scream and despair of his orgasm. For jazz is orgasm, it is the music of orgasm, good orgasm and bad, and so it spoke across a nation, it had the communication of art even where it was watered, perverted, corrupted, and almost killed, it spoke in no matter what laundered popular way of instantaneous existential states to which some whites could respond, it was indeed a communication by art because it said, "I feel this, and now you do too."

Mailer is half right. The man has to go to the boy for his balls, just as he used to go to Harlem for his drugs and a little uninhibited (as he thought) fun. He has, in other words, already accepted the terms that "American" culture imposed on his existence. Fucking is slumming. So he goes around compulsively in the company of prize fighters (Mailer), bullfighters (Hemingway) and hot little numbers to assert his machismo. He is—in this particular case—no longer just a Jewish boy from Brooklyn: he has now made it in the world of WASP (white?) emasculation and has been sufficiently acculturated to require a sexual recharge from blacks, or from his fantasy of what blacks are like. Which is not to suggest that Jews have no hangups (or to deny that they are the analyst's best clients), but only to say that the search for what Mailer calls the good orgasm seems, in his description, to have little to do with the tenacity of Jewish upbringing and family life, or with the demands of a Mrs. Portnoy who fears that her son might get a disease, and a lot in common with the fantasies of a deputy sheriff in Mississippi. That Mailer should regard the problems of depersonalization as anything but a matter for males is beyond the bounds of reasonable expectation. That he might recognize in the life of the Jew special frustrations and special strengths (even for the assertive, ego-tripping male) is inconceivable. The world screws men (white) because it keeps them from properly screwing women (black, white and other). The good orgasm. For men only. Mailer thinks he is Hemingway, and Hemingway thought he was Natty Bumppo.

Still, it is undeniable that much of the new energy and material of American culture now comes from black people and—for related reasons—from other minorities. The primary legacy of the American cataclysms that followed World War II was the discovery that we were no longer the special children of Providence, that we were not exempt from tragedy, mortality and despair, that we were capable of systematic violence (and subject to it) and that we were, therefore, going to be sharers in the general human condition. Minorities were better prepared for that condition than WASPs because they had never believed—or had not believed as fully—that they were completely "American," had always lived with some sense of limited possibilities, with some equivocation and without the illusion of historic and social omnipotence. Having been the tenants of American culture, they were better prepared to be the tenants of fate; at the same time, their position as outsiders gave them something in common with people outside America, and made them, in the gut if not the head, a little more cosmopolitan. Hemingway (among others) understood that existential condition, and kept saying it in his novels, but he was incapable of doing more than clenching his teeth, looking tough and hanging on. In the end, he couldn't even manage that. Death in the afternoon. Those of us who grew up in the thirties and forties relished *A Farewell to Arms* and *For Whom the Bell Tolls;* now many kids find Hemingway stupid, boring and vulgar. Humphrey Bogart is camp.

Whatever the resources of black people and minorities, they clearly extend beyond the qualities that Mailer's hipster found in the Negro. To some degree, in fact, they contradict them. "The American Negro," wrote Baldwin, "has the great advantage of having never believed that collection of myths to which white Americans cling: that their ancestors were all freedom-loving heroes, that they were born in the greatest country the world has ever seen, or that Americans are invincible in battle and wise in peace, that Americans have always dealt honorably with Mexicans and Indians and all other neighbors or inferiors, that American men are the world's most direct and virile, that American women are pure." The tendency of Negroes, said Baldwin, was "to dismiss white people as the slightly mad victims of their own brainwashing." The recurring theme of blackness—and often of other minorities—in relation to the new forces in our culture is the honesty of human experience.

Behind what we think of as the Russian menace [Baldwin again] lies what we do not wish to face, and what white Americans do not face when they regard a Negro: reality—the fact that life is tragic. Life is tragic simply because the earth turns and the sun inexorably rises and sets, and one day, for each of us, the sun will go down for the last, last time. . . . It seems to me that one ought to rejoice in the *fact* of death—ought to decide, indeed, to *earn* one's death by confronting with passion the conundrum of life. One is responsible to life: It is the small beacon in that terrifying darkness from which we come and to which we shall return. One must negotiate this passage as nobly as possible, for the sake of those who are coming after us. But white Americans do not believe in death, and this is why the darkness of my skin so intimidates them. . . . White Americans have supposed "Europe" and "civilization" to be synonymous—which they are not—and have been distrustful of other standards and other sources of vitality, especially those produced in America itself. . . . What it comes to is that if we, who can scarcely be considered a white nation, persist in thinking of ourselves as one, we condemn ourselves, with the truly white nations, to sterility and decay, whereas if we could accept ourselves *as we are*, we might bring new life to the Western achievements, and transform them.

The resources are not simply those for a personal foray into new possibilities, material to do, as Mailer says, "what one feels whenever and wherever it is possible," but the promises for a life in which suffering can be tolerated and love is possible. Quoting Baldwin again: "Love takes off the masks that we cannot live without and know we cannot live within. I use the word 'love' here not merely in the personal sense but as a state of being, or a state of grace—not in the infantile American sense of being made happy but in the tough and universal sense of quest and daring and growth." The white man, in short, cannot free himself by stealing something else from blacks; the price of his transformation is "the unconditional freedom of the Negro." Mailer writes as if the fact of sudden death had materialized only yesterday through the invention of atomic bombs and totalitarian states, and as if only Negroes (male) had been required to live a mortal life in this country. The choice: "One is Hip or one is Square, . . . one is a rebel or one conforms, one is a frontiersman in the Wild West of American night life, or else a square cell, trapped in the totalitarian tissues of American society, doomed willy-nilly to conform if one is to succeed."

It all sounds a little silly now, the image of the Negro is quaint, and the hope is vain. While the twin possibilities of total destruction and total repression have undoubtedly become major elements of consciousness in the relatively affluent West since 1945, and while the impact is tremendous, the nonconformist response is not to accept the facts of collective annihilation in the search for forms of private hedonism. "If the terms are death," said Jean Malaquais in response to *The White Negro*, and if the hipster accepts them, "if he so to speak naturalizes the terms generally prevailing for his private use, why, he conforms nice and clean, he is at the avant-garde of conformity." Baldwin, among others, knows that people died in America before 1945, even if the majority of Americans denied it, and that they will continue to do so, no matter what happens in technology and politics. He knows that the real sources of strength available against the fact of death are not solo tickets of temporary escape but the grace, poetry, dance, music and love of life that can enrich an entire culture, can possibly even save it from itself. He knows the blues, knows that "something very sinister happens to the people of a country when they begin to distrust their own reactions as deeply as they do here, and become as joyless as they become," that "the person who distrusts himself has no touchstone for reality—for this touchstone can be only oneself." Most of all he knows something about the underside of history and understands that white men must now learn it from blacks. History. Not the official history of Western superiority or of WASP achievement, but that history which derives from a gut sense—accumulated and studied over the collective centuries—of how people behave, of realities behind façades, of power. Beyond the novels, the poetry, the dance, the music of black Americans, there is simply that collective memory which is probably the most important thing that any black person possesses, that most WASPs do not, and that many other people have either ignored or forgotten. Mailer once said to Baldwin: "I want to know how power works, how it really works, in detail." And Baldwin, writing about Mailer, answered: "I know how it works, it has worked on me, and if I didn't know how power worked, I would be dead. And it goes without saying, perhaps, that I have simply never been able to afford myself any illusions concerning the manipulation of that power. My revenge, I decided very early, would be to achieve a power which outlasts kingdoms."

The new fashion of black culture in the sixties created vast opportunities, not only for scholars and writers and poets, but for all sorts of hustlers and pitchmen peddling black rhetoric to people who couldn't tell junk from soul. And because there had been too many Toms, and too much brainwashing, even some otherwise sincere people got the message confused: If white history was a fraud, if white men had cheated and robbed Negroes for centuries, there was no choice but to return to African sources—real or imagined—start the whole journey over again, and recapture the traditions and heritage that white men had stolen from blacks. The white-devil theory of the Muslims was nothing more or less than a myth of creation and plunder which made it impossible to regain one's full dignity without a symbolic return to the tribal home. The Jews had Israel, so black men were going to have the kingdoms of the Nile. When Malcolm X made his African visits, he managed—apparently without much effort—to see feudal Arab sheiks and petty potentates as men of high culture presiding over happy societies of dignified people. There was no mention of African slavery, exploitation and corruption (or of oil royalties), and no anticipation that Yorubas might, in a few years, practice genocide on Ibos. Malcolm—who later changed his views—was simply reversing the historic American assumption that the Old World was corrupt and backward while America was the garden of the West. In his search for black dignity he began by accepting the idea that since the Negro was not a WASP he was not an American at all: the Negro would have to reinvent or regain things he had lost centuries ago—would, thereby, become a new man.

It was, finally, an American myth, despite all its costumes and rhetoric, and almost every American Negro who has gone to Africa or to China or to Cuba has discovered just how American it was: eventually almost every one of them comes home. Although the myth served to generate black pride, black styles, black awareness, it required—perhaps necessarily

—the long route to get there. The Muslims themselves are as puritanical as Cotton Mather and as entrepreneurial as Babbitt; their racial separatism is not so different from the religious separatism of Roger Williams or of the Pilgrims who came to Massachusetts Bay: they preach self-reliance, enterprise and nineteenth-century Protestant virtues, while Malcolm himself talked about how "Allah would be more inclined to help those who help themselves," about the virtues of women who wore ankle-length gowns and no makeup, and about the vices of America, "where scarcely any moral values are left." He imagined, finally, that paradise would be "wherever material progress and spiritual values could be properly balanced." An eighteenth-century conservative. In rummaging through Africa and inventing the Nation of Islam, Malcolm and the Muslims managed, really for the first time, to color Americanism black; the triumph of Malcolm's hustle was his ability to make some people believe that the stolen goods from Franklin, Carnegie and Emerson were really new.

What was new, of course, was the discovery of things that had been there all along. In the introduction to *Shadow and Act* Ralph Ellison describes some of the imaginative play of his childhood in Oklahoma City fifty years ago:

. . . fabricated our own heroes and ideals catch-as-catch-can, and with an outrageous and irreverent sense of freedom. Yes, and in complete disregard for ideas of respectability or the surreal incongruity of some of our projections. Gamblers and scholars, jazz musicians and scientists, Negro cowboys and soldiers from the Spanish-American and First World Wars, movie stars and stunt men, figures from the Italian Renaissance and literature, both classical and popular, were combined with the special virtues of some local bootlegger, the eloquence of some Negro preacher, the strength and grace of some local athlete, the ruthlessness of some businessman-physician, the elegance in dress and manners of some headwaiter or hotel doorman.

In the generation since World War II—and partly because Malcolm helped dispatch the embarrassment—all that material returned to the surface. It was neither purely black—certainly not African—nor purely anything else. It was an American composite. In art, in sports, in the ordinary transactions of the street and home. Black athletes have nearly taken over professional sports, *our* sports—they dominate the statistics and the imagination—not merely because they are the latest minority to use sports to make it, because white boys won't come out, but because they are more interesting, more elegant, more stylish, because people like Willie Mays and Walt Frazier play the game with a flow and a freedom that few white athletes can match. Their presence enlarges the games they play; they provide excitement beyond competence. Anyone who has ever watched a basketball game in a Harlem playground, or even a checker game, who has heard Dionne Warwick sing or Charlie Parker play or Martin Luther King speak, who has read Baldwin or Ellison or Cleaver, or simply watched the scene in Central Harlem on a Saturday afternoon, has to be struck with the concern for style itself, for elegance, for performance. "Around here," says the hustler, "they got guys that can sell you anything, and if they got nothin' to sell, they'll try to sell you nothin'. They have this con; they learned it from the masters." Not even the worst dressers in Harlem, said Albert Murray, the black writer, "are indifferent to high fashion. They are *overcommitted* to it." The artists, the musicians, the dancers are improvisers; life is in the style of the improvisation, in the tradition of the blues, playing, as Murray said, with "the possibilities that are also there." Largely they work in the media of the West; they create American music and poetry, use materials of Western thought and art (and sometimes African and Oriental as well), but return them enlarged. You learn to play changes. Which is to say that they are Americans, not Africans; are, as Murray said, "Omni-Americans" who are, at least at this moment, more able to say things of value—beyond the issue of race—than almost anyone else. The point of *Invisible Man*, one of the best American novels of the last twenty-five years, is not the invisibility of the Negro protagonist but his symbolic assumption of the invisibility of all men, the black as everyman—asking, in the last line, "Who knows but that, on the lower frequencies, I speak for you?"

Much of the confusion over what goes on not only in the counterculture but in America generally derives from the dichotomies between hipsterism and hustle and a larger comprehension of the available resources. Do we save it or tear it down? Do we bring bombs or flowers? Are they pigs or fellow victims of the system? Do we march again or burn, or just drop out and turn on? When Mailer wrote *The White Negro* (1957) it was impossible for him to anticipate the black revolt of the following decade or the other movements that would come in its wake. But he—and all of us—might have anticipated that the anxieties of square life would, in the not too distant future, invite a whole range of reactions and counter-expressions, create new heroes, and generate new art and new myths. Most of us gave the system as we saw it in the fifties too much credit for coercive energy, too much cultural veto power, and it was therefore too easily possible to see the hipster and his cohorts—Teddy boys, Hell's Angels, beatniks—as cultural gunfighters hounded by the nervous posses of conformity. The fact, as it turned out, was that the posses were lazy and tired; they had guns (and are now using them), but they just couldn't capture anybody with Lawrence Welk and Norman Vincent Peale. Black people broke through the illusion, and then others followed. By the early sixties, students, sensing that something was happening in North Carolina, and then in Alabama and Mississippi, did borrow from the courage and vitality of Negroes and, as long as they were allowed the partnership, found new meaning in the values of freedom and equality that older WASPs had forsaken. Kids who had been dragged to Sunday school by suburban parents found themselves on their knees in Southern cotton fields echoing the cadences of Baptist preachers and learning the tunes of refurbished hymns they never knew existed. The villains were distinct and the heroes shiny, and the cause was as American as the textbook. Freedom Now! When? Now! For six or eight years, probably as late as the Chicago convention of 1968, many Americans enjoyed a hiatus of optimism, a temporary revival of belief that the older WASP virtues—not those of conformity and caution, but those of ebullience and hopefulness and even work—might still be worthwhile. What was the Peace Corps but the ultimate in enlightened missionary projects, and what were the New Frontier and the Great Society but efforts to bring everyone into the mainstream on classic terms? TR would have loved it. Here were Head Start and Upward Bound, compensatory education and equal opportunity (in education and employment) and a hundred other projects and programs and calls to action, all of them designed to give the deprived, the poor, the black, the Spanish an even shot in the race. (It didn't sound like a pun at the time.) For the first time a man might say his beads in the White House and a Negro sat on the Supreme Court. There was style in Washington again—and energy; Frost read poems at the Inaugural, and Pablo Casals played the cello in the East Room, and every night the lights burned late while the hotshots from Harvard and MIT engineered their programs and their reforms.

We all know what happened to it; there is no point in reciting again the history of a despair that refuses to fade from memory. But despair is not all that was left. Even with the failures of the sixties the genie wouldn't go back into the bottle. Black Power was emulated by Puerto Rican Power, the Panthers (succeeding the Muslims in the nightmares of J. Edgar Hoover) were emulated by the Young Lords, and by a series of other newly self-conscious ethnic movements. Bilingual classes (in English and Spanish) had become fashionable not only in the major cities but in parts of the Southwest, black studies were a fact (if sometimes also a travesty), and the sachems of culture were predominantly people of a new breed. Most of all, the young had suddenly become a force. If the sixties taught us all about the inadequacies of the old mainstream without solving them, the decade did send people marching to a new tune and, most of all to a new beat. It became fashionable again to be different, to be distinct, ethnically, socially and personally. We sang not about love and marriage, paper dolls, kissing at the garden gate, and the girl next door, but about society's child, Lucy in the sky with diamonds, and how I'd love to turn you on. The unvarnished brutality and overt sexuality of Elvis Presley and the hipsterism of the fifties were tamed and civilized by the Beatles, who mixed and refined what existed before with material from every conceivable source: jazz and blues, Indian music, electronic music, the brass band, serious poetry, fairy tales and much else besides. The Beatles, as Nuttall said, "robbed the pop world of its violence, its ignorant self-consciousness, its inferiority complex. They robbed the protest world of its terrible self-righteous drabness, they robbed the art world of its cod-seriousness." For the first time white men, mostly kids, took black idioms and transcended them, which is to say that they created as much as they borrowed, and more, producing a vital, individualistic, assertive international culture that came not from the top but from the bottom. If the strong sense of new social and political possibilities of the sixties was nourished largely by young men and women, the new cultural possibilities were even more obviously a product of their efforts. Within a few years kids—black and white—seized the initiative from their parents, and the whole country began to look to children for its news; Margaret Mead calls ours a prefigurative culture in which the children are natives and the adults immigrants. The beat of rock made Glenn Miller and Lawrence Welk sound pallid, and its message rebuked the plastic world even more effectively than the official social critics. ("We gave her everything money could buy," goes the voice. "Fun money can't buy," comes the response. "She's leaving home after living alone.") Rock 'n' roll, said an underground writer in Detroit,

is the most revolutionary force on earth—it blows people all the way back to their senses and makes them feel good. That's what the revolution is all about. . . . Actually [he added] we co-opt their media, not vice versa. Just like we co-opt their kids. When the son of an industrialist big shot starts smoking dope and dropping acid and digging hard-core rock and roll music and taking the money from his father's system and bringing it into our economy, we don't say he's co-opting the free thing—we have to say that we've copped another of their replacements.

The music and the drugs created a new community, defensive at first and patronized by the rest of the world, but the attraction was irresistible; kids who were later to be radicalized through confrontation with cops, school principals and other agents of authority were first put into positions of conflict through the music they heard and the musicians who played it. They became (or elected themselves) honorary Negroes and made a pamphlet entitled "The Student as Nigger," one of the most widely circulated documents of that phenomenon that became known simply as "the movement." It was not—and is not now—a political revolution that brings kids into conflict with their elders; it is their culture. The kids are not sanitary; they offend with their looks, their language, their dancing, their drugs and their sensuality. "They couldn't care less," said Cleaver, "about the old, stiffassed honkies who don't like their new dances: Frug, Monkey, Jerk, Swim, Watusi. All they know is that it feels good to swing to way-out body rhythms instead of dragassing across the dance floor like zombies to the dead beat of mind-smothered Mickey Mouse music." Sex is no longer that grim act of aggression, the dusky slumming that Mailer's hipster seemed to think it was. It is no longer hedged with puritanical restraint or with that super-WASPish effort in determined anti-puritanism to fuck, *Playboy*-style, Without Inhibitions. Sometimes the cultural offense is calculated: filth becomes a premeditated reproach against the establishment, and tight-assed sanitation politics is met with anal freedom of expression. The Chicago cops who beat demonstrators in Grant Park and on Michigan Avenue during the week of the 1968 Democratic convention did not pursue peaceniks or political revolutionaries; they pursued hippies with long hair who used foul language; and if, on occasion, there were assaults with stones and bottles, and cries of "Kill the pig," they seemed hardly comparable to the offense of bad manners and bad speech. It may even be said that the whole significance of the counterculture—its prime offense—is that it so often tends to be nonviolent, and that the people the authorities face on the streets or in the classroom are behaving in the one way that really exasperates the man with a club. He can deal with overt violence, but how is he to respond to girls passing out flowers and, in his imagination, offering the kind of openness that he must not allow himself to entertain? Violent acts—by Weathermen and others—thus tend to represent a form of relief, the sort of behavior that justifies his violence and enables him to act in the manner of his custom.

The crime is compounded by the apparent rejection of the second of the major Puritan virtues: work. Dirtiness is permissible in the process of making it, and foul language is acceptable in the precincts where making it takes place. You can cuss in a steel mill or a warehouse or an Army barracks, can even tell people to go fuck themselves in the homosexual camaraderie of a Legion bar or a Sunday-morning softball game. But such manners invariably require the justification of exertion in conventionally accepted activities. The students, by virtue of their class, are supposed to have made it and must, therefore, not act like truck drivers at the urinal. But what then? The Puritan ethic is so involved with work, with upward mobility, that it leaves little for the next step. There are, of course, the rhetorical obligations to God and your fellow man, and the kids, it goes without saying, often try to honor them. But what if those responsibilities lead to the discovery that the economic and political system is destructive and that the payoffs—the automobile, the suburban life and the status of an executive position—are not worth the rat race, are, indeed, corrupt and empty? If the students did not learn that lesson from their own experience, they could not have helped learning it from Paul Goodman, David Riesman, Edgar Friedenberg or any number of the other social critics who now form the basis of intellectual self-definition in American life. The Puritan ethic, the rat race, the life of conformity are exposed almost in the first moments of awareness; criticism often precedes the literature of affirmation in formal classes, or, if not there, then certainly in the music and in the pages of *Mad* magazine. It is almost as if, on occasion, the kids envy the squares their illusions and detest them as much for that as for their hypocrisy, and as if the passion for blue jeans and denim shirts represents, more than anything else, some effort to return to a world in which work was worthwhile.

The collapse of the Protestant ethic leads, necessarily, to a search for something new, to a new quest. The never-ceasing question "What do the kids want?" is unanswerable. What they want, one might say, is illusions, heroes, myths: Gene and Bobby, Malcolm and the other Bobby, Abbie and Jerry, Huey and Cleaver. In *The Graduate*, which became the biggest money-making film of the sixties, a whole generation went riding with Dustin Hoffman (Ben) on that bus to nowhere, lighting out again for territories that no longer exist. The film, finally, is a fraud, not because it misrepresents the desperation and vacuity of the life of plastics, but because it offers that phony resolution. In the conventional girl–boy story, Ben and Elaine Robinson would have been meant for each other; it was only the guilty and corrupt interference of Mrs. Robinson, Elaine's mother, that made the outcome a close call, requiring Ben to rescue Elaine—at the altar—from marriage to a fraternity ass man who was an obvious double of her father. What saved the film, apart from its representation of a situation that a lot of kids recognized and understood, was Dustin Hoffman himself. Ben is not a Boy Scout, not a blond, blue-eyed WASP itching with ambition and facile with the social graces of suburbia; he is, miraculously (for the son of smooth California squares), awkward, dark, and more than a little Jewish—about as much at home in a Berkeley fraternity house as an Orthodox rabbi in the Union Club. But it is not his ethnicity that matters; it is his style, a style that, despite the plot, repudiates almost every quality of the conventional hero. He does not speak plain or shoot straight, has no idea what he wants—certainly not plastics—and isn't about to use his fists on anybody. Despite that last-minute rescue—employing a gilded Christian cross to ward off the hysterical members of the wedding—Ben is not really a protagonist, not even Huck Finn, but a victim whose humanity is itself a force and therefore an offense. He invites aggression from uptight people almost, it seems, by scent, an innocent victimized by the most American of Americans. Ben is Billy Budd against Mrs. Robinson's Claggart.

Under the surface of *The Graduate* and of the "road" films which followed (*Midnight Cowboy, Easy Rider, Five Easy Pieces*) there are bushels of sentimentality about lone travelers in denims and buckskin ranging the country in search of open spaces. (Or freedom, or identity, or whatever.) The riders are still innocents even if they plan to make it in New York as prime Texas-grown grade-A studs, hustling Park Avenue chicks who are tired of the faggoty screwing offered on the local market. At the same time there is, under much of the broader rebellion, a lot of communal passion for handicrafts, organic vegetables and more primitive ("meaningful") forms of work. Shades of Leatherstocking; echoes of Brook Farm; artifacts of *The Blythedale Romance*. Weavers, leatherworkers, jewelers, carpenters, readers of *The Whole Earth Catalog*, sifters of seeds. It is all very American and sometimes veers to the far side of Calvinist purity. But Thoreauvian rebellion on communes and lone-ranging on six-lane highways are obviously limited; only a few can play, and fewer still win. If the rednecks don't get you with their shotguns the state troopers will bust you for pot, and even if all the necessary personal compromises can be made, the long winter, the cold, and plain lack of bread are likely to tear the noble experiment apart. It's a good fantasy—and totally American, even if history honors only the limited dissent and deviation of those who will later write it, but too often it excludes the assumptions of triumph and justice which John Wayne carries into the mainstream. Wayne is the agent of the cosmos; his six-shooter is labeled progress, civilization, growth. Our man. The kid in denims wears the garb of repudiation. If his statements about the world are to be persuasive, it is almost necessary that, somewhere in the last reel, the bad guys shoot him down. In New York, when the heroes of *Easy Rider* came to their final denouement, the kids walked out of the theater talking about the shitty system. In Arkansas they cheered.

The tendency to romanticize underdogs is hardly new, either in America or anywhere else. But the pursuit of myth and meaning has now reached the point where the underdog is loved not for his aspirations, for the odds against his acceptance into the system, but, ambiguously, for the purity of his alienation. If the pirate captain allowed himself to be knighted in the last reel for his services to the queen he would be regarded as a copout. King Richard does not return to claim his throne; the villainous John reigns forever and Robin Hood stays underground. The separatism of the Panthers and the Muslims is honored above the black capitalism of the Urban League, and Cesar Chavez is supported more for his resistance and his earthy Chicano image than for the middle-class aspirations of the United Farm Workers.

The white race [said Cleaver] has lost its heroes. . . . Its heroes have been revealed as villains and its greatest heroes as the arch-villains. The new generations of whites, appalled by the sanguine and despicable record carved over the face of the globe by their race in the last five hundred years, are rejecting the panoply of white heroes, whose heroics consisted in erecting the inglorious edifice of colonialism and imperialism. . . . They recoil in shame from the spectacle of cowboys and pioneers—their heroic forefathers whose exploits filled earlier generations with pride—galloping across a movie screen shooting down Indians like coke bottles.

Understandably, the old liberals were horrified by the cults growing up around the figures of Castro, Guevara and Ho Chi Minh, and by the conversion of Latin-American guerrilla manuals into domestic texts of revolution. Hip audiences cheer whenever a French policeman is assassinated in *The Battle of Algiers*, one of the most artful and successful propaganda films ever shown in America. Perhaps they also imagine themselves killing cops and planting bombs in restaurants. (And, needless to say, some of them do it.) But it is far more probable that, for most of them, the revolutionaries of the Third World tend to be cultural figures of reproach—symbolic ways of saying "Fuck you"—and not the leaders of a disciplined movement. The American Stalinists of the thirties took orders from Moscow and imagined that they had a clear vision of the future. The kids of the late sixties and early seventies have no such discipline, no clear program, just a vast, unceasing strategy of reproach; theirs is the offense of style. Instead of cutting up the pigs and taking over the power plants you cut up the flag. You smear shit on the walls of the establishment. Revolution for the hell of it.

The manifestation of style is performance, and the material of that performance is, in this revolt of culture, the denial and refutation of WASP with-it-ness. (Even among the children of solidly middle-class Protestant families—perhaps particularly among those children—the guilt of being a WASP is sometimes too much to bear. People are constantly looking over their shoulders at their black or their Catholic and Jewish friends to ask how they're doing.) Performance: in the East Village, at Woodstock, in Hashbury, and on the streets and in the Federal District Court of Chicago. There is a Conspiracy —ironic, mocking, playing with its tormentors, tormenting with play. We'll put LSD in the water supply, liberate the public toilets (because everything should be free) and nominate a pig for President. The Yippies against the war machine, Abbie Hoffman against Julius Hoffman. After the demonstrations at the 1968 Chicago Democratic convention eight men were put on trial, each of them a symbol of one phase of the revolt: Yippies, an old-line pacifist, an SDS organizer, a Panther (later removed from the case by Judge Hoffman for special handling at some future date). They had little in common, but what the dissidents couldn't put in one bag the government did for them. The Chicago Seven, on trial for conspiracy to foment a riot. Is a culture a conspiracy? Do rock and pot make a plot? Maybe yes, maybe no. But the culture was in contempt of this honorable court. Five months for saying "bullshit"; fifteen days for laughing; one day for blowing a kiss to the jury; fourteen days for applauding; four days for baring body to the jury; five days for insulting the judge; six days for insulting the judge in Yiddish.

The strategy of the defense at the Chicago trial (two Jewish lawyers, William Kunstler and Leonard I. Weinglass, facing an Irish prosecutor, Thomas A. Foran, and a Jewish assistant, Richard G. Schultz) was not merely to explain and justify the position of the counterculture or to repudiate the establishment, but to play it out, to perform, to have Allen Ginsberg chant Indian mantras (he was allowed three Oms by Judge Hoffman), to have Pete Seeger and Arlo Guthrie and Judy Collins sing, to put the defendants into bizarre costumes —judicial robes, headdresses, beads—to have Abbie Hoffman ask the judge for permission to go to the bathroom, to bring a birthday cake into court, to have Hoffman identify himself as a citizen of an entirely new nation:

A. My name is Abbie. I am an orphan of America.
Q. Where do you reside?
A. I live in Woodstock nation.
Q. Will you tell the court and jury where it is?

A. Yes. It is a nation of alienated young people. We carry it around with us as a state of mind in the same way the Sioux Indians carried the Sioux nation around with them. It is a nation dedicated to cooperation versus competition . . .

Q. [Judge Hoffman] Just where it is, that's all . . .

A. It is in my mind and in the minds of my brothers and sisters. . . .

The festival of life that the Yippies had planned for Chicago during the 1968 convention was intended, obviously, as a political act: any form of cultural affirmation was bound to be political. "It was very important," said rock musician Country Joe MacDonald at the trial, "that we try to do something in Chicago which would be positive, natural, human, and loving, in order to let the people of America know that there are people in America who are not tripped out on ways of thinking which result only in oppression and fear, paranoia and death." Jerry Rubin, said Mailer on the witness stand, believed that "the presence of a hundred thousand young people at a festival with rock bands would so intimidate and terrify the establishment, particularly the Johnson war establishment, that Lyndon Johnson would have to be nominated under armed guard. Rubin said that 'the establishment is going to do it all themselves. We won't do a thing. We are just going out there and they won't be able to take it. They will smash the city themselves. They will provoke all the violence.'" The program was to freak everybody out, to blow their minds, and although it failed on the streets in 1968, it succeeded admirably in court during the gloomy winter of 1969–70.

Because the trial became guerrilla theater, it inevitably turned into a landmark for the movement, filling the underground papers, nourishing new myths, creating new heroes and reinforcing youth-cult attitudes with an official imprimatur that no street demonstration could have achieved: This time they had to watch; they couldn't turn it off, because it was happening in their court and before their judge, who was —appropriately, as Abbie Hoffman noted—a Jew. Judge Hoffman's schoolmasterish pomposity, his vindictiveness, and his arrogant pride in his own ignorance, not only about youth culture but about much else that was happening in America, made him a perfect foil for the contretemps of the kids and their lawyers. (Not that the defendants were all kids: David Dellinger, a lifelong pacifist, was fifty-three, and Tom Hayden, one of the founders of SDS, was over thirty. But it was the culture of the kids that was on trial—or, rather, that had come onto this stage for its performance.) At moments, as in his studied inability to get the name of defense counsel Leonard Weinglass right (he called him Weinruss, Weinrob, Weinstein, Feinstein, Weinberg, Weinramer), Hoffman's insecure establishmentarianism skirted overt anti-Semitism. He appeared deliberately to be trying to deny not only identification with kids but his own Jewishness. They seemed, at times, to represent similar (or even identical) crimes. The link was hardly precise, yet it had symbolic validity in a society that had always made it difficult to be totally American and totally Jewish at the same time. Abbie Hoffman understood. "Your idea of justice is the only obscenity in this room," he shouted at the judge. "You *schtunk. Vo den. Shanda fur de goyim.*" For insulting the judge in Yiddish (accusing him of shameful behavior on behalf—and in the eyes—of WASPs), six days.

For the defense, playing against Judge Hoffman, this trial, unlike Benjamin Spock's in Boston, was not designed to vindicate free expression and assembly through established processes. It was almost the opposite. References to constitutional rights may have been appropriate in a child's world—and often that is what it was—but they were patently absurd in Judge Hoffman's court. What the defense sought, and achieved, was an official hearing for the underground, which was not something which could be vindicated in conventional terms. To win—to carry off the show—convention had to be embarrassed. Revolution is in your head, Abbie had said before the Chicago demonstrations began. *You are the revolution. Do your thing. Do your thing. Do your thing. Do your thing. Do your thing. Be your thing.* It was one of the first public ceremonies of nonassimilation held in modern America, and its ethnicity was almost as important as the conflict of age and style: it made national figures of Kunstler, Hoffman, and Rubin—those three well above the rest—put them on hundreds of campus platforms (a necessity, given the costs of the trial), and it kept alive a movement that had all but foundered in the days between the moratorium of November 1969 and the killings at Kent State the following spring. The dagger of affront, looking ever like an extended middle finger, was pointing at the heart of America. Not Mark Rudd country, not Mario Savio country, not the country of James Simon Kunen or Paul Krassner, but the America of aspiration and clean.

"Whatever the hopeful future of individual writers," said Irving Howe in the late sixties, "the 'school' of American Jewish writing is by now in an advanced stage of decomposition." Given the command that Jewishness now holds over certain sectors of the American imagination, those words can be attributed only to a charter member of a club whose doors had lately been thrown open to any klotz who cared to join. How else, asked Howe, could one explain the attention that Jewish writing has lately enjoyed? Or the appearance "of a generation of younger Jewish writers who, without authentic experience or memory to draw upon, manufacture fantasies about the lives of their grandfathers? Or the popularity of Isaac Bashevis Singer who, coming to the American literary scene precisely at the moment when writers composing in English had begun to exhaust the Jewish subject, could, by dazzling contrast, extend it endlessly backward in time and deeper in historical imagination?" But after saying all that, Howe offers a convincing explanation of why Jewish literature should be thriving:

We were living directly after the holocaust of the European Jews. We might scorn our origins; we might crush America with discoveries of ardor; we might change our names. But we knew that but for an accident of geography we might also now be bars of soap. At least some of us could not help feeling that in our earlier claims to have shaken off all ethnic distinctiveness there had been something false, something shaming. Our Jewishness might have no clear religious or national content, it might be helpless before the criticism of believers; but Jews we were, like it or not, and liked or not.

To recognize that we were living after one of the greatest and least explicable catastrophes of human history, and one for which we could not claim to have adequately prepared ourselves either as intellectuals or as human beings, brought a new rush of feelings, mostly unarticulated and hidden behind the scrim of consciousness. It brought a low-charged but nagging guilt, a quiet remorse. . . . We could no longer escape the conviction that, blessing or curse, Jewishness was an integral part of our life, even if—and perhaps just because—there was nothing we could do or say about it. . . . I cannot prove a connection between the holocaust and the turn to Jewish themes in American fiction, at first urgent and quizzical, later fashionable and manipulative. I cannot prove that my own turn to Yiddish literature during the fifties was due to the shock following the war years. But it would be foolish to scant the possibility.

Howe is most upset with "a new phase in our culture, which in motive and spring represents a wish to shake off the bleeding heritage of modernism and reinstate one of those periods of the collective naïf which seem endemic to American experience. The new sensibility is impatient with ideas. It is impatient with literary structures of complexity and coherence, only yesterday the catchwords of our criticism." (Who, I keep wondering, is *us?* Which is *our* criticism?) The new sensibility, adds Howe, "breathes contempt for rationality, impatience with mind, and a hostility to the artifices and decorums of high culture. It despises liberal values, liberal cautions, liberal virtues . . ." The bad guys are taking over the club—which most people didn't know existed until a few years ago, and about which they may still not know very much—and everything is coming apart. But it is the kind of coming apart that fattens publishers and makes the serious idiom of Jewishness—not just the Jew as comic—a larger ingredient of American consciousness. The main literary contribution of the New York milieu, as Howe pointed out,

has been to legitimate a subject and tone we must uneasily call American Jewish writing. The fiction of urban malaise, second generation complaint, Talmudic dazzle, woeful alienation, and dialectical irony, all found its earliest expression in the pages of *Commentary* and *Partisan Review*—fiction in which the Jewish world is not merely regained in memory as a point of beginnings, an archetypal Lower East Side of spirit and place, but is also treated as a portentous metaphor of man's homelessness and wandering.

Jewish writing, it goes without saying, has been part of the American scene for more than half a century, but in the virile years before World War II it tended to keep its distance (or change its face)—existed, that is, in its own ghetto—and was not often treated as fully American. The idiom was so emphatically hyphenated that, with few exceptions, acceptance was possible only at the price of self-mockery and denial. We were ready to accept Sammy Glick or the lovable old pawnbroker, but Alexander Portnoy was inconceivable. At the same time the learned professors were willing to invite a Jewish writer to lecture—to have him perform—but the anti-Semites of the

English department continued to believe firmly that, for the long run, only a WASP could understand English literature. All that began to change with what Howe calls the European holocaust, with the war, with the decline of older American regions, and with the acceptance of the irreversible facts of technology and urban life. In the last twenty years a lot of people other than Jews were Semitized, became, in one way or another, immigrants to those places and states of mind which Jews had inhabited for centuries. What we learned was that Jewishness is in itself a place, a nation more permanent than Abbie Hoffman's Woodstock and, in its American identification with New York, more resilient than any region except (or perhaps including) the South. The Jew (unlike the Negro, who is the only other American to be cast in the role of universal sufferer) is preeminently an urban dweller; where other people migrate he has been all his life. That all of this can produce the most bizarre forms of provincialism is undeniable, but it also creates, perhaps through good fortune if nothing else, the best preparation for that combination of sophistication and paranoia which constitutes the prime defense for life in the city. To become a Jew in America meant growing up with the belief that they were out to screw you. It is, thereafter, easy to translate the goys into "the system" or "the establishment" and even easier to transfer your loyalties from the nation of Jews to the nation of Woodstock.

The point is that Jewishness has become fashionable. In New York, which is where the soapboxes are kept, it is the goy and not the Jew (or the Negro) who feels defensive. Half the major book publishers are Jewish and probably more than half the art dealers, the music managers (booking agents, publishers, Tin Pan Alley flacks) and the senior brass of network television. And yet there is no establishment: The lit crowd on the Upper West Side is as divided into factions as a Polish gov-

ernment in exile. There is no love lost between the Jewish socialists who trace their heritage to the struggles of the twenties
and thirties and the New Left radicals who hustle bread for
the Panthers and the Chicago Seven. What they have in common—beyond ethnicity and a contentious intellectual tradition—is a deep sense, subtle and sometimes almost uncon-
scious, that they are still outsiders even if events have now
given them a central position in the culture biz. At the same
time, they enjoy the fashion, know that they are well dressed
in their Jewishness, that Gimpel and Mr. Sammler and Herzog
are their people, that Leonard Bernstein is their man and that
—if they care for such things—Barbra Streisand is their girl.
In the last twenty-five years a lot of people have become honorary Jews: the Jew has become a symbol not only of "man's
homelessness and wandering" or of the resilience that permits
survival in a hostile environment, but also of the articulate
outsider in an age when to be out is to be in. The holocaust
put a little of the spirit of the Jewish Defense League into a lot
of people who had never wanted anything more than assimilation, and the creation of the state of Israel made it possible for
every Jewish kid in the Bronx to imagine himself a gunfighter
mowing down Arabs in the Negev or (more lately) along the
banks of the Suez Canal. Most of all, the events of World War
II and the postwar years broke the hyphen; they removed the
necessity to wear masks of impotence and gave every Jew
who wanted it a preeminent citizenship in the universe of
systematic destruction and impersonal annihilation. Jews,
branded at Dachau and Auschwitz, could welcome goys to
the club of nuclear destruction, and could, with Howe, arro-
gate the word "holocaust," part of the general rhetoric of the
atomic presence, to themselves.

And so Chaim Potok and *Our Crowd;* so *The Joys of Yiddish* and that incessant flow of books about rabbis; so Franny

and Zooey and the Glass family, and the stories of stickball games on the streets of New York; so John Updike, the best of the younger WASP novelists, imagining himself as Bech, a Jewish writer; so Philip Roth and *Portnoy's Complaint*, a book which would have been inconceivable (and incomprehensible) a generation ago, and which seems to me as important culturally as any novel published in the sixties. The issue is not whether *Portnoy* is a "good" novel or whether it will last—who is to know?—but that it grew out of one of the few surviving American regions in which idioms, styles, manners and traditions remained sufficiently strong to produce material worthy of an *American* novel. (A few months after it was published an editor in New York rejected a manuscript with a note that "no one is interested in reading novels about WASPs.") Roth did not simply lay to rest the schmaltzy joke about the Jewish mother, the overshoes, the broken glasses, the chicken soup, and in the process flush out the horrors on its dark side, he also created a character—for good or ill—who will ride over the horizons of American terror like some latter-day Holden Caulfield graduated from Pencey Prep into a higher order of emasculation. The Catcher in the Bed. When the book was published, some people in New York called it anti-Semitic; Portnoy, they said, could have been anybody, could have been the child of an uptight Irish Catholic family which doggedly justified its sex with the number of babies produced; he could even have been a WASP; and, anyhow, Jewish mothers weren't different from all other mothers, so why pin this on the Jews? Why make a *Jewish* boy masturbate on the 109 bus or have him spread his sexual hangups over 274 pages distributed in half a million copies? *Because there is no WASP voice, no WASP language, no WASP idiom in literature in which these things can be said.* The Boy Scouts jerk off—that's where a lot of them learn it—but there isn't a language in which they can discuss it except pornography. When James Gould Cozzens tries to describe sexual acts he comes out with an instruction manual for a Newtonian machine which clanks and grinds and thumps; and when sex is described in the average novel of suburban hanky-panky, the ingredients of the martinis and the optionals on the station wagon embody more seductive appeal than the *accouchements*. It is obviously true that all the things that Portnoy does other people do—and, more important, that the conditions of his life are the conditions of other lives—but they cannot express them. On the way to the mayor's reception, Portnoy, the Assistant Human Opportunity Commissioner of the city of New York, to the Monkey, "who sucked me off before she even knew my name":

> ". . . for Christ's sake," I tell her, "don't say cunt to Mary Lindsay!"
> "What?"
> "You heard right. When we get there don't start talking about your wet pussy to whoever opens the door! Don't make a grab for Big John's *shlong* until we've been there at least half an hour, okay?"

Anybody can say cunt and pussy, but who can talk about grabbing for Big John's *shlong*, can think (or speak) that explicitly about Big John's sexuality at all? Big John is supposed to be sexy, but is there any way other than this of making it concrete, of making it a little less mystical, without becoming pornographic? How do you bring that WASP attractiveness down to size—how does one say everything in a moment? Again—the Pumpkin, the healthy WASP girl from Iowa:

> *She never raised her voice in an argument.* Can you imagine the impression this made on me at seventeen, fresh from my engagement with The Jack and Sophie Portnoy Debating Society? Who had ever heard of such an approach to controversy? Never ridiculed her opponent! Or seemed to hate him for his ideas! Ah-hah, so *this* is what it

means to be a child of *goyim*, valedictorian of a high school in Iowa instead of New Jersey; yes, this is what the goyim who have got something have got! Authority without the temper. Virtue without the self-congratulation. Confidence sans swagger or condescension. Come on, let's be fair and give the goyim their due, Doctor: when they are impressive, they are very impressive. *So sound!* Yes, that's what hypnotized—the heartiness, the sturdiness; in a word, her pumpkinness. My wholesome, big bottomed, lipstickless, barefooted *shikse* . . . Oh perfectly ill-proportioned girl! No mile-long mannequin you! So she had no tits, so what? Slight as a butterfly through the rib cage and neck; but planted like a bear beneath! *Rooted*, that's what I'm getting at! Joined by those lineman's legs to this American ground!

The Pumpkin is nothing more than a female version of Christopher Newman, but it seems hardly possible to describe her in Henry James language (or in Cozzens language) without turning her into a cigarette commercial or worse. The all-American girl, symbolic winner of all the blue ribbons, "in your halfslip and brassiere, with flour in your ears and your hairline damp with perspiration—remember? showing me, despite the temperature, how real bread should taste?" This is not the immigrant boy mesmerized by the stylishness of the goyim but the Jewish writer removing that style from its ineffable mystery, making it speakable and therefore manageable. *When they are impressive, they are very impressive. So sound!* Almost ten years ago Roth published a piece about the difficulties of writing fiction in America: the country had become too bizarre—hopelessly absurd and corrupt—for imaginative literature; there was no base of manners or tradition that did not satirize and traduce itself every day in the newspapers, no set of conventions against which the novelist could play. But it is still possible to use what in this case is the best of all possible devices, the established "foreign" idiom (Jewish or black), not only to portray WASPs but to create transcendent American characters and situations: Portnoy is no less everyman than the protagonist of *Invisible Man;* obviously his "region" creates limitations, but without that region there would be no base at all.

III

The shocks that followed the Second World War sent people scurrying in every conceivable direction, searching, searching, and retrieving from the American WASP tradition itself material that had almost been forgotten. *If a man does not keep pace with his companions perhaps it is because he hears a different drummer. Let him step to the music which he hears, however measured or far away.* Good stuff. Where was all that disobedience? What happened to self-reliance? What had we done with Thoreau and Tom Paine or even Sam Adams? The distortions of history seem almost inevitably to associate cantankerous individualism with shotguns and six-shooters, and not with ascetic figures who refuse to pay their taxes or with otherwise ordinary people who say no by climbing aboard atomic submarines or throwing themselves in front of defoliating bulldozers. History celebrates winners and the rhetoric of victory; it honors dissent only in theory, rarely in practice. And yet there are people in this country who were, one way or another, born to dissent, and for whom dissent and measured disobedience are not so much matters of learning or intellectual orientation as they are elements—God help us—of breeding.

We have never quite known what to do with the Quakers or Tom Paine or Henry David Thoreau. Everything would be simpler had Thoreau never lived (or if he would just stay out of the way), but there he is, rambling around the place like an eccentric uncle of history, making introductions necessary, requiring attention and, from time to time, even a salute from official company. Very American; very Yankee; very self-reliant. Very. *All right, so we put his face on that postage stamp, but did they have to make him look like a goddam hippie?* In the avalanche of militant anti-Americanism that accompanied the revolt against the world of uptight, the nuts-and-berries asceticism of Walden Pond and the disciplined, muted disobedience of its inhabitant were bound to seem a little thin and tough: they required conditioning, and not merely adoption at will. The romance of Walden and the philosophy of civil disobedience demanded more than beads and feathers in Washington Square. But the people who had been raised to them, or who had studied and practiced them long enough to make them second nature, enjoyed a kind of moral immunity that couldn't be embarrassed by love-it-or-leave-it: they knew that this was their place, and that what they were doing was as American—as White Anglo-Saxon Protestant American—as the log cabin and the DAR. Hell-no-we-won't-go obscured a lot of young men—and some who were older—who regarded resistance as their American birthright and whose protest was consciously mined from the traditions of WASP experience. "I believe," wrote Timothy Zimmer, a conscientious objector who was jailed for refusing to cooperate with the Selective Service System,

that the state does not have the right to compel an individual against his will to serve the society in a positively and explicitly defined role. The state may not command the individual to spend a part of his life working at a job which the state has chosen and imposed upon him.

It is the duty of the state and the function of law to define what actions the individual may *not* take with impunity. The state may say what the individual may not do: he may not violate the rights of others, he may not harm the lives or property of others. But beyond this . . . the state has no right to go further and say what an individual *must* do.

The pacifist is the inevitable critic in any political context, for the business of politics is power . . . and the use of power against humanity is the definition, by contrast, of pacifism. Criticism is valid only when made with love. . . . I find it easier to love the New Left critically than to love the establishment at all.

Thoreau and the Quakers make radical action conservative. The man who resists the draft or advises resistance becomes not an enemy of tradition but a defender; establishment bishops can condemn the fundamental Christianity of Catholic radicals, and the nativists of Middle America can dismiss it as alien, but what are they going to do with Benjamin Spock, Staughton Lynd, William Sloane Coffin (other than calling them intellectuals), and how are they going to deal with Quakers or with seventy-year-old Yankee ladies named Peabody who get busted in sit-ins? It helps to have them around; they are the nearest thing in America to Lord Russell, and they make any demonstration respectable.

But the radicalism here—however measured—may not be as important as the conservatism itself. On her side of the stream Rachel Carson was working the same territory as Spock and Coffin, and if ecology might now keep Teddy Roosevelt from shooting moose and antelope, the hesitant practices of conservation—birds, forests, air or even the English language—have been almost exclusively the work of WASPs. WASPs dominate the ranks of the conservationists, the birdmen, the Sierra Clubbers, the librarians, the lexicographers, the antiquarians, and it can only be WASP inspiration that prompts people to stick plaques on every decaying barn to proclaim that General Washington had once picked his teeth near this site. Which is to say that WASPs have become the caretakers of what they regard (with some dispute from the Indians) as their special heritage. Once it was all theirs, the land, the streams, the language, and they—shocked by the depredations of technology

and the travesties of language—are trying desperately to preserve it. Clearly there are others involved—Jewish automobile
dealers from Cleveland, Japanese landscape architects from
San Francisco—but it is hard to imagine the movement without WASPs, hard to visualize a Jewish Roger Tory Peterson
or a black president of the Izaak Walton League. Ecology is
their revenge, a cultural counterattack that is at once modern,
necessary and, above all, clean. Its targets are the uncouth
boors, upstarts who roar down the highway and litter the
roadside with beer cans, people who want amusement parks
and ticky-tacky developments on remote hillsides heretofore
accessible only to dedicated hikers with the energy and time to
slog up the slopes, newcomers to the neighborhood who have
neither the resources nor the aesthetic sensibilities to build on
three-acre plots. It is like a huge suburban zoning meeting,
concerned with the preservation of the things people have, but
innocent of the requirements of people who have not. Ecology is making amends for Grandfather's plunder without
returning the swag. The crusade of Clean.

And yet, in the contemporary circus of culture, and against
the incessant assaults of people who are trying to put things
down, the value of conservation and the conservatism of values—whether ornithological or constitutional—are obviously
significant. After five years as master of Pierson College at
Yale, the novelist John Hersey took pains to remind dis-
traught Yale alumni that if their education had any value it
rested in their ability to distinguish bullshit from reason, to
understand, for example, that the inflated rhetoric of students
or Panthers had to be sifted for what it said and what it obscured. I take this to mean that genuine cultural conservatism
does not concern itself with the repudiation of new ideas and
voices, or with condemning bizarre styles of expression and
behavior, but rather with the affirmation of old ideas and tra-

ditions that seem worth keeping. Yale is no longer a private preserve, but the skills and attitudes and learning (if any) that it provides are the irrevocable possessions of the individual. The American WASP who understands his own heritage—the Quakers and the Thoreauvians, the Coffins and the Lynds, the Rachel Carsons and the Ramsey Clarks—must feel that the decline of his own cultural preeminence does not necessarily mean the fall of all, that there are elements in his own system which will allow him and almost everything else to coexist. Given the state of American politics and culture, that may be an illusive hope, but anyone with a shred of historical memory knows that the country has survived other invasions of dirty people and uncouth boors. The fact that WASPs no longer enjoy exclusive control of the country and the universe should now make it possible to manage and nurture more intimate cultural resources, to do your inherently WASP (or other) thing, and to let the shit flow into a common sewer. Minorities enjoy a certain freedom, a release from responsibilities, that the man in the mainstream is denied.

Despite all that, however, it is unlikely that the major WASP contributions to contemporary culture will soon begin to transcend social arbitration and spectatorship. Andrew Wyeth, the most fashionable of our painters, can make technical perfection overwhelm the sentimentality of his ideas and the chilly tone of his descriptions, but his work almost inevitably puts the museum on the canvas, which is to say that he pickles feeling safely in the formaldehyde of retrospect. This obviously appeals to museum directors and trustees, most of them still WASPs, who specialize in the pickling business and who are, as a group, probably the coldest fish in the world of art, but it doesn't do much to revitalize styles or create new energy. It puts feeling into the rear-view mirror of historical distance, of time remembered, of things which can be confronted only because they are no longer there—appeals, in other words, to a high-cult voyeurism which creates its thrill without much need to be engaged.

For those who prefer their stuff in more contemporary modes, the fashion runs to George Plimpton, perhaps the leading WASP purveyor of with-it-ness, a twentieth-century salonist on the fringes of every form of fashionable involvement: friend of the Kennedys, pal of Mailer and Capote, host to the striking grape workers, patron of the stylish poor. Plimpton, not content with mere journalism, casts himself into the arenas where the action is, fights Archie Moore, pitches to the Yankees, plays football with the Detroit Lions, all activities saturated with ethnics, with people who are still making it, and with those for whom there cannot be any compromise with style or demonstrable superiority. Plimpton is the arch voyeur; as a Jew he might have played schlemiel in a jockstrap, but as a carrier of every form of WASP privilege—Exeter, Harvard, Paris, the whole bit—he can do no more than represent the man whose dreams have long turned sour, for whom there is no viable form of future achievement, and whose greatest moments come from watching someone else do something well. While Wyeth looks through the windows of time, Plimpton takes himself through the lens of the camera and not only becomes a proxy for personal experience but makes the feelings of others surrogates for the unattainable realities of feeling for oneself. It is always done well—Plimpton is a superb writer—and it is undoubtedly done with sincerity, but it is, at the same time, a confession that real style, real life and real experience are beyond one's reach. The uncouth boor has taken over. He controls the imagination while the rest of us watch from a safe distance and send our man Plimpton to report back on how it feels. Wyeth and Plimpton—among others—are our secret agents; one has been sent to investigate the ruins of WASP memory, the other to let us know how it feels in those precincts of action which seem forever beyond our reach. At one time the underprivileged pressed their noses against the windows of fashion. Now the fashionable send their spies over the fence because life on the inside is too empty and dull to sustain without some help from beyond.

3

WHO RULES AMERICA?

I

Some hardhat was carrying the sign on lower Broadway while his buddies were chasing longhairs and other ill-fitting types up the street: GOD BLESS THE ESTABLISHMENT. God bless the who? The Queen and the House of Lords? Jackie Onassis? Richard Nixon? The nearby bankers of Wall Street? The Chase Manhattan Bank? The Ford Foundation? Mario Procaccino? George Wallace? The Pentagon? The State Department? The president of the union of construction workers? Yes and no. More likely I am thinking of a red-white-and-blue chimera with slipstick shift and four hundred horses, or of reliability, law and order, good contracts and pensions, a nice lawn and no shit from nobody. *God Bless the Establishment.* A Catholic boy, no doubt, who has learned well from the sisters that somebody else knows best and that grace is hardly distinguishable from obedience. Get those lazy sons of bitches with their dirty hair. Hippie bastards who don't do no work and carry Viet Cong flags. We think the President knows best and we don't believe people should be burning the flag of their country. Commie fags. *God Bless the Establishment.*

There is in America a subtle relationship between people of

privilege and people who long ago gave up any hope—or indeed never entertained any hope—of achieving wealth, fame and power. This may be the case in any class society—which means every civilization on earth; perhaps things have not changed all that much from the Middle Ages, perhaps the workingman still depends on the nobility for protection and stability and for the management of certain rituals. But the relationship is more complex here because American rhetoric has always claimed that we have no classes, that we are immune from all the nonsense of rank and status, and that we have, for all practical purposes, no elites. Americans are often accused by Europeans of not knowing how to treat their servants—a charge that I think is true—because they expect them to do dirty work while they pretend to treat them as equals, a practice which is unfair and confusing at both ends of the line. If employer and servant are equals, why is one going out to shop at Cartier's while the other is mopping the floor? There are payoffs for both: each can pretend that in all respects but his (or her) employment the servant is as good as the employer, could even, in some hypothetical world, achieve the employer's status and position, thus freeing the employer from any concern about the servant once the wages are paid and they have jointly swindled the Social Security Administration and the IRS out of their cut, and allowing the servant to maintain his belief that he/she is a full-fledged citizen who has managed to delegate the real dirty work to someone else. The servant may never have heard the word "establishment," but he must believe in the benevolence of those who rule, must believe that someone is taking care of him, that there is something on which he can depend.

The confusion derives from the excessive expectations of those who are not members of the establishment. For us the first great disillusionment came in 1929 when the rulers of

America appeared unable to fix things up and we could watch them—almost daily—as they jumped, physically and figuratively, out of Wall Street windows. Franklin Roosevelt helped to restore some semblance of confidence—enough confidence, anyhow, to make a lot of people believe that the only individuals who stood between the common man and chaos were the very people who had mismanaged the situation in the first place. The officers who command lifeboats are generally the same men who have put the ship on the rocks; their stupidity, at least for the moment, rather than reducing the dependency of the passengers on their skills, enlarges it. In America, however, the illusion of equality reserves to every man, no matter how untrained, the power to act unilaterally; if the rulers of the country won't beat up those goddam hippies, *we* will. And yet the fear created by the depression transcended the confidence inspired by the New Deal. It did not create more independent citizens. If anything, it achieved the opposite.

Ten years ago Richard Rovere, tongue partly in cheek, wrote a piece called "The American Establishment" in which he listed the leading personalities and described the major requirements and characteristics of what, in the sloppier language of sociology, has been called the ruling class, the power elite and other reverential names. The establishment, he said, is "a more or less closed and self-sustaining institution that holds a preponderance of power in our more or less open society. Naturally, Establishment leaders pooh-pooh the whole idea; they deny the existence of the Establishment, disclaim any connection of their own with it, and insist that they are merely citizens exercising citizens' rights and responsibilities." Its power, he pointed out, is not always decisive, but its influence is pervasive; it has connections in the higher reaches of banking, government, the foundations and the universities, and its most representative—its penultimate—manifestation is the Council on Foreign Relations. When he wrote the piece, Rovere, tongue still partly in cheek, concluded that its chairman was John J. McCloy,

chairman of the board of the Chase Manhattan Bank; once a partner in Cadwalader, Wickersham & Taft, and also in Cravath, de Gersdorff, Swaine & Wood, as well as, of course, Milbank, Tweed, Hope, Hadley & McCloy; former United States High Commissioner in Germany; former president of the World Bank; liberal Republican; chairman of the Ford Foundation and chairman—my God, how could I have hesitated—of the Council on Foreign Relations; Episcopalian.

The problem with listing credentials and characteristics is that neither background, affiliations nor any other simple catalogue will suffice. The tendencies are too complicated, the permutations too involved. Not all foundations will do, not all big bankers belong, not all universities are indicative. (It is not even enough to specify categories of institutions, since the Ivy League, for example, is not universally a plus; to be a dean at Dartmouth is not half the qualification of a professorship at Chicago—for the right man in the right department: more qualifications. By the same token Ford and Carnegie and Rockefeller are prestige foundations, Danforth is marginal, and Field, which is probably the most socially alert and vital of the lot, does not rate at all.) The choices as to position in the establishment always required a certain amount of *feel*— the same kind of feel, I imagine, that makes for success in the stock market, but given the volatility of contemporary conditions any reading may be deceptive. Since the establishment feels shakier than ever, the level of a man's membership tends to change rapidly. University administrators, for example, are highly vulnerable; by itself the presidency of a college will not suffice for a high establishment position, but a campus disaster may jeopardize a man whose rank is based on other (or additional) qualifications. I suspect that since he was fired by

Ronald Reagan from the presidency of the University of California Clark Kerr has slipped, even though he still heads a Carnegie Foundation study commission. Undoubtedly James Perkins, former president of Cornell, is suffering a similar fate.

The best current indicator of establishment rank is the degree of reverence displayed by the *New York Times*, the establishment's newspaper. When the *Times* treats a fatuous statement with extended courtesy, if it plays political and social platitudes into front-page news, if it gives their authors a "Man in the News" sidebar, then a high establishment figure is almost certainly involved. But even the *Times* is now misleading, because the establishment has lost so much clout; the *Times* knows who is supposed to be pushing the buttons, who talks to whom, and who thinks what of which one, but so often these days when the buttons are pushed no bells ring and the lights don't even flicker. Yes, there is still an establishment, but it is becoming, every day, a little less than the House of Lords.

Although Rovere asserted that the executive committee of the establishment "is carefully balanced religiously as well as racially," it goes almost without saying that it is overwhelmingly WASP. Rovere, in listing what he called the Founding Fathers of the establishment (he was writing in 1961), included one or two Jews like Oscar Straus; but there were no Negroes and few Catholics. Cardinal Cushing may have been a member of the Boston establishment, may indeed have held more power in Boston than the mayor or the president of Harvard, but his eminence as a national establishment figure was limited by his ethnicity; he was, moreover, too political and therefore unclean. Father Theodore Hesburgh, the president of the University of Notre Dame, on the other hand, is considerably more of an establishment figure, because he is, in his national positions and affiliations (as chairman of the U. S.

Commission on Civil Rights, for example) sufficiently liberal, un-Catholic and *sound*. A token Catholic. To become a cardinal or an elected politician or a nouveau-riche businessman requires too much obvious effort, it involves too much ethnicity and too much dirt—and too much push; the typical establishment figure reaches his position without apparent effort— almost, it seems, by inadvertence—and he rarely involves himself in partisan politics except at the very highest levels; committees, trusteeships and appointed public positions are his specialty. My own favorite example is Francis T. P. Plimpton, the former president of the New York Bar Association and former deputy ambassador to the United Nations. From *Who's Who:*

PLIMPTON, Francis Taylor Pearsons, s George Arthur and Frances Taylor (Pearsons). b NYC Dec. 7, 1900. A.B. Amherst 1922; LL.B. Harvard 1925; LL.D. (hon) Colby Coll 1960. Delta Kappa Epsilon; Phi Beta Kappa; Kappa Beta Phi; Delta Sigma Rho. prep Browning Sch NYC; Phillips Exeter Acad. Lawyer; assoc Root, Clark, Buckner and Ballantine NYC 1925–32, in charge Paris office 1930–31; gen solicitor RFC Wash DC 1932–33; partner law firm Debevoise, Plimpton and McLean, NYC 1933–61; Deputy U.S. Rep to UN with rank of Ambassador 1961–63; member U.S. delegation to UN 15th and 16th Gen. Assemblies. Trustee U.S. Trust Co. NY, Bowery Savings Bank; Teachers Ins and Annuity Assn; pres of trustees TIAA stock and Coll Retirement Equities Fund Corp; trustee Amherst, Barnard Coll (v-chmn), Union Theol. Sem., Phillips Exeter Acad (chmn), Athens Coll (Greece), Lingnan Univ (China). Dir. Philharmonic-Symphony Soc NY, Roosevelt Hosp, Amer-Italy Soc. Former director of trustees Greater NY Fund, Foundation for Youth and Student Affairs, Morningside Heights, Church Peace Union, Municipal Art Society, Dalton School, grad faculty New School for Social Research, Judson Health Center, Practicing Law Inst, etc.; f Amer Bar Found; mem Amer Law Inst, Bar Assn NYC (Exec com 1940–45), NY St Bar Assn (Com on Corp Law), Cncl on Foreign Relations, Foreign Pol Assn (dir. 1939–45), Acad. of Pol. Sci, Inst. of Pacific Rels, Soc Mayflower Descendants, Colonial Soc. of Mass. Clubs: Union, Century, Brook, Down

Town, Coffee House (NYC); Piping Rock, Cold Spring Harbor Beach (LI); Metropolitan (Wash); Ausable (Adirondacks); Mill Reef (Antigua BWI) m. June 4 1926 Pauline Ames, dr. Oakes Ames, Boston. ch. George Ames, Francis T. P. Jr., Oakes Ames, Sarah Gay. Rs. 1165 5th Ave NYC and Chichester Rd. West Hills Huntington LI . . .

The style here is responsible worldly involvement, directing institutions which nourish and somehow mediate American culture: schools, universities, hospitals, the Council on Foreign Relations, the United Nations, the Church Peace Union, the missionary college in China, the Philharmonic. Whatever one's private prejudices, one learned to deal graciously with all sorts of exotic personalities, learned, in other words, to make diplomacy a style of life. At the same time one also learned to behave—again almost casually—as if the Century, the Union, the Piping Rock were as accessible as Nedick's or the A & P, as if any good fellow could amble over for a drink or a game of squash, or whatever the place offered. One treated the world, in other words, as if everything were nicely manageable, all doors were open, and all things available without great effort: *now, says the establishment voice, we've got this little war in the Middle East; let's just call up old Jack McCloy (or old David Rockefeller) and see whether there isn't something we can do.* Real establishment influence was never official, it traveled without effort through clubrooms, directors' meetings and casual chat on the telephone or at the Century, and its spirit was always that of the amateur. You fix up a war or a million-dollar grant with the nonchalance of a Willie Mays catching a fly ball; even if the thing involves work it must look easy. It is, in short, the ploy of the aristocrat.

At one time the words—that ambience—would have sounded splendid. It is B. Devereux Barker III, chairman of the Race Committee of the New York Yacht Club, discussing the response of the competing America's Cup skippers to the committee's decision to disallow protests in the first of the 1970 races. "There's a great deal of discussion during a protest meeting," said Barker (Dev for short), "and the committee will always remember the really splendid way Bill and Jim conducted themselves. No harsh language, gentlemen all the way. Sitting side by side with so much at stake, they were an inspiration for us. A lot of what goes on in the world today could take a lesson." Or Seymour St. John, headmaster of the Choate School, quoted in Peter Prescott's book *A World of Our Own:*

> On values—we always look for values that we like, that we stand for, that we believe in; we do not go out of our way to find boys with very different values from ours. . . . If you don't have a certain type of environment, you don't train boys in the same way that you do if you have one. If the values are so disparate that there is no general consensus, then you don't accomplish one of the things that you hope to accomplish. Not inculcation, but rather a gradual understanding of a close relationship with other people who have the values that we have accepted as our values. . . .
>
> Do we hold to standards? Do we say: these are our values? Or do we roll with the punch? Personally, I'm concerned enough about our standards and values in our country at large to feel that if we have to be, as we were twenty-five years ago, a last stronghold in the world, then we had better be the last stronghold. I don't want to be stuffy about that. And I don't feel that we have the only answer. I do feel that we must stick with certain basic values of Western civilization and the Judeo-Christian tradition and while we keep our minds open to all the ephemeral questions that arise, underneath we stand by and hold to and insist on for our students the kind of values that I think you recognize I'm talking about.
>
> In admissions, we have looked for this kind of value in student background.

The language was explicated by a teacher at Choate who pointed out (this was 1967) that "among the intangibles we are going to need for the future are the traditional strengths that are always in danger: friendliness, courtesy, respect, good humor, concern for each person, honesty, integrity, reverence for God and man." B. Devereux Barker all the way. One of the marks of a traditional gentleman is that he cannot understand the difference between behavior at the New York Yacht Club or the Century and proper decorum in a police raid or a welfare office. One of the handicaps of a contemporary gentleman is that no one seems any longer to care. For fashionable prep schools like Choate or Lawrenceville or Deerfield, which once knew where they belonged, and where the rhetoric was reinforced by the WASPiness in the woodwork, the playing fields, the dormitories, even the pictures on the wall, the impact is traumatic. The kids should have the stuff in their blood, are not supposed to ask why, what does it mean, are supposed to understand that they have been born into special places in the society, and that the school will—without question—train them to the manners which their place demands. The Judeo-Christian tradition? The West? The WASP? Over and over there is talk about values, and the values are supposed to justify the endless impositions, the lack of privacy, the lack of time, and the structure that runs kids from required class to required athletics to required chapel, and that tries to teach them that the one thing privilege cannot buy is honest self-expression. But they do not want to join: first they shuffle their feet in chapel, then they try a little grass and a decorous protest, then they revolt or simply stop coming. There is talk about reform or a new headmaster or student committees, but the applications keep going down and the barriers keep getting higher. "Is there something in the atmosphere that is not conducive to openness?" St. John wonders. "Perhaps some of the communication gap comes from each generation; and we need hard to fill it in, to make contact."

But even if men like St. John could actually listen—and some probably can—it would be impossible for them to understand what they heard. The Choates of this world grew great when the social assumptions on which they operated were taken for granted, when the students, the school and the parent agreed (at least on the surface) on where the kid's place would be, on what sort of world it was, and on how he should be trained to get there. The school depended on a larger set of assumptions not only about America or the West (or the Judeo-Christian tradition) but about the special place of its students within them. Now both are shattered. The kids begin to understand what is happening; the best law students do not want to join the downtown firms (not one 1970 law-review graduate of the Harvard Law School entered private practice); the brightest college seniors disdain business, and nearly all those who are, one way or another, angry about this country have lost faith in the beneficence of manipulation in high places. At places like Lawrenceville, the older hands still speak about "opening the place up," about bringing in more blacks, more Jews, more of the "disadvantaged." They still believe that they are offering something that people want and that they represent a gate to a place where kids will someday want to be. But that assumption is no longer justified. If they open things up, the school may blow; if they do not it will become increasingly stagnant. Either way you lose.

It is always dangerous to underestimate the power of WASP resources and institutions; WASPs do, after all, control the banks, the foundations, the corporations and—with a growing number of exceptions—the universities. The WASP establishment, moreover, still retains considerable mystique and money, each of them a commodity much in demand during periods of crisis, especially those which are economic in nature. They can still *buy* things. And people. And yet there is growing reason to doubt. In the spring of 1970, when thousands of individuals descended on Congress to protest the invasion of Cambodia, a group of Wall Street lawyers who made the trip identified themselves as members of the establishment, a self-refuting claim if ever there was one. No real member of the establishment ever admits his membership—certainly not to the press; the admission itself is grounds for disqualification. The old establishment style prohibited overt lobbying; you called up old Jack or old Bill or old David, and you discussed it. To proclaim your involvement to the public is either a confession of impotence or a cover for other, more complex, objectives. I found it admirable that Francis Plimpton himself spoke forcefully on the matter of police repression, and that he made the journey to Washington on the issue of Cambodia. But both indicated that the normal establishment circuits were no longer effective; old Dick, old Spiro and old John Mitchell are hard to reach.

According to the best indicators, the establishment's fair-haired boy is now John Gardner, former president of the Carnegie Foundation, former Secretary of the Department of Health, Education and Welfare, former co-chairman of the Urban Coalition, and now head of Common Cause, an organization that describes itself as a "Citizens' Lobby" in the Public Interest: "an effective force in rebuilding America . . . not a third party but a third force . . . which will uphold the public interest against all comers . . . to revitalize politics and government . . . with an overriding interest in the well-being of the whole society." Common Cause, as much as anything, may indicate what has happened to the establishment and to those who depend on it for leadership. Common Cause is the creature of a mitotic split from the Urban Coalition, which Gardner had taken over after he left HEW in 1968, and which was itself a product of the panic ensuing from the ghetto riots of the preceding summers. By that time Gardner had already become a philosopher-hero to those in the establishment who were trying to dream modern. A Californian with a Ph.D. in psychology, and once, we are told, a champion swimmer, he had done all the proper things, had taught at Mount Holyoke College and at Connecticut College for Women, served in the Marine Corps and with the Office of Strategic Services in World War II, and joined Carnegie as a staff associate in 1946. In 1955 he became president of Carnegie, and in 1965 Lyndon Johnson named him Secretary of HEW. There were other qualifications. For fifteen years Gardner had been an apostle of Civic Responsibility and Leadership and Excellence. He had written about Tasks for the Tough-Minded and Self-Discipline, about the Aims of a Free People and the Recovery of Confidence, trying always, it seemed, to resolve the contradictions between the elitist impulses of establishment intellectuals and the democratic professions that the fifties and sixties seemed to require. Gardner's contention, in a book called *Excellence*, that a plumber with pride in his craft and a commitment to the highest standards is as noble a creature as a nuclear physicist or a neurosurgeon was received like revelation. Here was a man whose democratic heart led him precisely to the kind of social selectivity (based on merit, of course, and not on class privilege) that corporate intellectuals already practiced.

All the causes were precisely right, the rhetoric well balanced, the tone exquisitely modulated. Gardner, moreover, was a kind of nonpersonality, a man untouched by scandal or gossip or even by idiosyncrasy. He was not the kind to talk about his aches and pains, not a whiner, not a joker. He was what the enlightened WASP would regard as Class, and he thus became a logical establishment figure to take on for the newly organized Urban Coalition the task of midwife for the bankers, corporate executives, union leaders and ghetto activists in what was regarded (depending on your point of view) as a collaborative effort to facilitate communication among urban groups and pour private money into the ghetto, to clean up the corporate image of the Chase Manhattan Bank, to energize the establishment in solving the problems of the cities, and—most immediately—to cool the angry spades. The Urban Coalition was created at a moment when otherwise sober individuals were certain that hordes of blacks were about to march down Fifth Avenue and Michigan Avenue and Market Street to loot every shop, trash every bank and burn every corporate office in sight. Gardner said that he learned a great deal in those Urban Coalition meetings— learned to listen to militants and militant language, and to understand why the brothers had trouble getting jobs, decent housing and all the rest. But the Coalition, despite its occasional successes in sponsoring programs of ghetto rehabilitation and in prying loose a few big-bank dollars to finance minority businesses and housing, grew limp and moribund. Its most visible manifestation was the ubiquitous slogan "Give a Damn" which appeared on subway placards, billboards and television public-service announcements and which was directed, presumably, to all the unmannered honkie slobs— Poles, Irishmen, Italians—who were then regarded as the prime cause of the problem. These were the people who wouldn't integrate their schools and neighborhoods, who supported all-white unions, and who produced racial friction in the cities. Give a Damn. Be nice to the nigs, said the Responsible People.

There is no telling now whether the frail performance of the Coalition reflected the impotence of its corporate members— whether even David Rockefeller, for example, couldn't give the Chase Manhattan Bank a corporate conscience—or whether the inability (or unwillingness) to deliver what the original Coalition rhetoric had promised was merely a sign that the urgency of the crisis had been quickly reconsidered and demoted from an apocalypse to a problem in public relations. At any rate, just at the moment when the Coalition was falling into its impotent funk it spawned an internal twin called the Urban Coalition Action Council, a political arm not dependent on the separate initiatives of its various members. UCAC lobbied for welfare reform, against the nomination of G. Harold Carswell to the Supreme Court, and for the extension of the Voting Rights Act, which the Administration had been trying to water down. In the fall of 1970 Gardner escalated UCAC into Common Cause.

The original benefactors of Common Cause—the providers of what the philanthropy business calls seed money—were, by and large, the same blue-chip individuals who had helped support the Coalition: John D. Rockefeller III, John Hay Whitney, Norton Simon, Roger Stevens, Arthur A. Houghton, Jr., Howard Stein, Andrew Heiskell, Roy Larson, Tom Watson, Jr., Morris Hadley, Mrs. Arthur Hays Sulzberger, plus organizations like the Ford Motor Company, United Artists, the United Steelworkers of America, Time, Inc., and the International Union of Electrical Workers. But their support was regarded as a one-time proposition; Common Cause was to be a membership organization relying not on a few large donors but on the fifteen-dollar annual fee that each of a hundred thousand concerned citizens would contribute. The idea was not simply to mitigate the charge that the Action Council–become–Common Cause was an organization of fat cats, but also to create, to find or (more significantly) to *imagine* a constituency not concerned with its special interests, one that is not political in the ordinary, scruffy, sense, but will be political only in the Public Interest. It requires a special imagination and background to believe that a particular constituency and a certain kind of leadership can rally "against all comers" in Its Name. Common Cause suggested that the thing called the Public Interest is distinguishable (to certain people) from *particular* interests; the Public Interest, moreover, was more noble than particular interests and, almost by definition, could be articulated only by those who have no overriding special interests to defend (since the special interests would, logically, one might assume, tend to cloud their view)—those, in other words, who were already sufficiently secure or established (or saintly?) to be incorruptible and selfless. Such people must necessarily be individuals who place themselves into an "American" tradition that is beyond class or race or time, beyond the pressing business of making it, beyond even the memory of having made it. It is only the establishment which can deny the possibility that the Public Interest is simply an arrogant misunderstanding of its private concerns, however selfless it may regard them. It is only the establishment which can toss out the word "we" as if it meant everybody, as if there were no "us" and "them." The crisis (real or, again, imagined) which gave impetus to Common Cause is the breakdown of that "we"; it is the dawning realization that when someone says "we" as if it did mean everybody there is a cacophony of count-me-outs.

The creation of Common Cause generated no end of speculation. It does not require a great deal of cynicism to wonder what, beyond ingenuousness, lies beneath this unprecedented effort in public virtue. A plot by the Eastern Establishment/ liberal Republican/Council on Foreign Relations/Ivy League axis to grab national power away from the boors of the Nixon Administration? The Last Hurrah of the Old WASP? John Lindsay's national machine for 1972? Gardner's campaign organization? The possibility that Common Cause was an establishment plan to make Gardner President would indicate even more political ingenuousness than its declared objectives. A cloudy historical memory may suggest that once, long ago, statesmanship was created out of the untainted unpolitical souls of public saints, that in Platonic states philosopher-kings might be crowned by acclamation, but any contemporary politician worth his ward knows that virtue is hypocrisy unless it has been dragged through the muck of contention, and Gardner has always been clean.

Most likely, Gardner was running for something higher than the Presidency, something more noble and important, perhaps, in the hearts of his constituents. What does a man do after he has written about "tasks for the tough-minded," about "values in action," "shared visions" and the "opportunity to serve"? What place can he hold if he can write—not in 1870 or in 1914, but in 1970—words like the following?

> We are not at our best when the battle is won; we are strivers, at our best when the goal seems nearly unattainable. That is our nature. And it fits us well for the world in which we find ourselves. There are inescapable features of the human condition that guarantee the continued struggle . . .
>
> We will not accomplish the exceedingly difficult tasks of redesign that lie ahead without a combination of commitment and cool intellect. Intellect alone won't generate the courage and determination necessary to cut through the obstacles. But the contemporary fashion of ardor without intellect is even more inadequate. Accomplishing social change is a task for the tough-minded and competent.
>
> We shall accomplish none of the significant tasks if we count our short-term comfort as more important than our long-term future, if we are unwilling to tax ourselves, if we lack the courage to demand disciplined behavior of ourselves and others.

Where can he go if he has already risen to—and beyond—the pinnacle of big-time philanthropy, both public and private, and if he wants to regard himself as a "philosopher who doesn't hesitate to get his hands dirty in the rough and tumble that advances social policy"? Most probably, if he is not to repudiate his past, he will create Common Cause, will try to organize something that is political but regards itself as above ordinary politics, a movement that is part lobby, part citizenship training and part moral rearmament: "We will lobby in the public interest at all levels of government, but especially at the federal level. We will press for a reordering of national priorities. We will also press for the revitalization of the public process, to make our political and governmental institutions more responsive to the needs of the nation and the will of its citizens." He will, in brief, not found a church but lead a revival, will be a super-philanthropist working the biggest cause of all.

Common Cause, now established in a suite of Washington offices (foundation modern crossed with political-precinct functional), employs a staff of a dozen professionals, many of them former second- or third-echelon hands in the New Frontier or the Great Society and all but one of them white, and a growing number of volunteers who man telephones, stuff envelopes and try to rally Common Cause members Out There to write or call their Congressmen on specific issues. The style is moderate-corporate, the political tactics are conventional and the objectives are middle-of-the-road liberal. The members, who are overwhelmingly white, middle-class, and college educated, regard the Vietnam War, governmental reform, the environment and poverty as the most pressing national issues, but their letters to Common Cause suggest that their distress has more fundamental roots, that here are thousands of displaced people whose malaise goes beyond issues or politics, people too "responsible" or decorous for picket lines and sit-ins, but certain nonetheless that they have lost control over those things that they used to regard as their most special possessions. Responsiveness and Accountability are the rallying cry of the displaced middle:

If it is any inspiration to you, I thought you'd like to know that you are my only hope for the future.

The Masses have most of the votes and are gaining more. The members of all our legislatures listen to groups with the majority vote. In other words, the masses control our destiny. That makes us socially a backward nation . . .

Our support isn't much but as long as your cause remains honest, genuine, dedicated and unselfish in the interests of this nation we will do what we can to support it in word and work.

I'm a middle class, middle age, middle income bourgeois and love it. It appears that this comfortable little world of mine is coming apart at the seams. Why?

If you read that mail long enough you are left, somehow, with the perverse thought that here are people who never had all that much confidence in the democratic process and who never believed it could survive outside the small town and the village council. By and large they are people who once regarded the nation and its ideology as comfortable preserves, the small-town landlords of American culture, who took it for granted that to be white and Protestant was to be the preeminent American, and who never felt easy about the ethnic upstarts, or about noise and contention and the uncertainty of real partisanship. There is something here that smells of sanitation and zoning, that has the suburban suspicion of anything labeled political, and that has always been committed, above all, to keeping the place clean of beer cans and undesirable elements (and that nowadays calls itself ecology). Here are people caught between their sense of crisis and their absolute inability (out of propriety or apathy or simple lack of imagination) to act as if there were one. Give us something to do, says the mail, tell us how we can be effective; but do they really want to know? The fee for Common Cause, the fifteen dollars, is a kind of poll tax, and the people who join—many of them—seem to regard it as an opportunity to make the politics of Bronxville and Winnetka into the politics of Washington.

Common Cause appeals to large expectations, not only because that is the way its literature is pitched but because Gardner himself has come to symbolize the abstractions of High Purpose and Great Objectives. The only qualification in the nearly unanimous Gardner-reverence of the press concerns his effectiveness: Can he get anything done? Common Cause is therefore caught in a set of semantic and practical traps from which there is no escape except, perhaps, to ever-higher levels of abstraction. Great promises, small steps; great battles, small casualties; central objectives, peripheral villains; vast rigid institutions, conventional weapons. The focus at the close of the Ninety-first Congress was on support of welfare reform; early in 1971, as the new Congress convened, it was abolition of the seniority system and reform of campaign practices. The members of Common Cause were urged to write or wire their Congressmen, the staff lobbyists called on uncommitted and friendly members of the House, and Gardner from his corner office phoned his friends in the legislature and tried to coordinate the Common Cause effort with other groups committed to the same side of the same issues. More radical action has not been contemplated; it is not the kind of thing in which "the members feel comfortable." People who are attracted to Common Cause because government is unresponsive are then asked to do the very things—write your Congressman—that presumably failed in the first place. The problem is compounded by the ambiguity of the Public Interest. The very process of choosing issues and positions (either by polling members or by decision of the directors and staff) makes certain that every common cause will be something that has already been certified as acceptable to proper people; it will already have been approved by the *Times* and other "responsible" publications, and will already have been labeled consistent with that view of the Public Interest to which the members and leaders of Common Cause subscribe. Which is to say that it will be fashionable.

It is hard not to be sympathetic. If Common Cause represents any portion of the People it is the incipient minority of decent WASP-minded individuals who once took their hegemony for granted and now feel besieged. Nixon is not their man, although his offenses may have more to do with style and manners than with policy. At one time in the past—real or imagined—these WASPs *were* the Public Interest and the country was theirs. Seventy-five years ago, as the Irish politicians started to take over the cities, their grandfathers created municipal-reform leagues and good-government associations (later labeled Goo-goos by the likes of James Michael Curley of Boston) to press for civil service, the merit system and other measures to keep the schools (or the police, or the awarding of franchises) "out of politics" and to curb the power of the ethnic upstarts. Now, as displacement in other forms—technological, psychological and institutional—has become not only national but, in a sense, cosmic, as the People are losing control not only in Washington but in the special institutions they helped establish (including, among other things, the universities and the civil service), there are new forms of goo-gooism, and Common Cause is one of them. Common Cause is the shadow establishment. It was born not of strength but of weakness. Gardner is the first to point out that the institutions the goo-goos created to curb or circumvent the urban politicians have themselves become rigid and unresponsive. The crisis, therefore, is not simply that politics will not work; unpolitics won't work either. The people who invented "nonpolitical" forms of public administration are no longer able to manage their own instruments. Fifty years ago civil service and "scientific management" were their answer to corruption; the civil service and the institution were the Public Interest. Now the institution is also unresponsive. *Everybody's organized but the people.* The WASP is a refugee in his own country.

Maybe there is no language to describe Gardner's kind of commitment other than what he used in his books and speeches: a dose of Teddy Roosevelt, a dash of Parson Weems, a pinch of Kipling. The writing speaks of "the demands that history has placed upon us," about responding "with vigor and courage and dedication" to those demands, about the ability to survive as a nation "if enough Americans care enough," and he uses that resplendent "we" with the assurance of a man whose mortgages have long been paid: he knows who "we" are and whose history it is, but does he really understand that the cause of all that disaffection among black people and blue-collar workers, among students and now, increasingly, in the bourgeois middle may be nothing other than the growing suspicion that his version of history, government and institutions is a lie? Does he understand that his history is not necessarily my history and certainly not the history of an angry black person in Harlem? Everything is sensible—the observation that there is no way for a society to operate without "responsible" people, the conviction that someone or something has to replace the establishment (though, God knows, it isn't the masses), the idea that institutions are always in incipient decay, that every generation has to do the job all over again—but what am I to do with all that? It is always the same moral lesson, the same subtle preaching, the same mission. It always smells of "public education," us and them, missionaries and cannibals, "Americans" and immigrants. Is this all that a good WASP can do? Is this the only thing left to a person who means well and who, as much as almost any man, can still call the rich and powerful? It is hard, he wrote somewhere, "for Americans to realize that the survival of the idea for which this nation stands is not inevitable." Does the Public Interest have any meaning except as the injunction of an elitist, the self-serving statement of someone who thinks he knows better? Is the Public Interest the last cry in the wilderness?

The creation of Common Cause was similar in spirit to another WASP effort to confront social breakdown in the late sixties—the attempt by John Lindsay and McGeorge Bundy of the Ford Foundation to teach the slobs of New York some manners. In the process they almost managed to blow the place apart—managed, indeed, to create so much ill-will that only the monumental ineptitude of Mario Procaccino, Lindsay's opponent in the 1969 election, saved Big John, another of the fair-haired boys, from a humiliating defeat. It was, moreover, something just this side of sheer luck that kept the Jews and the blacks from slicing each other up with something more lethal than invective. What Lindsay and Bundy set out to do was to sell the city on the virtues of school decentralization and local control, a highly admirable objective considering the self-serving rigidity and brutality of the downtown school administration, but a complete reversal of form for the historic WASP advocate of clean who was perennially trying to make government more efficient and professional, to take it away from the ethnic ward politicians, not hand it over to them, and whose forefathers (if not he himself) had always preached such goo-goo virtues as civil service and the merit system. (Lindsay himself, in his efforts to reform city government in New York, had tried to centralize all municipal departments other than the schools into a handful of superagencies.) On that score alone, then, school decentralization was something spooky for the liberals of New York. But the offense was compounded by an unmatched imperiousness of style: it assumed that the city's teachers and administrators are as secure in their profession and possessions as any Park Avenue patrician, and it ignored the fact that most of the city's sixty thousand teachers learned long ago that their most valuable property is not their skills (and certainly not their bank accounts) but the job itself. What the American teacher (or any other civil servant) owns is points, ratings, credit, seniority. If the system changes he is likely to lose the things for which he has worked all his life—things which cannot be exchanged, which have little marketability, but which were given meaning by the very people who were now treating them with so much contempt. His resistance was therefore ascribed to bigotry (which, of course, it often was), thus reinforcing the hostilities between the Jewish teachers and the black parents, persuading each that the other was indeed the enemy: if he was a good teacher, the black or Puerto Rican community leaders who would take over the schools would be happy to hire him, and if there was some uncertainty, a little fussing, in the process (or in integrating his neighborhood, or any other act of social conscience) he should please be a good fellow, be a brick, and behave like all other patricians and give a little, give a damn. It never occurred to the establishment devotees of excellence, with all their good intentions, that standards did not matter at all, did not matter to the teacher or the system—that all that counted was *points* (and, at an advanced age, some peace and quiet, steady pay, vacations and predictable increments in salary and pensions). It did not occur to them that the majority of Americans do not feel, as John Gardner put it, "so blessedly comfortable," and that easy living was not a narcotic but a frightening, haunting dream that spun like a tornado out of the memories of the depression. In trying to integrate the schools or the neighborhoods or the unions, the spokesmen of the establishment were trying manfully to correct historic injustices—injustices which were obviously there, but injustices which the establishment itself had helped create and justify, and for which it was now asking the slobs to pay the bill. In the middle sixties people who sent their children to St. Mark's and Groton were asking the Irish of South Boston to integrate their schools; in the early seventies they were asking them to integrate their unions even though the unions, kept tight to protect the wages and perquisites of membership, had been established on the same terms of nepotism and personal acquaintance as the banks and trusts of the privileged.

II

There are, depending on how you count, some eighty million of them: the forgotten man, the silent majority, the blue-collar class. Their family income is somewhere between five thousand and twelve thousand a year—truck drivers, millworkers, stevedores, mechanics, ironworkers, steamfitters, meat cutters, packinghouse workers: people who, despite the verbal categories, are more likely to wear green pants and shirts than blue (hippies and convicts wear blue), put decal American flags on the rear window of the car and a plastic figure of Jesus on the dashboard, bowl every Tuesday and go to the trotters as often as the wife allows, drive from trailer park to trailer park "camping," take their moonlight pay in cash, call for law and order and think themselves affluent. Most of all they are intimidated by the American dream—are haunted by it—and believe firmly that not to have made it is not to be fully American at all. While they cheat and hustle, holding second jobs or sending the wife to work, they continue to rely on the predictability of the system they are cheating, and are convinced that, by and large, their failures are their own, not those of the technology, the economy or the political structures of American life. Many of them never finished high school and are therefore consigned to the dead-end jobs that such educational failures teach men to accept, but they learned well the lessons of civics-book Americanism: the importance of hard work, just rewards, clean looks, Victorian morals and victory in war. They learned, moreover, that the nation was supposed to honor its traditional virtues and the people who try to live by them, that the price of citizenship itself—whether you were a honkie, a Polack or a wop—was, if nothing else, the lip service and costume of WASP tradition.

Which is why they feel forgotten. For a decade the journalists of elegance, the sociologists, the politicians divided the country between the affluent and the poor, disregarding what used to be called the common man and confronting him with the unsatisfactory choice between, on the one hand, living far above his economic and moral means and, on the other, being classified as a nigger. If he was not affluent and secure, could not manage the *noblesse oblige* of integration and social justice, then he must be poor, must, that is, be classified with the colored people. He was obviously unwilling to do the second (would often, indeed, refuse to accept welfare, even when he was fully qualified, because welfare was for shiftless blacks) and yet unable to do the first. For himself there was no voice, no category, no political leadership, no place in the equation. He had to call himself affluent, yet knew at the end of every month that even though he had worked his tail off he just managed to stay even. Twenty years ago his father was earning five thousand a year; now the son was earning ten thousand—plus a little more on weekends; obviously those must be the wages of affluence (who could have imagined so much money?), and yet it never came out right.

All around were the ghosts of the depression and the memories of struggle—breadlines and foreclosures, unemployment and insecurity—and you therefore armed yourself with the instruments of economic and social resistance. To the extent that younger men had learned to take their steady jobs for granted, to the extent that the tribal memory had been forgotten—to that extent they had also (perhaps without knowing why) begun to discover the ragged edges of their fathers' dreams. Development houses were not little palaces; the pay was good but the job demeaning and the psychic payoff marginal. The specific anxieties of unemployment were replaced by the vaguer and more terrifying existence on an economic plateau where inflation tended to cancel wage increases, needs always exceeded resources, and automatic machinery destroyed even the mythology and confidence of tough work in ugly places. No fashionable issue here. The liberal wisdom about Vietnam, racial injustice, poverty and student protest was relevant only in creating contempt; what mattered instead were the barriers and protections that had been established through a generation of struggle: union seniority, the civil-service bureaucracy, the petty sinecures of particular ethnic groups, and the "good" neighborhoods and classrooms which still remained uncontaminated by blacks. If you ask about schools in the suburbs, people speak about the kids who are going on to Harvard or the number of National Merit finalists; if you ask in Bethlehem or Daly City or Parma, they will answer that they haven't had any trouble yet—meaning that there has been no change, that the blacks haven't moved in, and that drugs haven't taken over. For a man who learned at twenty-five (or at eighteen) that opportunities are limited— that, as Robert Wood once said, "the frontiers of his career opportunities have been fixed [since] he found out that he had too many obligations, too much family, and too few skills," it is stability that counts, stability in the job and the neighbor-hood, stability in home and church and friends. Change is al-most inevitably for the worse; celebrating Sunday mass in English, revising the liturgy and bringing guitars into church are no more welcome than black children in the local school and the first Negro family on the street. A man of wealth or education has other places to go, can move physically or intel-lectually, but the man in the lower middle has none.

In the last few years his world has slowly started to come apart. He still has *Reader's Digest,* "The Lucy Show," *True Grit,* the track, the lake, the Sunday ball game, but his most important possession other than job and home, his bourgeois pride, is up for contempt. The smart people are putting him down; while their well-heeled kids are tearing up the cam-puses and burning the flag he is being called a redneck and a bigot, being told that America is a sick society, and being cas-tigated for not giving up things he cannot possibly do with-out. He was supposed to work for everything he had, to pay taxes, to send his kids to school, to obey the law (and that, being the American way, was all right with him); it was even acceptable to him that poor people get special training—at least to get them off welfare—but he wasn't about to tolerate special privileges in *his* union or *his* schools, wasn't going to pay *their* bills, and couldn't understand why everybody was coddling a bunch of pot-smoking freaks who had never done a decent day's work in their life. It wasn't surprising, then, that he started to look for a man with a club, or to do a little clubbing himself, why he flirted with George Wallace, elected an ex-cop mayor of Minneapolis, cheered Nixon and Agnew when they talked about campus bums, effete intellectual snobs and other liberal lowlife, flew the American flag on his house and car, and applauded whenever the cops started beating up on freaks or shooting up a Panther office. Whatever law and order means to a man who thinks his wife is unsafe on the street or whose kids get shaken down in school—and it obviously means a lot—it also contains the overtones of something like normalcy, a demand that everybody play it by the book and that things shouldn't be as they are but as one imagines they used to be. All his life the man in the blue collar believed in his lessons—lessons taught not only by schoolteachers and establishment flacks but also, and with immense effect, by the Catholic Church. There is no way to estimate how much the incessant injunction to respect authority—the authority of priests and nuns, the authority of superiors, the authority of Authority itself—has conditioned the current belief, especially in the lower middle class, that the President knows best. In America, perhaps because of nineteenth-century nativism, perhaps because of the Puritan atmosphere, the American Catholic Church developed a habit of rendering unto Caesar more than his due. The Church taught people to accept, to work hard, to love their country, and not to complain. To prove its Americanism it carried the flag higher than anyone else. Now the very people who represented temporal authority—the wealthy, the people of class and learning—are telling the man in the lower middle that it was all Mickey Mouse, that Americanism wasn't what he thought it was, and that everything he had been doing wasn't worth it. (The Church itself has created enormous resentment by changing its rituals, demoting certain saints and Anglicizing the mass. That too jeopardizes stability.) Nothing is safe or sacred. Italian parents who were finally convinced that they should send their children to college saw the colleges blowing up; people who had learned to defer to erudition found the erudite negotiating with the freaks; and ethnics who had learned to dream about suburbs and green lawns were told (or learned for themselves) that their version of the good life contained a strong dose of drugs, adultery and fear. After all that work, all that sublimation, all that Americanization, the establishment was deserting them; the tenants of the culture were discovering the neglect of the landlords, knew vaguely that a bargain had been broken, and were ready to start taking matters into their own hands.

It was a complicated bargain. Most people in the lower middle class have few illusions about upward mobility; somewhere, probably as early as grade school, they learned about folks and began to understand the subtle distinctions of manner, fashion and language between themselves and those who hold positions of esteem. They learned that expectations were limited, that they lack a certain style, that they aren't one of the "bright students," and that their academic failures are, on the one hand, justified by specific personal limitations and, on the other, mitigated by certain forms of compensation: athletic skill, popularity, a little fun. They expected the schools to teach order, discipline and a certain set of "good" manners, not to produce candidates for the university and the executive suite. At the same time they were convinced that those positions were justified by the attributes and behavior of those who held them. Black parents in the early sixties assembled the hard data to demonstrate what many had suspected for years: that the schools systematically discriminated against minority and underclass children, that it was the schools which failed, not the students, but most whites never came to the same conclusion; the system still teaches them to accept the idea that they had their chance, that they are deserving losers, and that the distinctions the schools and society make are founded on objectively valid criteria. At the same time they develop certain expectations: that the elite will not tolerate certain transgressions in its own ranks, that standards of behavior will be self-enforced, and that there will be at least token deference to the workingman and to work in general. It was also expected that the elite would help police the lower orders and permit the agents of the common morality broad latitude in cracking down on freaks, drifters, homosexuals, vagrants, radicals and other violators of middle-class belief. The tyranny of the majority may be not nearly as extensive as Tocqueville believed; it is not able to crush all things in its path, because it is too often divided or apathetic, but it nonetheless expects no interference from the elite in trying to enforce its will on unpopular minorities. For its part, the elite was expected to justify its privileges by being *classy* and by avoiding offensive acts and gestures. Individual playboys were tolerable, occasional eccentrics were amusing, but eccentricity on a class basis was forbidden and the flaunting of bad manners impermissible. You do not make fun of the servants in public.

It has frequently been said that the American democrat never took to socialism because he imagined himself to be an incipient capitalist; expecting someday to be wealthy himself, he was not about to jeopardize the property and position of others. When the intimidating talk of universal affluence began in the fifties, and when easy credit began to foster the illusion of a "better life" for all, a large number of Americans mortgaged their fantasies to the system, began to think of themselves as consumers and property owners, hustled off to become middle-class sharers in the boundless cornucopia of development housing, supermarkets and discount stores and began to complain about taxes, welfare and "hippies who fart around the streets and don't work." They sounded not like union men demanding a bigger share of the profits but like a petty bourgeoisie fearing most the things it had barely ceased to be. (Their rightful forefathers, as Andrew Hacker wrote, "are not the middle class but rather the peasants and proletarians of an earlier time.") For such people the most threatening act is not the socialist's attack on real privilege but the blasting of fantasies: the reminder that one's status is still limited and one's position still insecure. Every college rebel and every hippie freak therefore symbolizes not only heretofore forbidden forms of elite behavior but, at the same time, proclaims to every *Untermensch* the existence of class distinctions and personal failures not repealed by the façade of discount affluence. When the official agents of the establishment—the college president, or John Lindsay, or the liberal press—fail to punish freaks and dissidents (when, indeed, they seem to honor them), then the man in the blue collar is forced to face the limits of his affluence, his security and his Americanism, and the bargain has been violated. If the elite aren't punishing their kids for bad words, long hair, sex and drugs, how can anyone hold out? If they do not honor the manners and mythology of Americanism, then what was all the work for? A rich man can permit his children to run around, but for a family on the margin of security such a luxury is beyond the bounds of possibility. We had never been entirely unequivocal about the symbolic patricide of Americanization and upward mobility, but if at one time mobility meant rejection of older (or European) styles, it was at least done in the name of America. Now the patricide is being carried on under a wholly new set of labels, unpatriotic, un-American and incomprehensible. Even though the rebelling students are attacking the establishment, they still represent, in the eyes of people at the bottom, the establishment itself.

Leonard Kriegel, a teacher at the City University of New York, revisiting his old Jewish neighborhood in the Bronx, a place that had, in its own time, been as saturated with trade-union radicalism and socialism as any in America:

> The neighborhood is not yet a slum. It may never become one, although one suspects that its days are numbered. Nor is it a place where politics is taken as seriously as it once was. Even among the grand-fathers of the revolution that never came who wait for death on the sidewalks of Mosholu Parkway, there is little talk of politics. History, we have been told, has many strange twists. Can anyone blame these old people if they do not understand life-style radicalism as what they had in mind when they launched their own struggles? When I talk to their grandchildren at City College, I frequently find myself thinking that they are right to have cashed in socialism for sun on a park bench. In any case, they do not believe that they have any choice.
>
> For they have been forgotten—by their children, who betrayed them to begin with, by their grandchildren, who never bothered to ask who or what they were, by the Left, by New York, by time itself. Perhaps that last is the greatest of all betrayals, for when time robs you of your dignity then memory itself becomes treacherous. And they are now the enemy, inhabitants of the country of the faceless. They are not willing to pay the price because they insist that the fault is not theirs. And they insist, in however inarticulate a fashion, that we radicals look at ourselves as we really are, nothing extenuated. The guilt, they claim, is not theirs, although they are once again being made the scapegoats of a society unwilling to face up to the dictates of its fears or its conscience and pay from where the larder really is overstuffed.
>
> "Give a damn!" one reads on the buses of New York. "It's still 1930 in the ghettos." This is real enough, despite one's knowledge that, to the man who wrote it, 1930 means *Bonnie and Clyde*, a dreamy tech-nicolor landscape filmed through the haze. But it is not merely in the ghettos that 1930 is still alive. For 1930 is, as much as anything else, a particular consciousness of history. And we have forgotten how real

1930 is to people such as those in my neighborhood. For the neighborhood suffers from a sense of impending poverty, a feeling that the wind has once again shifted and that events are out of control, that time and power and calculation are rallying against them, that there is no one to listen to them, no one to speak for them, nothing against which they can protest. And so their world is to be forfeit, their reality to be surrendered, while they themselves will be cast aside, dry bones and dry souls, for one or another slogan that is simply a distortion of the truth they once viewed as elementary. Men suffer and men die. *All* men. No, they do not have to be told that it is still 1930 in the ghettos, for it has never been anything but 1930 in the neighborhood. They were not born to rule; they would settle now merely to be told that they were not born to suffer excessively either.

No place, apparently, has been reserved for them in the apocalyptic future. What they need is an Orwell whose honesty has thrust up from their own midst. What they have gotten are the barbs of swingers and the friendship of such as Mario Procaccino, and while the one may be a testimony to their virtue the other is an indication that fate, too, has settled for a quick laugh at their expense. "With friends like you," the old saying has it, "I don't need enemies."

But the truth remains, and the truth is that they are not the racists, not, at least, if that term has any meaning beyond that of being the most available pejorative whip for anyone in the radical circus eager to try his luck as ringmaster. For the rhetoric of radical and liberal righteousness is being created at their expense. They have been lashed by the tongues, minds and pens of their Fire Island betters—and they are now beginning to stiffen with the helpless self-defensive anguish of the victim suddenly accused of being a victimizer. And can those of us who have created our virtue at the expense of their reality escape the whispers that tell us that they, too, are suffering, that their terror and fear, like the terror and fear of the black dispossessed, are something against which, in our shame, we should protest? For my uncle is right. Poor is poor. And the brotherhood, ultimately, is not of the skin.

In the period of a few years all the rules seemed to change and things that had presumably been accomplished decades ago were found still undone. All that rhetoric about "regardless of creed or color," all that prattling about equal treatment, all those words about the melting pot and opportunity. In some mythic prehistoric era before the textbooks were written and the self-praise meted out, most of us (if not all) had presumably made it, had begun to trade the tenuous security of the ethnic neighborhood, the familiar faces and accents, the native-language churches and the old-country food for full-status Americanism. But there they still were, the Irish in South Boston, the Slavs in Pittsburgh and Cleveland, the Italians in the Bronx; here were people still going to the Ukrainian Club and holding their weddings at the Polish-American, reading *El Tiempo*, *Il Progresso*, the *Irish Weekly*, the *Staats-Zeitung* and a hundred others in every conceivable language; here were priests still offering to hear confession in Italian, Spanish or English, or even in Polish and Croat; here were men still jamming the bocce courts and following the international soccer scores. In the wake of Black Power and in response to the new signals about ethnic pride we found them again, and they found themselves: Italian-American Unity Day, Polish Power, Ukrainian Power, the Jewish Defense League. Suddenly the Poles demanded equal representation on the school board, the Slavs called for action to "make up for lost time," and the Italians picketed the newspapers to stop them from associating Italian names with organized crime.

Since the whole country had been certain that only black and Spanish-speaking people were poor, the poverty programs rarely represented white ethnics, many of whom were, for similar reasons, too proud to use them. What had happened, of course, is that the problems which were supposed to have been solved eons ago had not been solved at all. Behind the millions who have moved to the "affluent" suburbs there are several million others who have never moved at all and who now find themselves caught between presumptions about their own success (or assumptions that they simply do not exist) and the hard facts of retardation. In the old neighborhoods of the cities the incessant depredations of the bulldozer, the incursions of supermarkets, the decline of ethnic stores and churches and clubs, the destruction of familiar places, were always hard to take, but the justifications of progress and Americanization that once accompanied them—the faith that there was a place worth moving to, that there was, indeed, a kind of American imperative to move—have become more doubtful. For the first time the signals from above are indistinct. Exposure to the modern has always been disturbing, but now it leaves some people on the verge of hysteria because the one-time exemplars of the culture, the models of Americanism, offend the very things on which working-class identity is built and repudiate precisely those values which made change bearable. Perhaps the option of becoming a WASP ("American") is no longer as attractive as remaining a hyphenated Pole or Italian; a lot of third-generation Americans, moreover, are trying to reclaim the religious and ethnic affiliations which their fathers tried to disown a generation ago. At the City University of New York, Jewish undergraduates who stumbled through their perfunctory bar mitzvahs are demanding more Hebrew studies, and on the streets of Boston and Chicago Irishmen who had never done more than wear a green tie on Saint Patrick's Day are reclaiming spiritual loyalties with demands for the independence of the northern counties. (What a blow it must be for second- or third-generation suburban Irishmen to hear someone like Bernadette Devlin, in a perfect brogue, come to the defense of the Panthers.) But even for those who live in the spirit of the melting pot, the WASP option remains thinkable only in the obsolescent terms of another age. The incomplete Americanism of the ethnic neighborhood cannot conceive of any fulfillment which doesn't wave the flag and support our boys in Vietnam; it cannot establish itself without the symbols that tradition forced upon it. The rich and wellborn have their privileges, but even a first-generation Italian can have the flag. It is all he has, all that he was offered in exchange for his own culture. Everything else has been corrupted or compromised.

People have been displaced without moving at all—culture shock without the promised payoff—in a forced migration to regions of the mind and spirit which demand more responsibility because they do not offer the security of familiar patterns, and yet provide little if anything in the way of a better existence. Not just ethnic minorities but a lot of others—cops, firemen, schoolteachers, clerks, and vast numbers of people left stranded by the inadequate values and resources of the past. The cop, said Dick Gregory, "is the new nigger." They share —or used to share—almost total dependency on the cultural and moral certainty of their class superiors; dirty workers were willing to execute the unpleasant tasks of keeping vagrants out of the nice neighborhoods, wiping the noses of little children, and settling the domestic fights of "troubled" homes because the establishment—indeed, the whole society—gave them its blessings for this "important work." Now they are being treated as if they had violated their social instructions, as if making life miserable for people on the wrong side of town hadn't been part of the deal at all. Weren't they supposed to shoot looters and beat up drunks? Weren't they supposed to enforce middle-class standards of cleanliness, punctuality and deference to those who were older and presumably wiser? Weren't they supposed to make the clients of welfare buy milk and shoes rather than wine and television sets? New signals again, confused and indistinct: cultural pluralism, welfare rights, community control. Don't impose your values on them. Whose values? Your values. Cops are pigs, school principals are fascists, social workers are imperious little agents of the state snooping around the homes of the poor for violations of the rules. As a consequence, the dirty workers, knowing no other role, are beginning to act like independent agents of authority, are organizing unions and lobbies, and are carrying out the instructions of the past and not the orders of their immediate superiors. Which is to say that the old WASP values, always more relevant to those trying to make it than to those who have made it, seem now to survive primarily in the ranks of the lower middle and in the independent bureaucracies of the state: the schoolteachers, the cops, the FBI, the social workers, many of them organizations dominated by ethnics from the cities and by people no more than a generation removed from the rural regions of the South and the Midwest. At the same time, however, the submerged pressure to revert to ethnic patterns (partly in response to the respectability of Black Power) begins to mount: the ethnics are fighting for the remains of the WASP-abandoned culture and the WASP-forsaken neighborhood; Tony Imperiale negotiates with LeRoi Jones for control of the streets of Newark; the Indians occupy Alcatraz; and John Lindsay, despite his mistakes, is reelected mayor of New York because the city's Jews, although suspicious of WASP imperiousness, trust that tough-talking Italian Procaccino even less. The ethnic vigilantes are out, sometimes in uniform, sometimes in yarmulkes and rusty Chevrolets, patrolling their turf, protecting their women, and knowing that the establishment, whatever its pretentions, is too weak to protect anything but itself and sometimes can no longer manage even that. Park Avenue is under siege.

III

The film was called *The Brotherhood of the Bell*. *Glenn Ford is this big-shot college professor, see, and his father is a rich construction-company president who used to be a ditchdigger and thinks he made it all on his own. But twenty years before, Glenn, who went to this exclusive College of St. George, joined a secret society run by fancy people who were trying to take over the country, and who threw a lot of deals to Glenn's father, and that made him rich. But he didn't know that, only Glenn knew it, because he was in with them. Follow? Like bankers and big lawyers. Not Italians, stupid, but Americans, WASPs. Since Glenn's father was Irish it doesn't say how Glenn got in, but he did, and once he was in he had to keep the secret and do what the Brotherhood wanted. If he didn't they'd get him. They made him blackmail another professor named Horvathi and finally drove this other professor to suicide. Killed himself. That really shook Glenn up, because he liked this guy, so he decided to warn the country about the Brotherhood and its secret power. No, they didn't dump him in the river, but they ruined his old man's business and his wife left him. He held these press conferences and went on TV to tell about it, but nobody would listen. They all thought he was crazy, and sometimes he really seemed to act a little crazy. Some black guy on a TV show said he knew all about the conspiracy, and said that his people had known about it for hundreds of years, but that they called it the United Racist States of America. He thought it was just a white man's plot. And a woman who just called herself a patriot said that it was really the international Jewish conspiracy, and that Glenn*

*Ford himself was a Jew, and she told how you could find out
all about it by writing to this post-office box in Pasadena, California. But nobody believed that the Brotherhood was made
up of those fancy people who looked too classy to be crooks.
Finally Glenn found a student at St. George who had signed
up with the Brotherhood and who was willing to talk; in the
movie they don't really tell you what happened then or
whether the Brotherhood collapsed, or even what most of the
guys had done, but you have to guess that they finally got
caught and the whole thing got exposed. If you ask me I think
the picture was a little dull; those big shots didn't look like
crooks; they just looked like big shots. . . .*

We all need to believe in an establishment. Paranoia, the belief that *they* are fucking things up, is the first line of defense
against the suspicion of chaos. If there were no establishment
we would invent one or would, in another age, create epic
dramas populated by gods on Mount Olympus who juggle the
fates of men to suit their personal vanities, settle their disputes
and satiate their lusts. The ascendancy of Richard Nixon and
his gray men of low profile was an obvious signal to the pur-
veyors of political platitudes that what used to be called the
Eastern Establishment has lost its hold, and that the national
center of gravity had swung from the Ivy League, from Exeter and Groton, from Wall Street, from the Century and the
Piping Rock, to the haberdasheries of Main Street, the country clubs of Arizona, and the real-estate brokers of the sun-
land. Many of those whom Rovere specifically excluded from
the establishment (Nixon, Billy Graham, Norman Vincent
Peale) are now in positions of official respect, while the Cabinet itself is composed of people too obscure (then or now) to
be considered even for the list of rejects.

And yet we still speak of the establishment, or speak of a
new establishment, or speak as if two giant tribes were en-

gaged in mortal combat for dominion on the Olympian Heights. In most of these discussions there are several kinds of fantasy, most of them coming from people who cannot conceive of themselves as anything but outsiders. It does not matter to them that they themselves may be in high cultural fashion, or that in the role of New York publishers or black militants they can intimidate any ordinary WASP from Minnesota. Norman Podhoretz, the editor of *Commentary*, for example, is persuaded that despite its temporary exile from Washington, the WASP patriciate (his phrase) is busier than ever arranging to recapture its traditional preserve, either in 1972 or 1976.

In 1964 they were humiliated by a new crop of Robber Barons who used Barry Goldwater to take over the Republican Party; in 1968 they were again humiliated by the same forces, this time operating through Richard Nixon. Now they are readying themselves either to challenge those forces in 1972 if things should go badly for Nixon, or to succeed them in 1976 with a candidate of their own who will be presented, just as their last successful candidate was in 1952, as a man above politics and above party. I would guess from the regularity with which Tom Wicker, James Reston, and their colleagues on the editorial page of the *New York Times* have been puffing and pushing John W. Gardner in the past year or two . . . that he is probably the current front-runner in the race for the candidacy, especially since John Lindsay's clumsy handling of the New York school strike all but eliminated him from contention.

Perhaps he is correct, and yet every Podhoretz reference to the WASP patriciate has about it a touch of an ancient hangup which sees an anti-Semite in every woodpile and which cannot imagine America without a permanently established Brotherhood of the Bell. The Goy Complex. It was, and sometimes still is, a healthy defense not only against the real anti-Semites —at least for the moment in disrepute—but also against a great many non-Jews who are no more sensitive to anti-Semitism than they are (or were) to those pervasive forms of racism which infuriate their black brothers. But sometimes it reaches into a realm where nothing is quite what it seems, saying, for example, that the effort to make special provisions for black students at Harvard is a veiled act of anti-Semitism because it jeopardizes the places of Jews who have, in the last decade and a half, finally managed to get in without quotas; it asserts that any tampering with "merit" is, in effect, the reimposition of quotas and that the prime target of the quota is always the Jew. The fact that many people—goys and Jews—don't understand is simply evidence of the subtlety of the danger and requires, for that reason, all the more vigilance. During the school controversies in New York, the Jewish teachers were thoroughly persuaded that the "merit" system of grades and tests was absolutely impartial, and not just a means of bureaucratic self-perpetuation by which one generation rewarded those who had most faithfully learned its lessons and most accurately reflected its style and background. Nonetheless they regarded attacks on the system as veiled attacks on themselves and therefore as anti-Semitic. (Perhaps they were persuaded that "impartial" always meant that Jews had an advantage.) The WASPs were, as usual, sacrificing the Jews (for whom they'd never done anything anyhow) because, under circumstances like this, that is what goys always did. It did not occur to most of those who complained that goys like Lindsay—that the whole WASP patriciate—have less control over the lower echelons of the public bureaucracies than the Jewish president of the United Federation of Teachers or the Irish president of the Patrolmen's Benevolent Association or the Italian president of the sanitation men. But the goy complex says, nonetheless, that at the heart of things there is a WASP patriciate which, if it so desires, can manipulate all the lesser goys (Italian, Irishmen, whatever) to make them do its bidding. The establishment is Father, and you need Father even if you don't want to do anything more elegant than kick his ass.

In the last twenty-five years dissecting the establishment has become a highly popular academic endeavor. C. Wright Mills (among others) took it on in *The Power Elite*, E. Digby Baltzell in *The Protestant Establishment* and G. William Domhoff in *The Higher Circles* and *Who Rules America?* One might suspect that the very existence of these studies indicates that the subject bears more resemblance to a carcass than to a living body, even if it is being embalmed without regard to cost. One could ask, moreover, whether its economic and political power is still matched by a corresponding cultural and moral force or whether the studies tell us more about the past than about the present. But leaving all such questions aside, it is still worth asking whether these serious, documented versions of *The Brotherhood of the Bell* take sufficient account not of structure and possessions but of substance. Let us grant the existence of the military-industrial complex; accept the fact that two thousand retired military officers are now working for major defense contractors; that the CIA had its finger in the National Student Association and dozens of other "cultural" groups; that shirtsleeves to shirtsleeves in three generations is a myth; that inherited wealth can be exchanged for degrees in the prestige universities and then reconverted into more wealth; that 200,000 families control twenty-two percent of the wealth in America and sixty-five percent of the corporate wealth; that corporations, foundations and universities are linked through interlocking directorates; that the elite, through the Council on Foreign Relations, the universities and the foundations, try to make foreign policy; that Wall Street runs the Securities and Exchange Commission, the networks dominate the decisions of the Federal Communications Commission, and the private utilities control the Federal Power Commission—let us accept these things as true, which, indeed, they generally are. It is then easy to speak about a vague yet monolithic *them* where the same people can function in different roles without changing costume: the white power structure, the WASP patriciate, the liberal establishment; or—in the short form—militarists, racists, colonialists, male chauvinists, capitalists, anti-Semites and reactionaries. (On the other side Communists, Jews, radicals, and revolutionary conspirators.) It is striking indeed how the same people and institutions can become acceptable targets for the Right and the Left: McNamara, the State Department, the liberal churches, the courts, the universities, the unions, Rome, Israel and foreign aid. Obviously all of these fill, as the professor said, a much-needed gap. They keep us, among other things, from the undemocratic idea that repression, corruption and violence can be acts of the popular will and from the even more terrifying suspicion that the CIA, the military, the corporations, even the universities seem to have become self-actuating organisms subject to no elite, no class and no establishment other than their own bureaucrats; that the "system" more nearly resembles a machine than an oligarchy—that, finally, no one is in charge. Baltzell, if I understand him right, is himself an elitist, he objects not to the establishment but to its practices of ethnic exclusion, and he fears that because of such exclusion the establishment is losing its energy and turning into a caste without legitimate right to rule. Domhoff, a disciple of Mills, is trying, more than anything else, to expose the structure and practices of the higher circles, but he clearly is not interested in abolishing them. It would, indeed, be hard to imagine any academic person who is not, by his very profession, an elitist. In his secret heart every one of them must know that his existence depends on some establishment, that only establishments stand between himself and a mob.

Which may be why, so far, none of them has fully faced the more fearful possibility that the patriciate controls very little, that it is striking its colors and is acting—or beginning to act—like another minority. To any self-conscious member of a minority group, whether black, Jewish, Italian or "intellectual," the traditional mode of identification was based on the assumption that primary responsibility for the country and the world was with "them" and that your own people were limited in power and had little access into the higher circles. College professors who spend too much time around the White House or the State Department begin to smell peculiar to their former colleagues, partly as a result of envy, but partly also through the conviction that if power corrupts, it corrupts no one as foully as a scholar. As a consequence the suspicion that "they" don't control very much, either—which should be a welcome surprise—tends to threaten not only the case of the outsider but his very identity. Which is to say that the same sense of abandonment which afflicts those who shared the ethic and aspirations of the mainstream, and who supported the establishment, can and does afflict people who identified themselves as its critics or simply as outsiders. Sartre once said that "it is the anti-Semite who creates the Jew," but it can just as easily be said, at least in America, for a lot of others. Ethnic identity is partly forged out of discrimination; life for a black man may be more comfortable in New York, but the definitions of his blackness are more secure in Georgia or Mississippi. The hard-shell Baptists and the Pentecostals cannot understand how the liberal denominations can bring themselves even to entertain the demands for "reparations" presented by the black militants or how the National Council of Churches can support the World Council, to which it belongs, in its efforts to provide relief to North Vietnam. Isn't the National Council supposed to be on *our* side—isn't it at the very heart of the establishment? Isn't North Vietnam the enemy? Despite the fact that many right-wingers have had flirtations with anti-Semitism, people like Billy James Hargis (who has turned his right-wing fundamentalism into a multi-million-dollar enterprise) regard the State of Israel as "the most anti-Communist country on earth"—meaning that it is, from the perspective of Tulsa, Oklahoma, the most American of all nations. In the same moment that Hargis accuses NCC of being all-powerful he also charges it with capitulating to the weakest people and the most unpopular causes.

The panic comes from the weakness of the establishment, not its strength. The WASP elite still controls its own corporate offices, its board rooms, its banks and its foundations, but its power is limited not only in the streets but in the mines and factories it is theoretically supposed to manage, in the college dormitories it has so generously erected and in the bureaucracies it established to do its work. The Attorney General of the United States cannot persuade the Irish mayor of Chicago to give the 1968 convention demonstrators a permit; the WASP mayor of New York cannot control his Irish cops; the establishment president of Columbia University cannot manage his students; and the whole power of the United States is insufficient to deter Arab hijackers from seizing airplanes flying the American flag and detaining their passengers. As a consequence the same liberal professors who made their reputation as critics of the shabbiness of mass culture or as cheerleaders of the "consensus" in American belief are ready to call the cops to clear their offices and classrooms of militant students, relying not on the vast moral and social power of university trustees, presidents and deans, or, God forbid, on consensus, but on the unequivocal force of lower-class Italians and Irishmen equipped with guns and Mace. While academicians who made their names as socialists ally themselves with a President of the United States who made his reputation as a witch-hunter, the ethnics are arming themselves with clubs, and the hardhats, cheered by the antiestablishment rhetoric of the Vice-President, take over the streets shouting "God bless the establishment!" The establishment is dead. Long live the establishment.

The ruling class of America maintains power—what it still has—because it does not know how to let go and because most people *believe* it still has it. Buffeted by organized outsiders, by ethnics, by cops and civil servants, by unions, by students, by politicians, and hemmed in by its own technology, it can make deals catch as catch can—with teamsters, with university alumni, with the military or with the brokers of local power. It can occasionally buy off black ghetto militants (with jobs or just plain cash) to keep things cool in the city, pay off union leaders to keep the trucks running, hire Filipinos and Thais to fight in Vietnam and maintain the "free" world, manipulate Latin-American politicians, "reform" university governance to placate students, bust the demonstrators to placate the legislature, and promise investigations of police brutality to mollify liberals, then forget the promises to appease the cops, but there is hardly anything it can still initiate or run by itself. In the new industrial state it is hard to tell the hostages from the jailers: does the government have to save Lockheed from bankruptcy because of the capitalists or the workers who depend on it for their jobs? Was the war in Southeast Asia merely an act of military and economic imperialism or also a way for boys with no other place to go to establish their manhood and independence? Is the corporation an organism responsive to its managers and owners or simply a mindless monster that is beyond the direction of mortal man? Wealth there is, and occasionally power, but both are losing the legitimacy and even the energy on which their perpetuation depends. Thirty years ago manufacturing automobiles was self-justifying; the car was a sacred symbol. Now it is becoming a symbol of dirt, noise and destruction, and the whole romance of "production" has turned contemptible. The good life has become polluted and the folks who promised to bring it to you are defensive and confused. The moral and social credit of the American "ruling class" is almost exhausted, and the only thing that prevents any formal transfer of responsibility to someone else is the pressure of competing groups and the complexity of the monster itself. You can't officially give it to blacks or kids or workers. So you do nothing while, with each passing day, they try to seize it for themselves. America in the early seventies looks more like the country of factions that Madison described in *The Federalist* than the monolith of C. Wright Mills and G. William Domhoff.

IV

Who rules America? Given the breakdown of social and cultural consensus, any person who wants to "rule" (or simply survive in office) has two options. He can try to manufacture a sort of *ersatz* Americanism which most people will hopefully salute, and which will create some semblance of "common values," or he can become a figure of repression, can lead the strong against the weak and launch pogroms against the most threatening and/or vulnerable elements, or he can do both. The problem is the same for any public executive whether he is the school principal or the President of the United States: proclaim the blessings of freedom and citizenship, search the gym lockers, bust the Panther offices, infiltrate the Left and, most of all, talk to the powerful as if the weak were strong and the strong were weak. The politics of paranoia is not new in America, but it is new in the Presidency of the United States.

In his piece of ten years ago, Rovere called Nixon the leader of the organization—meaning that Nixon was the ultimate org man, a person whose antennae were always tuned to the drifts of opinion, but he could not then appreciate the depths of Nixon's talent or—in all fairness—the strange circumstances of his Presidency. Nixon is the man from nowhere, the first American President who has no special place, no accent, no style. We know little about his convictions, his hobbies, his passions, can understand only that his campaign and his behavior in office reflect the corporate-organization-man residue of WASPiness and the insecurity of the mainstream culture. Is he from California or New York? Is he a conservative or a liberal? If he represents the new millions of the Southwest, the retired suburbanites of Scottsdale and Anaheim or the oil barons of Oklahoma, what is he doing in a Wall Street law firm or a Fifth Avenue apartment?

There is a forlorn air to arguments in favor of Nixon's leadership [said Garry Wills in *Nixon Agonistes*]. There may be things wrong with the American spirit, men grant, but Nixon can at least deal with the authentic national character. He knows it. Here is one thing we can rally to when the nation seems agreed on little else. Nixon can "bring us together again" because he can find the ground where we last stood together years ago. . . . The new liberalism has a cowed apologetic air. Even things that were once sources of pride have a faded mousy look. Things like Hannah Nixon's undemonstrative piety and sensitive concern for others. . . . Or homely uncomplaining industry, a quiet patriotism running deeper than xenophobia. Or a "Faustian" willingness to take great risks on the chance of making great progress. Traces of all these qualities are left in Nixon, in the new Americanism. But they are a residue only, dilutions of what had once been strong. Weariness and compromise—the workings of the Mix-master "market"—have pureed all Nixon's separate virtues into an un-offending mush.

When he was first elected in 1968 he brought to Washington that Cabinet of nonentities selected, it seemed, to illustrate the fix the country was in: Clifford Hardin, Maurice Stans, Wal-ter Hickel, Winton Blount, the old Agnew. (The exceptions —neither was then a regular Cabinet member—were Daniel Patrick Moynihan, an Irishman, and Henry Kissinger, a real-politician from Central Europe who learned his stuff by study-ing the diplomacy of Metternich.) Most of them were men without visible personalities, without place or class or style. We had had something similar in Washington during the era of Eisenhower, but the atmosphere at that time was tempered by an older set of convictions, by a legacy of place and, finally, by the smell of principle. The principle was often pig-headed and obsolescent: John Foster Dulles, like the ghost of Woodrow Wilson, prattling about the free world and massive retaliation, always certain he could tell the good guys from the bad; Engine Charlie Wilson believing that capitalism was the salvation of America; and Eisenhower himself, convinced that most of the country was populated by small-town boys from Abilene or Emporia. But if they were dangerous moralists playing brinksmanship while the rest of us hid in the saloon or the dry-goods store, they were not plastic. Nixon did not bring with him any Jack McCloy, any Francis Plimpton, let alone a General George C. Marshall or a Henry Stimson; he did not speak in the accents of a Hudson Valley patrician or a Harvard Irishman or even in the cadences of a small-town shopkeeper from Missouri; he was not a regional man, had no place, and no special sense of himself except perhaps that ceaseless depression anxiety, the corporate drivenness that never abates because it has no tangible goals, no job to be

168

finished, no product to be made, no pride of craft—a driven-ness that seeks only the abstractions of success itself. By in-stinct Nixon must have had considerable empathy with all those people who were never convinced—despite all their rhet-oric—that they had really earned what they had, that they possessed any skills worth having, and who were, therefore, forever anxious that it could all vanish in a flash. Most of them had always spoken of their own independence as if they actu-ally believed that the major beneficiaries of all those govern-ment handouts—farm subsidies, social security, oil depletion allowances, cheap land, tax write-offs—were people other than themselves. But they knew it wasn't true.

There are advantages in Nixon's politics. Gray men are not crusaders; they don't speak about massive retaliation and final solutions (or about the Great Society, the New Frontier or Making the World Safe for Democracy). They tend almost inevitably to be tentative people who leave the exits clear and the rhetoric ambiguous. In the first months after the 1968 election it was almost funny: who were those guys anyway? Would Agnew ever be more than a household yuk, would Nixon fill those high jobs with real people, was someone gin-gerly knocking on the door of the President-elect at the Hotel Pierre every morning to remind him that he really had won the election? Maybe, in fact, Nixon never really wanted to *be* President; he only wanted to *become* President so that he could tell Pat he'd been promoted and soak up the congratula-tions of the people at the country club. We were (remem-ber?) going to tone down the rhetoric, were going to speak softly so that we could hear each other without shouting; we were done with crusades for a while, were not going to make promises we could not fulfill and therefore were not going to extend any promises at all. Since the sixties had been marked by frustrated hope, hope would be suspended. There had been something ominous in that talk about law and order (Richard the fascist?), but even that could be played for laughs: Nixon, we said, was running for sheriff. The most lethal possibility in the first months of 1969 was not nuclear annihilation, civil turmoil or even an American Gestapo. It was death by boredom.

And yet the same gray men with penchants for the tentative and the cautious, men who cannot imagine themselves in Napoleonic roles or even in the limited parts of New Deal reformers, men with the souls of school principals and insurance clerks, men for whom storm troopers are too much and dictators too indecorous—these men especially are likely to regard any noise as offensive and possibly even dangerous. They are offended by protest and dirt, by kids and Black Power, by rock and drugs and shit—are, indeed, more than offended; they are scared. For the first time in our history, certainly the first time since the 1920s, the majority has begun to act like a minority, the strong are paranoid about the weak, and people who never thought of themselves as anything but "Americans" began to act like Italians and Greeks who had learned through bitter experience that there wasn't anybody you could really trust. We should have known that Nixon (even more than Wallace) was made to be their man. Sentimentality and paranoia had always been two of his strongest suits; he had the manner of a loser, was better in the role of victim than protagonist, better at bleeding than laughing, more at home, it seemed, in defeat than in triumph. In the era of the Kennedys it was not Teddy who was the runt; it was Nixon.

Society's child. Epitaph: He caught the drift. Beyond the pragmatic imperatives to solve problems (or to pretend they don't exist) there exists an even greater compulsion to stay on the track, no matter what. The WASPs of earlier times brought their own gyroscopes to the Presidency; Nixon, deprived of such equipment, faced the unpleasant task of being an organization man in what is probably the only government job in which the organization style won't work. The office was constitutionally designed to be a one-man job; it was invented for stylish men, and if some of them compromised their principles to be elected they nonetheless had principles to compromise. For many of them, style itself mitigated the failures of specific political decisions. Kennedy managed to do very little, but he did it with flair. In almost any other job a man can look to the other members of the executive committee for style and attitudes, but there is no track for the President except the one that he sets for himself. The buck, not only of decision but of style, stops here. Nixon came to the job because the better men were destroyed, because there seems to be something in contemporary America that no longer tolerates genuine stature in public office. It was clear in 1968 that only a runt could be elected: Johnson, the Kennedys and King had all been victims of their own overexposure, targets of vanity, and Nixon was there, sitting on the bench at the opportune moment when there was no one else left to go in. He could play any position. His television campaign in the fall of 1968 was not so much a matter of cleaning up the image—of selling the *new* Nixon—as of manufacturing an image from scratch. "It was," said Joe McGinniss in *The Selling of the President*, "as if they were building not a President but an Astrodome, where the wind would never blow, the temperature never rise or fall, and the ball never bounce erratically on the artificial grass." It did not matter whether Nixon really existed at all, or that, as Pat Nixon bitterly confessed to Gloria Steinem, the Nixons had always been too busy scrounging to read or bother with ideas; what did matter was the image, and the image only. "The response," said Nixon's chief speechwriter, "is to the image, not to the man," and the image was that of a loser. "Nothing can happen to you, politically speaking," said one of his campaign advisers-to-be in 1967, "that is worse than what has happened to you. Ortega y Gasset in his *Revolt of the Masses* says, 'These ideas are the only genuine ideas: the ideas of the shipwrecked. All the rest is rhetoric, posturing, farce. He who does not really feel himself lost is lost without remission.' You, in effect, are 'lost'; that is why you are the only political figure with the vision to see things the way they are and not as Leftist or Rightist kooks would have them be. Run. You will win." In another age, had they thought of it, they might have sent the man to a good shrink. But in the age of Nixon they hired him for the campaign staff and made him, in January of 1969, a speechwriter in the White House.

But if the task of becoming President is primarily a matter of image, the job of being President is not—or at least not yet. The man in the White House can command endless hours of television time; can use its vast resources to announce the invasion of Cambodia one day and the withdrawal from Cambodia a few weeks later with equal conviction; can call press conferences when the spirit is upon him and avoid them when it is not; can appear at Billy Graham revivals and Southwest Conference football games according to need or plan, and plead more pressing commitments when time, place or event are not propitious. But he cannot forever evade the demands of decision and style that the constitutional office imposes: he must not only make political decisions, must not only demonstrate his own tastes, his likes and dislikes (football versus golf, Mantovani versus Casals, cottage cheese against barbecued beef), he must also lead the nation in its collective rituals and ceremonies, decide when to weep and when to cheer, when to send condolences and when to issue praise. One way or another he has to Be Somebody.

It has been fashionable in the proper circles of invective and innuendo to characterize Nixon as a psychotic who thinks of his own life in terms of "crises," escapes compulsively from the White House for retreats to San Clemente or Camp David or Key Biscayne, tells the press, "You won't have Richard Nixon to kick around any more," shifts his eyes and wrings his hands in press conferences like an unlicensed sidewalk necktie peddler who has spotted the cops coming around the corner, and is invariably more comfortable when he has cause to feel sorry for himself. In 1970, after two years in office, Nixon campaigned as if he had lost in 1968, as if someone else had been President. He was still the loser. Yet most of that behavior is undoubtedly attributable to the pressures on a man who, as McGinniss said, knew that "his soul was hard to find." He is, said Wills, "the least authentic man alive, the late mover, tester of responses, submissive to the 'discipline of consent.' There is one Nixon only, though there seem to be new ones all the time—he will try to be what people want." Nixon has no style because he has no convictions. When it comes to style he plays the role of secret agent, taking on the coloration of the moment, the place and the environment. Given the choice between trying to synthesize a social and political consensus and leading the repression, Nixon (characteristically) is trying both. It is not enough to say that Agnew has become Nixon's Nixon, because Nixon is also Nixon's Nixon. He is not Eisenhower, 1970 is not 1952, and the old establishment is only a shadow of its former self. In 1952 Nixon and Joe McCarthy were attacking people and institutions which, despite their near-fatal lack of courage, finally put them down. Against their gutter politics stood the benign principle of the old war hero, mauling his syntax, unable to distinguish good politics from bad, but nonetheless holding to his convictions. In 1970 the attack is largely directed from the inside: Agnew and John Mitchell *are* the government and they have the confidence of the President; their targets are the black and the young, not university presidents and former secretaries of state, and the mediating institutions—courts, universities, the press, even Congress itself—tend to be unacceptable to either side. Nixon is supposed to be a symbol for a nation in which he himself has only marginal confidence and in which the most talented people and the brightest hopes hold him in the highest contempt. Nixon can stage triumphal appearances at the University of Kansas and the University of Tennessee, but he cannot risk a visit to any prestige college in the country of which he is supposed to be President. It is no longer safe for him to attend the graduation of his own daughter or his own son-in-law; it is no longer even possible—to avoid embarrassment—for them to attend their own.

Play it both ways. *On this side plasticulture*. Mister Clean. A Muzak-playing, Mantovani-loving, two-stepping, tube-watching, breakfast-praying, Bob Hopeful, Norman Vincent Pealing, air-conditioned, polyethylene-sanitized, pastel-tissued miniexistence imitating life, imitating art, imitating the terrorized dreams of the depression. Daddy, says Tricia, likes to have a fire in his room even if he has to crank up the air conditioning to be comfortable. Does Mother cover the dining-room table with a plastic cover? How about one of those little ceramic figures of Black Sambo holding a light to welcome the folks home? On the White House lawn. Something for everybody. Passions sliced, bottled and purified; nothing too revealing, please, nothing too joyful, too sad, too expressive. Nothing for Somebody. This side for Everybody.

On that side the heavies. Unleash Spiro, unleash John. Get out some more feds for the freaks, for the subversives who don't dig plastic, for the kids and the spades and the funky noisemakers running around the streets. If the revolt is cultural, the counterrevolution will also be political, physical and violent. A police action featuring law and order for people inside polyethylene bags. If the limousine liberals have guards and doormen, why shouldn't the people in the developments? That's democracy. John Mitchell will talk to the police chiefs, the prosecuting attorneys, the judges. Spiro will talk to the nation, will make one country of us by sending all the rotten apples into exile or to jail or simply into that oblivion which exists beyond Executive Acres and Homogeneous Heights. He is the perfect man: second-generation Greek Orthodox Democrat turned third-generation suburban slick Republican, a man who can make paunchy country club Republicans with fat pinky rings feel like street fighters at the urinal, and who knows how to call a fag a fag in the special language of a Middle American golf-course bar. Agnew's identity card is valid in any precinct dominated by men who doubt their own virility—in the new developments of Phoenix and Tulsa and Jackson, Mississippi, in the nervous neighborhoods of the inner city, and in that vast territory of Holiday Inns, automobile dealerships, hunting trips and bowling leagues which extends from sea to shining sea. It is hard to overestimate the unifying capabilities of a person who can locate the hidden frustrations that cut across class lines, and give them expression in that vulgar language whose most common denominator is obscenity repressed. *The Christine Jorgensen of the Republican Party; effete impudent snobs; nattering nabobs of negativism; hysterical hypochondriacs of history.* The appeal is to those who regard themselves as liberated modern men because they feel free to tell dirty male-chauvinist jokes in mixed company, jokes in which male prowess is always established through the ease of the seduction. Agnew's rhetoric expresses the common theme with variety: They—the liberals, the college freaks, the dissidents—are queer, unmanly and effeminate. It is hardly surprising that there is mutual admiration between Bob Hope and Agnew, or that Agnew frequently adapts Bob Hope jokes for his own performances. Essentially the joke is always the same: the male is exploitative, and his fundamental humanity is established by the fact that he is, at heart, a dirty old man. What makes him funny are the rhetorical taboos which make it necessary to express that dirtiness in circuitous terms, usually in double entendres. Thirty years ago Hope got into radio trouble with a line (to a girl) which went something like "Meet me in front of the pawnshop and kiss me under the balls." In the late sixties there was another line, indicating how the double meaning had become political: "Lyndon Johnson should get the Church to make Martin Luther King a bishop. Then he'd only have to kiss his ring." Agnew, from all reports, and according to considerable overt evidence, likes that stuff. Most of it would be unseemly for the Vice-President of the United States (or even for public use by Bob Hope), but there are enough cues in the speeches to indicate at what level Agnew is trying to communicate. The real men against the fags:

Today's breed of radical-liberal posturing about the Senate is about as closely related to a Harry Truman as a Chihuahua is to a timber wolf.

There will be no amnesty for draft dodgers. There are great choices in life. Millions of young Americans chose the path of courage, and more than forty thousand of them died for their decision. The few hundred slackers who chose another path are just going to have to live with the consequences of their decision.

This little band [of radical liberals] is guided by a policy of calculated weakness. . . . They were raised on a book by Dr. Spock, and a paralyzing permissive philosophy pervades every policy they espouse.

When we allow a creeping permissiveness to permeate every aspect of our relations with our young people we are not helping them—we are harming them.

These politicians seem to think that by adding a soupçon of finger-wagging to their mixture as before, they can thoroughly dissociate themselves from the consequences of their previous tolerance [of campus radicals].

There have been many campaigns in which innuendos have been directed at the private habits of the opponent: Grover Cleveland's illegitimate child; Warren Harding's seduction of a White House chambermaid; the alcoholic consumption of a particular Congressman or Senator; Nelson Rockefeller's re-marriage and Adlai Stevenson's divorce. But with the possible exception of Joe McCarthy's attacks on State Department homosexuals the innuendos were used in specific political contexts and directed to particular people. None of them was an attempt, as in Agnew's speeches, to assemble a new political coalition on the basis of its sexual anxieties, to find, as it were, a common culture in the style of the dirty joke and in the communion of men—always men—who assert their virility over a beer in the saloon. The fact that Agnew plays a rotten game of golf or an awkward game of tennis is of no negative consequence; it tends to demonstrate that he is one of the boys and to suggest that if he had more time (away from the office, away from his responsibilities, away from the wife) his backhand would be better and his golf slice would disappear. We know that he is a real man because it is in his nature to call a person a Polack or a fat Jap, that he is one of us in his repressed desire (repressed by "liberals") to use ethnic labels without restraint, but that he regards, at the same time, any uninhibited expression of personal or sexual freedom as dangerous or effeminate. It is hard for him or his admirers to imagine life without chauvinism or exploitation, and it is precisely in the resulting anxieties that his constituency finds its common life and language.

The inconsistencies in Agnew's assaults lend them strength

rather than vulnerability. If the liberals and the freaks are so effeminate, so pusillanimous, why are they dangerous? And if they are not dangerous, why are so many people afraid of them? Agnew functions in part as a surrogate for the establishment, as a symbol of power attacking permissiveness and promiscuity around which anxious men can rally. But the anxiety is directed not so much at particular manifestations of violence (which should be welcome, since they can be handled by policemen and other armed people in the old-fashioned way) as it is at an intangible cultural threat whose magnitude cannot be calculated and which cannot be confronted by ordinary means. What that threat demands, most of all, is a cheerleader of cultural reaction, a man who will lead the counter-revolution and help drive the four-letter words and all they represent out of public discourse and back on the john walls where his listeners scribbled them in their adolescence. The attack on drugs and Agnew's belated discovery that there was some sort of connection between hard drugs and hard rock function as a ritual confirmation that a man's secret thoughts are properly secret, that what has been repressed is not "normal" and that the latter-day demons now abroad must be relentlessly pursued. It is the sort of declaration that—in more circumscribed terms—used to be expected of the establishment but which is no longer being delivered with sufficient frequency or amplitude. The rhetoric gives heart to right-wing politicians and brings joy to cops and free-lance agents of repression, but it functions also at a "higher" level—a casting out of witches which are all the more fearful for not being quite real. The threat of the young, of bad words, bad drugs, bad thoughts, bad manners; the fear of contamination at home; the mounting terror that your own children are more sophisticated sexually than you are, that they have found out the vulgarity of your desires, that they have somehow bugged not only your bedroom but the anxieties that fill it, that they understand your hangups while you haven't a clue about theirs—all these things are far more dangerous than "Communists in government" or the possibility that there are fairies in the State Department. The effete impudent snobs, the nabobs of negativism—all those weak, effeminate people—are not likely to attack the bridges, the power plants and the broadcasting stations (although some of their violent brothers may indeed try to blow them up); what most of them are assaulting are the mind and the gut, and that is where it hurts.

Agnew's attacks have other payoffs: They make Nixon's kitsch look decorous and even elegant; against the danger of all that filth plasticity can appear civilized; they generate, moreover, the *feel* of consensus among a "silent majority," and they keep Nixon's people distracted from the substantive ills which plague the country. The unemployed black man and the marginally employed white are, it goes without saying, common victims of a technocratic economic system which, all rhetoric to the contrary, continues to distribute its material payoffs with fantastic inequity and which assures neither of them anything even remotely close to the affluence that is commonly advertised. Agnew makes certain that the nonaffluent will keep fighting, or that some of them will remain so thoroughly persuaded that it is kids or revolutionaries or addicts who cause their problems that it will never occur to them that they are economic losers. In pop sociology a clerk earning $6,000, a steelworker making $12,000 and a physician who reports $80,000 are all "middle-class," but they do not share the same swindles, let alone a common level of comfort or common access to the "blessings of democracy." Agnew's task has been to make people with boring, marginal jobs in factories and used-car lots believe that they belong in the same economic and social categories as the men who manage the business, direct its legal affairs and sell its hardware to the Pentagon. The kids have often helped by vilifying the anxieties of blue-collar people, by forcing them to repress their insecurity and their state of nonaffluence. But Agnew and—in more subtle and polite forms—Nixon have turned confusion into fraud, have played to fear rather than aspiration, have mined hate and violence with a precision unimaginable from politicians who do not share the feelings they try to cultivate. The elite, said Agnew in one of his efforts to rally his constituents, "consist of the raised-eyebrow cynics [fairies?], the anti-intellectual intellectuals, the pampered egotists who sneer at honesty, thrift, hard work, prudence, common decency and self-denial." He proposed a test for the elite that included, among other things:

1. Do you walk around with an expression on your face that seems to say that the world smells a little funny?
2. Do you wish those great masses of people would stop questioning your right to determine public morals and public policy?
3. Do you think that a college education makes you not only intellectually superior, but morally superior as well, to those who did not have your opportunities?
4. Do you think that blue-collar work—like fixing an automobile or driving a truck—is not clearly as dignified or significant as pushing a pencil at a tax-exempt foundation?

Agnew's text, of course, could have come directly from John Gardner, who has made a career of pushing pencils in tax-exempt foundations. But leaving that matter aside, and leaving aside Spiro's attempt at humor (it is, after all, true that the world *does* smell a little funny, and that the smell itself—apart from the stench of dogshit on the sidewalk—has become a political cause, called ecology, that even Nixon supports), there remains the attempt to ally working stiffs with limousine reactionaries whose contempt for the masses is legendary, with suburbanites whose credit-card indebtedness has long made a joke of "thrift," and with an economy that would collapse if it depended on common decency and self-denial. As far as I know neither Agnew nor Nixon has ever repaired an automobile or driven a truck, but even if they had they seem to have forgotten everything but the manner in which mechanics and truck drivers are patronized by charlatans. In his heart almost every truck driver must suspect that his work is not as dignified as pushing a pencil and nearly every mechanic dreams (or used to dream) about sending his children to college so that they can get better jobs than he had.

American populism has always contained its share of bigotry, its hate and its violence. And it has always had, on the other side, its hope, its egalitarianism and its irreverence. After Bobby Kennedy was killed in June of 1968 thousands of his followers, perhaps several hundred thousand, became supporters of George Wallace, thereby turning (in the marvelous categories of political science) from democrats into reactionaries and bigots, and demonstrating again that the tone of leadership—the basis on which a man tries to establish "consensus" —has as much to do with "public opinion" as the demographic distinctions of pollsters, head counters, sociologists and people who write books called *The Emerging Republican Majority* or *The Real Majority*. Most people, I suspect, act out of their own sense of decency, and not because, somewhere, they have decided to play villains in the body politic. Agnew helps them forget that the jobs are lousy, that more and more people are out of work, that they don't have proper medical insurance and will go broke if they have to confront an extended illness, that it is the generals who are taking their tax money and not the poor, that "curbing inflation" means exorbitant interest rates and bank profiteering that borders on the obscene, that slobs with $10,000 incomes can't find decent housing, that hard work, thrift and self-denial *are*, under existing economic arrangements, so much hogwash, that their schools are as rotten as the ones attended by black kids, that their cars and dishwashers, if they have them, fall apart too fast and that the comforts which are supposed to come with affluence seem to be enjoyed by only a few. He makes them forget that if there is any elite in America, it is the elite of the gun, and that as the noncoercive attractions of "Americanism" fade, as the real establishment gets weaker, the society is ever more divided between new forms of culture (which are themselves sometimes crazy and violent) and people who pack pistols. The official rhetoric of the national Administration in the years since 1969 is not likely to reduce crime but to sanctify it, to enlarge the categories of criminality, to encourage free-lance and local vigilantism by prosecutors, grand juries and police, to undermine even further the crumbling confidence in the judicial system, and, by challenging the virility of dissenters, to tempt them ever more to demonstrate their strength through violence. It is striking that with all the national hysteria about drugs and crime the authorities never seem to manage more than scattered arrests of users, mostly kids, and not pushers, and that the "rings" which are broken up by federal agents tend as often as not to look suspiciously like collections of interlopers (a Frenchman, an Argentinian, perhaps a Costa Rican or a Honduran) who are moving into someone else's territory; that it seems almost impossible to convict any policeman of murder (or even manslaughter) no matter what the evidence against him; that the most conservative national commissions have found existing civil-rights laws neglected and unenforced; that the Justice Department has made it policy not to enforce the statutes against habitual and systematic industrial polluters of navigable waters; that the Administration resists effective gun-control laws, despite all that talk about violent crime; that the most important piece of national anticrime legislation of the past five years, the Omnibus Crime Bill, provides money for police hardware to the states (and therefore to small towns and cities which stockpile mace and bulletproof vests and riot guns they do not need and don't know how to use) and that the cities which need better police protection get virtually nothing; that the most compelling interest is in "habitual" criminals and in kids and blacks, but not in prison reform or rehabilitation, and that the most popular innovation in all this hysteria is the no-knock warrant, the wiretap and "preventive detention." Agnew does not like the word "repression," yet it is clear that the Administration's entire crime program provides weapons only against soft criminals—against cultural and social deviants, against dissenters who can be selectively busted for possession or vindictively indicted for conspiracy, and not against the hard-core managers of gambling, narcotics, bribery and extortion. The word "crime" in America now has a double meaning; obviously it means something to the person who feels unsafe on the streets or in his home and who feels vulnerable to muggers, burglars and random theft, but for him all the crime bills of the past two years have provided almost nothing. At the same time "crime" also means cultural, political and social deviance—and this is where the interest and energy of the crime fighters have gone. In the 1970 campaign Agnew's most extended attack on the drug culture was delivered in Las Vegas, Nevada, which represents, as much as any town in America, the lusts of an uptight society and the corruption of big-time hoodlums. Is Las Vegas Middle America? Is this the silent majority?

"We have given you the tools," said Nixon to Messrs. J. Edgar Hoover, John Mitchell and John McClellan when he signed his crime bill. "Now you do the job." What this bit of Churchillian rhetoric suggested was not merely pretentiousness (What embattled island did Nixon imagine he was de-fending? What heroism had already been acted out?); it was, more than ever, a call to arm against dissent, and, on its fringe, an official incitement to riot. If the resisters could be forced to arm, if they could be driven underground, or if they could be forced back into line, then there would be a new consensus—fatal, perhaps, but effective. Then any man would have to choose between their barricades and your barricades, and the cultural options, the economic choice, the joy, the hope—all of it—would vanish, leaving only the fissures and the violence. Up against the wall, motherfucker, the nice policeman said.

4

THE PLASTIC AMERICAN

I

In the last generation the country sorted itself out, hardened and broke apart. Much of Middle America became a sentimental fantasy, a colony of colonies, and the fissures were papered over with average-man statistics, Green Stamps and kitsch. Richard Scammon and Ben Wattenberg, in *The Real Majority*, hypothesized the average American voter into the forty-seven-year-old wife of a machinist living in a suburb of Dayton, Ohio—or was it Akron, or does it matter?—hardly aware, it seems, that the whole thing had become a parody twenty years before they set pen to paper. The anxious politicians of Washington took up the thesis of an electorate of the middle concerned about "the social issue"—meaning fear of crime, kids and Negroes—because it was the only thing they understood. The young, the poor, the black were to be banished as politically marginal people (which, God knows, they are), without so much as a question about whether everyone else, including the lady in Dayton, was not as marginal as the constituencies who were being prepared for limbo. What made *The Real Majority* so welcome was its reassurance that the consensus was already there, did not have to be re-created

—that there is a Middle America ripe for political plucking, anxious about crime and drugs and civil disorder, and ready to support anyone promising to restore normalcy, whatever that might be. For anyone prone to cynicism, the "social issue" sounded like a polite phrase for backlash. What made it into a dangerous fantasy was the fact that the politics of *The Real Majority* totally discounted the effects of rhetoric and leadership and fatally disregarded the possibility that the existing frustrations, anger and division could only be exacerbated by the politicians who followed the book's advice. Did Scammon and Wattenberg believe that it was possible to speak to the highest in America as well as the worst? Could they conceive of any American "majority" that could be rallied on the basis of things other than fear? In the fall of 1970 a newspaper in Dayton went out to search for the woman who might fit Scammon and Wattenberg's hypothetical description and found a person, Bette Lowrey, who conformed to the figures and—in some respects—to the attitudes. But in the flesh she also turned out to be more decent than the political projections, more complex than the statistics and more informed than Agnew and his speechwriters took her to be. "I wish," she said, "people would do more listening. All these kids wouldn't be rioting if they didn't have good reasons. Sometimes it takes rioting and dissent to bring change." Mrs. Lowrey, as it turned out, had a twenty-one-year-old son with long hair.

Of course they are still there, neither silent nor invisible, and still to be reckoned with as a political force: the men in their steel-rimmed glasses, their white shirts and subdued ties, the women with their short hair, clipped, teased and bouffed, testifying to endless nights more passionately devoted to home permanents and rollers than to making love, verifying the all-American triumph of the ego over the libido, the hair curler over the contraceptive pill. Was it possible to sleep in intimacy under a head of metal or plastic, was it possible to have hair so manicured after a night of screwing? What do those faces say? What does a man proclaim with a steady diet of white shirts and subdued plaid? Where, finally, are the dimensions of Middle America, where are its limits, and what is its common bond? Mailer described some of the older and wealthier among them at the Republican national convention in Miami in 1968:

Most of them were ill-proportioned in some part of their physique. Half must have been, of course, men and women over fifty and their bodies reflected the pull of their character. The dowager's hump was common, and many a man had a flaccid paunch, but the collective tension was rather in the shoulders, in the girdling of the shoulders against anticipated lashings on the neck, in the thrust forward of the neck, in the maintenance of the muscles of the mouth forever locked in the readiness to bite the tough meat of resistance, in a posture forward from the hip since the small of the back was dependably stiff, loins and mind cut away from each other by some abyss between navel and hip.

More than half of the men wore eyeglasses, young with old. . . . You could not picture a Gala Republican who was not clean shaven by eight A.M. Coming to power, they could only conceive of trying to clean up every situation in sight. And so many of the women seemed victims of the higher hygiene. Even a large part of the young seemed to have faces injected with Novocaine. . . .

In their immaculate cleanliness, in the somewhat antiseptic odors of their astringent toilet water and perfume, in abnegation of their walks, in the heavy sturdy moves so many demonstrated of bodies in life's harness, there was the muted tragedy of the WASP—they were not on earth to enjoy or even perhaps to love so very much, they were here to serve, and serve they had in public functions and public charities (while recipients of their charity might vomit in rage and laugh in scorn), served on opera committees . . . , served as the sentinel in concert halls and the pews on the aisle in church, at the desk in schools, had served for culture, served for finance, served for salvation, served for America—and so much of America did not wish them to serve any longer, and so many of them doubted themselves, doubted that the force of their faith could illumine their path in these new modern horror-head times.

There are other versions in other places: the noisy and wishful not-so-young flowing through the football stadiums of the South, moving like herds from Tuscaloosa to Knoxville to Athens to Oxford, weekend after weekend, with picnic baskets and pennants, screaming, exhorting, forgetting time, but remembering too, saying, "Those boys down there are fighting all our battles for us," the boys on the field, and the girls, sorority-fresh, pompomping across the fields, resisting not only niggers and change and the government in Washington, but the loneliness and the emptiness, resisting the irrepressible sense that the spectacle of Saturday afternoon—the contest, the courtship, the sound and fury—is the one great moment of life, a moment that once was truly your own and now must be borrowed or stolen from the young, week after week, to hold back the deepening wrinkles of the spirit. . . . Or Sunday dinner at the Holiday Inn, at a thousand Holiday Inns and Coach Houses and Valles—tables for six or eight where one young man is often missing and the grandfather stands in for the soldier in Vietnam, helping the mother with the high chair, ordering the predictable food, the roast beef, the baked potato with sour cream, the squishy rolls, the shrimp cocktail, undemanding, trying not to disrupt, trying not to be inconvenient, negotiating the meal like young children trying to prove that they are old enough, responsible enough, to eat with adults, always reverent in the presence of white cloth and thick goblets and the ubiquitous brass utensils and the fake wrought-iron heraldry and the synthetic carpets that tie the nation together; these are not Frenchmen or Italians making love to their food, enveloping it, surrounding and overwhelming it, are not the familiars of passion, but people who behave like trespassers on life itself, free men who expect to be driven off at any moment. . . . Or again the little clusters of men on Main Street, at the gas pump or the seed and feed or the luncheon cafés or the doors of the mill, comfortable and easy when place and subject and company are familiar, when the talk is about, well, about gaskets or valves or the high-school quarterback, yet inevitably awkward when that familiarity must be tested against some larger force, layoffs at the plant, mortgages, credit, war, when the intimate sense of what works and what doesn't must be tried against the abstractions of economics or politics and technology, when relativity overtakes mechanics, and when the comprehensible forces of the cosmos —floods and weather and drought—are replaced by even greater forces of economic or technical "control" and manipulation. What people learn in the small towns and cities is a trust in immediate transactions: if you call the mayor's office someone will answer and respond; if you go shopping there will be a place to park, a person to help carry the groceries, a clerk, a waiter, a cashier not habituated to sullenness. Decency is still practiced in the expected ways and courtesy extended to acceptable people; ordinary life has not been politicized, and paranoia remains only an affliction, not a common mode of personal defense. . . . But none of that can be applied to the larger issues; the White House will not respond, the local plant belongs to a national corporation, decisions are made elsewhere, or maybe nowhere. Middle America, sorting itself out, sends its most talented kids to the big cities, to the East Coast and the West Coast, while those who have been identified as losers stay home: Do "good" genes leave? And "bad" genes remain? Is every small town likely to become an Appalachian hollow or a ghetto of defeat? The very publicity of Main Street becomes a journal of anonymity—wedding announcements of girls just out of high school and boys who work for the mill or the railroad, or who are just about to be shipped to basic training, and who have little identity other than the parents they are trying to escape, the companies for which they work and the war in which they are about to fight. Secretly they dream of freedom, but it is a dream they have long ago learned to deny, and so they exchange almost everything they have—youth, expressiveness, skill—for something that is worth less than what they gave for it: a job, a marriage, a home, a car. Most of them are bad trades, because each imposes a mortgage with exorbitant interest; each puts the future in hock; little will come back, because the moral bankers of the local community and the commercial bankers of the national economy demand too much.

The political fiction called Middle America confuses ethnic and social groups which are linked primarily through that contemporary rhetoric which plays to fear and despair with a fantasy of old-fashioned Americanism. The hardhats of Gary or Bethlehem or Pittsburgh are far more likely to be Poles or Czechs or Hungarians than Middle American WASPs, more likely to be Catholics than Protestants, more likely to be children of the inner city than small-town boys. The rhetoric, obviously calculated, tries to make urban factory workers believe that the exurban plutocrat and the country-club broker is "one of us"; it attempts to link the elitism of reactionaries to the fears of people who cannot bring themselves to confess their fundamental insecurity or to declare that they haven't made it either. It makes them believe that they have things they do not have and that those unpossessed properties are being alienated or jeopardized by the black, the young and the poor.

But even beyond that confusion there is something else: The Middle America of sentiment—the culture of the small-town WASP—is becoming more myth than reality. There are at least two "Middle Americas," and the spread of the second has concealed the decay of the first. Underneath, the WASP values of the small town; above it, the plasticulture of Green Stamps. Because they sometimes coincide it is assumed that wherever there is kitsch there is also old-fashioned American-ism: Sunday church, apple pie, decency. Drive a polished sta-tion wagon and the police salute you; drive a beat-up Volks-wagen painted in psychedelic colors and the cops stop the car to search for drugs. If the prototypical forty-seven-year-old wife of the machinist in Dayton collects plastic lawn furni-ture, brass chafing dishes and curly-maple chairs she is, obvi-ously, one of us; but does that indicate that she is a Christian, a Republican or even a genuine constituent of Middle America? What if she is carrying on with the man next door? What if the salesman across the street, who lives in a house just like hers, goes from convention to convention (as he generally does) chasing ass? How applicable are her values—as stipu-lated in the catalogue of American virtues—when it comes time for the machinists' union to negotiate a contract with management? If you count the artifacts, look at the house, the car, the figures for income or the responses on the standard-ized opinion questionnaire, she will float somewhere in the suspended middle. But nobody has 2.2 children, some people are deeply in debt and some are not; some have extramarital affairs; some would love to have them if they had the courage or the opportunity; and some—a few—are happy with what they have. It is not Middle America that manufactures *Read-er's Digest*, "Mission Impossible" and "Playboy after Dark," yet all these things are manufactured with Middle America in mind. It is not Middle America that produces the television commercials, the political rhetoric and the funny papers. It is not Middle America that puts the dials and buttons and lights on the newest-model washing machines. It is not Middle America that devised the décor, the style and the practices of the Holiday Inn. Five seconds after the last desperate pass in the televised Sunday-afternoon football game twenty million Americans put down their beer cans, pick up the cluttered newspapers from the living-room floor and shuffle to dinner; it is not Middle America that chose this moment to eat; nor was it Middle America that decided to put the preservatives in the soggy bread, the polyethylene wrapper around the hamburger or the bland tastelessness into the tomatoes. Partly these things were determined by technology, sold by technology and distributed by technology; partly they are determined by people in air-conditioned offices who hypothesize statistical norms and call them Middle America; and partly they are determined by effete impudent snobs in editorial suites and television studios who, in trying to imagine what Middle America must be like, decide that it is a place of very square people who would like to be just like them. They do not sell thrift but credit, not independence but conformity, not possessions but things that turn out to be, on closer inspection, loans coupled to the inflatable desires of future consumption. *Trade up.* The heart of the pitch is a peep into the bedrooms and bathrooms of the affluent, a constant tour through split-level suburbs and high-rise penthouses, and a representation of life in which "modern" manners are sold not for what they are, but for what editors and producers imagine the rubes of the hinterland believe them to be. Middle America is the son of the minister dreaming about affluence, about forbidden things, saying to himself, "For once in a lifetime get into this world." Middle America—increasingly—is square life dreaming about other things and being offered plastic goods to furnish its reveries. Middle America—even if Spiro Agnew doesn't like it—may have its feet in church, but it has its head in *Playboy*.

If there is any single source of confusion about "Middle America" it lies in the inability of politicians, sociologists and journalists to distinguish the square from the plastic. Squareness implies a strong dose of personal and cultural scruple; plasticity is the attempt to be fashionable without paying the price. Going to church out of religious conviction, however understood (or misunderstood), may be square; going to church for social reasons is plastic. "God Bless America" and "Semper Fidelis" are square; Lester Lanin playing the Beatles is plastic. Lady Bird Johnson and Bess Truman are square; Pat Nixon is plastic. Busby Berkeley musicals are square; *The Sound of Music* is plastic. Billy Sunday was square; Billy Graham is plastic. The major attribute of the plastic world is its *ersatz* quality, a quality which is, in many cases, an economic or social necessity, but which, when it comes to dominate the surroundings, cheapens or deadens everything it touches. It has often been said—by John Kenneth Galbraith among others—that Madison Avenue and the industry it represents manufacture desires, that they do not respond to needs but create wants for the goods that are produced. It may similarly be said that the hucksters have manufactured an entire culture, complete with values, which is directed to squares but which in fact has enervated the square world—much of it, though obviously not all—of its old convictions. And it may even be said that once the pitchmen of New York and Chicago came around with their goodies Middle America cheerfully violated its scruples in order to obtain them. Middle America is often angry because the old virtues are no longer recognized and rewarded; but just as often the universality of those virtues is overestimated, because the plastic artifacts and possessions are confused with the values of the small town. The bankers, the brokers, the Rotarians still exercise local political and economic control; they decide who gets mortgages and who does not, they affect the configurations of neighborhoods and the decisions of the mayor and the police, and they may—with varying degrees of honesty—still profess the virtues of Ben Franklin and Horatio Alger. But the cultural signals and the basic economic decisions are not subject to local control. They originate somewhere else and they give the desires of Main Street an ambivalence which, while it has probably existed for a hundred years, has now turned the great fount of values into a receptacle and transformed the former entrepreneurs of morals and culture into subjects. Plastic holds much of Middle America together; old WASP virtues are replaced by synthetics, and the plastic WASP replaces the square.

The two great puritan entrepreneurs of culture in the twentieth century, Walt Disney of Disneyland and Hugh M. Hefner of *Playboy*, illustrate the transformation. Although they were born a generation apart, Disney in 1901, Hefner in 1926, and although they seem, at first, to be polar opposites, they came from similar Midwest WASP backgrounds and might, but for the accidents of time, have followed similar careers. Disney, the son of an unsuccessful Missouri farmer, took the square values of rural America—or what sentiment later imagined them to have been—cleaned them up and turned them into plastic. The barnyard was sterilized into clean mice, happy ducks and bourgeois pigs; the small town was idealized into a blessed valley, and the frustrating universe converted into the sanitary Magic Kingdom of Disneyland.

The word "dream" is often associated with Disneyland [wrote Richard Schickel in *The Disney Version*], particularly by its promotion and publicity people. It is, as they have it, "Walt's Dream" and a place that awakens the desire to dream in the visitor. But the quality of the dreams it represents is most peculiar—no sex and no violence, no release of inhibitions, no relief from real stresses and tensions through their symbolic treatment, and therefore no therapeutic effect. It is all pure escapism, offering momentary thrills, laughs and nostalgic pleasures for the impressionable; guaranteed safety for that broad spectrum of humanity whose mental health is predicated on denying that there is any such thing as mental ill health, or indeed, a mental life of any significance beneath the conscious level; guaranteed interest for the technologically inclined; guaranteed delight for those who like to prove their superiority to the mass of men by making fun of their sports.

The issue here is not vulgarity (although Disney had his vulgar—and his violent—streak); it is, rather, the subtle process in which the puritanical compulsion to order the world, to control, to clean up, is coupled to technology and thereby lifted to a synthetic realm in which new deities are created and old ones destroyed. What begins with "delight" ends with horror. For the Illinois Pavilion of the 1965 New York World's Fair, the Disney engineers created an animated Abraham Lincoln who came to represent the ultimate transformation. Richard Schickel again:

So Disney labored over Mr. Lincoln as he had not labored to bring forth his Mouse. "Imagination had to be tempered with authenticity," he told a reporter. "Drama must intertwine with serenity. Fantasy would be entirely abandoned, since its presence would defeat our purpose. Reserve was demanded but would have to take the form of subdued excitement. And dignity would have to be the constantly sounded keynote." Thus was the sixteenth president, martyr, hero and summary of the virtues of democratic man turned into a living doll, "capable of forty-eight separate body actions as well as seventeen head motions and facial expressions" (at least in 1965: there was a new, improved model a year later). Disney, caught in the grip of his technical mania and protected by his awesome innocence about aesthetic and philosophical matters, had brought forth a monster of wretched taste which, for all the phony reverence and pomposity surrounding its presentation, leaves one in a state of troubled tension. Are we really supposed to revere this ridiculous contraption, this weird agglomeration of wires and plastic, transferring to it, in the process, whatever genuine emotions we may have toward Lincoln in particular, toward mankind in general? If so, we are being asked to abjure the Biblical injunction against graven images and, quite literally, we are worshiping a machine that is no less a machine for having the aspect of a man. Perhaps, then, it is a form of art? But art is not imitation; its strength lies precisely in the art object's inability to speak or to move and the transcending compensations the artist makes for his inability. Take, for crude example, the Lincoln Memorial in Washington. The huge size of the figure, so often described as brooding, overpoweringly reminds the visitor of his own puniness of size and that Lincoln's spirit was alleged to have been similarly outsized in comparison to the ordinary. The silence of that massive figure encourages one's own reflections on the enigma of greatness. Surely, the atmosphere cues a quasireligious response, but it does not force a choice between the varieties of religious experience on the spectator as the Disneyland show attempts to do with its effects of lighting and music. Disney's Lincoln, for all its mechanical sophistication, reminds us that Lincoln was only a man; Daniel Chester French's Lincoln suggests that he might have been something more. But perhaps modern man is made uncomfortable by such suggestions. It is easier for him to live with the smaller "uneasiness" Ortega described some years ago when writing about the dummies at Madame Tussaud's. "The origin of this uneasiness lies," he wrote, "in the provoking ambiguity with which wax figures defeat any attempt at adopting a clear and consistent attitude toward them. Treat them as living beings, and they will sniggeringly reveal their waxen secret. Take them for dolls, and they seem to breathe in irritated protest. They will not be reduced to mere objects. Looking at them we suddenly feel a misgiving: should it not be they who are looking at us? Till in the end we are sick and tired of those hired corpses . . ." He adds: "The mob has always been delighted by that gruesome waxen hoax."

He should only have lived to see Abraham Lincoln rise up from his chair to mouth his carefully selected platitudes, with gestures— and is that a tear glistening in his eye as a mighty chorus of "The Battle Hymn of the Republic" swells behind him? Ortega would have been interested to hear of the curious fact that the "imagineers" discovered, quite by accident, about the plastic Mr. Lincoln's skin is made out of; after a while it excretes oils just as the human skin does and so "takes makeup wonderfully," as the press agent eagerly informs you. He would also like you to know of the interesting protection afforded Mr. Lincoln's electronic guts down in the basement. Should a fire break out, huge metal doors clang irrevocably shut in thirty seconds and the temperature drops instantly to thirty degrees below zero. A man tending the machinery could get killed, but the dummy would live—or exist, or whatever it does.

What can be said of Mr. Lincoln and of all the other human simulacra that are following him into Disneyland (not far away a group of pirates loots a town and rapes its women, who enjoy the process because, it is explained, they're all old maids) is that he stirs the observer to thought in a way that nothing else in the Magic Kingdom does. Here *is* the dehumanization of art in its final extremity, paradoxically achieved by an ignorant man who was actually, and in good conscience, seeking its humanization and who had, indeed, arrived at its dreadful solution, after a lifetime search for a perfect means of reproducing the reality of human life. At this point the Magic Kingdom becomes a dark land, the innocent dream becomes a nightmare, and the amusement park itself becomes a demonstration not of the wondrous possibilities of technological progress, as its founder hoped, but of its possibilities for horror.

If Disney's attempts to employ technology to create a Middle American utopia resulted in a plastic universe of dancing dolls, animated mermaids, shriveled heroes and, finally, an enervated and dehumanized world where technology was the only god, Hefner's parallel efforts to produce an antipuritanical freedom spewed forth a cornucopia of kitsch which was considerably less horrible only because it so often parodied itself. If you pass through the secret door in Disneyland you will in short order be among the Playboy bunnies. But it is still, somehow, the same place. What Disney did with sentimentality Hefner accomplished by inversion. As the son of a Nebraska preacher he grew up in the same landscape, learned the same lessons, and accepted the same descriptions of the good life. Then he reversed them, which is to say that he took the things that the puritan had always imagined joy to be, and which he had repressed, embraced them as healthy and valu-able, and advertised them as freedom and self-expression. Like Disney he is enamored of technology; like Disney he is a com-pulsive sanitizer; and like Disney he converted his puritanical hangups into a vast enterprise which flourishes on the cultural refugees of the land which formed him.

> Religious puritanism [Hefner wrote] pervades every aspect of our sexual lives. We use it as a justification for suppressing freedom of thought, expression and, of course, personal behavior. By associating sex with sin, we have produced a society so guilt ridden that it is al-most impossible to view the subject objectively and we are able to rationalize the most outrageous acts against mankind in the name of God. . . .
>
> The sexual activity that we pompously preach about and protest against in public, we enthusiastically pratice in private. We lie to one another about sex, we lie to our children about sex, and many of us undoubtedly lie to ourselves about sex. But we cannot forever escape the reality that a sexually hypocritical society is an unhealthy society that produces more than its share of perversion, neurosis, psychosis, unsuccessful marriage, divorce and suicide.

Scratch a puritan and you find a hedonist. Where it was once possible only to feel guilty about having sex, Hefner has now made it possible to feel guilty about not having it. The world of *Playboy*, with its pads, its gadgets, its plastic fashions and its always accessible girls, is as contrived as the world of Disney, as mesmerized by technology, and as free of blemishes as "Walt's Dream." Where Disneyland offers a mermaid with-out nipples, Hefner serves up his playmates without warts, birthmarks or pimples—either on the skin or underneath. Where Disney attempts to create a hermetic universe without sex, violence or release of inhibitions, Hefner's equally her-metic fantasies suggest that sex and gadgets will, by them-selves, represent all the answers to a man's prayers. (It goes without saying, of course, that *Playboy* honors most of the old fantasies of sexual exploitation, and that its women are presented as objects of consumption roughly on a par with tape recorders, lounge jackets, cologne and sports cars.) It does not occur to Hefner that sex might be as frustrating as repression and that in any case compulsive screwing, like compulsive consumption, is as likely to represent the end of experience and sensitivity as the beginning. "Being a romantic fellow ourself," he once wrote, "we favor our sex mixed with emotion. But we recognize that sex without love exists, that it is not in itself evil, and that it may sometimes serve a definitely worthwhile end." Good of him. Leaving aside that curious syntactical problem deriving from the editorial "we" and recognizing his disclaimer that one can get "so caught up in the trappings —both the form and the accouterments of living—that the real satisfactions become lost," it is still impossible to evade the recurring message: that "emotion" is of no central interest, that the "real satisfactions" are rhetorical abstractions beyond the bounds of Playboy-Disneyland, and that the mechanized male of Hefner's world imagines joy to be exactly the same thing as the uptight Puritan of his disdain. It is no longer done behind the barn but in a plush apartment; it is no longer condemned by fundamentalist preachers but blessed by psychiatrists; it is no longer dirty but healthy. But it is as uncomplicated as ever, and if you still feel guilty about doing it (or, more likely, about considering it) you can surround yourself with gadgets, crank up the hi-fi, and therefore remain as "Middle American" as the man who worships Disney. Hefner, said Rollo May, took the fig leaf off the genitals and put it over the eyes.

The heart of it is not freedom—as Hefner (and Disney) liked to claim—but the padded cell; it is what some behaviorists call "a responsive environment." Anyone who has traveled through Disneyland or reads *Playboy* knows that nothing is left to chance, that the good life has little to do with the unexpected, with the uncontrolled, with the messy, scruffy, untended, risky sides of existence. L. Rust Hills, describing the Playboy Mansion:

. . . Where business ends with Hefner and where living begins, it is almost impossible to say. The main feature is a vast "living room." There's a superb Kline on one section of the wall; a dreadful sculpture by Gallo on another; the wood paneling is dominated by the art and gadgets. The room is bisected by a counter-high electronics unit that does everything imaginable and there are speakers from all corners of the room; lights that swing out on cranes at the touch of a button and swing down to light a table in the middle of the room. Not just are there gadgets you haven't dreamed of, but everything *works*—two full-time repairmen, electronics experts, are on duty— that was perhaps the single thing that impressed me most, everything in my life being usually out of order. Downstairs there's a game room with a pool table surrounded by perhaps a dozen pinball machines— all of which work—and a Japanese game where you have a wheel that controls a car you see on a screen and the idea is you try to lap all these other cars that are always slowing down or speeding up so as to block the passing lane so you can't get by. . . . Then there's a bar downstairs with a window that looks out underwater into the swimming pool—this is all deep in the bowels of the mansion, got to by a narrow spiral staircase. . . . There were more rooms and bars and things than I could keep track of. I remember one that didn't seem to me to have much in it except a big rabbit (given to Hefner on his birthday) in a cage eating lettuce, but maybe that had the ping-pong table in it too; it was off the pool, I think, next to the sauna, on the side toward the room you only get to underwater, which of course I never saw. God's own amount of rooms are on all sorts of levels up and down the spiral stairs. All these rooms are open to the twenty-five Playboy Club bunnies (more or less) who live there regularly. I only saw one of these, a bunny named Avis, I think, who seemed nice enough, carrying a lot of clothes, exhausted from having just arrived here and from shopping to go on a thirty-five-day trip to Europe and Africa (and three days on a yacht in the Mediterranean) Hefner and a crowd of friends and six bunnies were beginning on the following Tuesday. There are also guest rooms and suites for distinguished visitors; the one I saw had, as well as a regular door, a secret-panel entrance that opened at the touch of a button concealed in the woodwork. Nowhere that I saw in this huge house was there a window that showed whether it was day or night, sunshine or rain, winter or summer, on the "outside."

Disney and Hefner dreamed together. The mechanized figure, "capable of forty-eight separate body actions as well as seventeen head motions and facial expressions," the Lincoln of the World's Fair, the dinosaur and the mermaid of Disneyland, the animated Mouse and the singing pig, the figure that speaks and dances on electronic impulse—all those creatures of "charm and wonder" are, after all, but the forerunners of the mechanized human, the bunny and the playmate, deblemished, cleaned up and nearly available, yet not to be touched (stay behind the ropes, folks, you can all see), or the airline stewardess programmed with preset announcements and cued responses and now the subject of endless fantasies of sexual exploitation (motels and airport inns), saying, perhaps in the tone of "Coffee, tea or milk?," "Oral or genital? . . . With the light on or the light off?" or "Sir, can I hang up your pants?" The fantasy of a night with this month's playmate or yesterday's stew on Eastern Airlines demands no more engagement with a real person than the mechanized Lincoln, and no more a confrontation of tensions and complexity than a trip through Disneyland. On one of Hefner's television programs "Playboy after Dark," the "guests" in the Playboy Penthouse, each guy paired off with a chick, are treated to a movie of the Playboy airplane (complete with bar, gadgets, etc., and an illuminated bunny on the tail) in which people just like themselves—Hefner, chicks *et al.*—are watching a movie, drinking Scotch and grooving in the skies over Los

Angeles. (I assume that the movie on the plane is another film of Hefner and guests watching a movie of themselves in which they are watching a movie of themselves . . .) It is all there at the touch of a button and it is the button itself that becomes the good life. Throw the switch and you have it—not real enjoyment or real people, but another button. The plastic world is not spectatorship so much as it is the opportunity to watch spectators. To the Disney fans, who see his works as the last bastion of order and decency against the floods of smut and pornography (not the least of which is represented by *Playboy* itself), the cheerful exploitation of sex is obviously to be envied and condemned. But that isn't Hefner's first love or his greatest interest. His interest is in that button; it is in power, control and clean. Walt Disney once told a reporter, "I don't like pestholes. I don't like pictures that are dirty. I don't ever go out and pay money for abnormality. I don't have depressed moods and I don't want to have any. I'm happy, just very, very happy." Hefner has often said the same thing. He doesn't like dirty pictures. He claims to be very happy. And he has developed the same means of getting there (or, if you like, of avoiding the issue). Thus the plastic representation of the things the Puritan is allowed to be happy about and the cosmetic versions of those which are forbidden come out pretty much as the same thing. You begin with the square, offer him a choice between the two forms of escape he understands and produce the mechanical figures that he considers appropriate. It doesn't matter much whether the machine looks like Lincoln or the Playmate of the Month.

When square turns into plastic, the vulgar and amoral disguise themselves as virtue, and the decisions that should, under older circumstances, require no end of moral agony become easy—are made, indeed, at the flick of a switch. We have no shortage of current examples—if there is "permissiveness," after all, it is not in raising children according to Benjamin Spock but in the constant invitation from Madison Avenue to indulge yourself—but one of the most obvious was the super-film *Airport*, a custom-made job for the Radio City Music Hall/G-rated/family-entertainment/All-American market. No four-letter words, no sex on the screen, no drugs, no debauchery. Family stuff: two divorces, two extramarital romances, one unmarried stewardess with child, one kook with a bomb, and lots and lots and lots of gadgets. Dean Martin, a married airline pilot, is the man who knocked up the stew; they don't have much in common (except vacuity), but he is concerned (Responsibility) and will Do Something, which, in the end, means leaving his wife for the chick. Burt Lancaster, airport manager at "Lincoln International Airport" (Chicago's O'Hare Field?), has a dual romance with his job and with Jean Seberg, an employee of Dean Martin's airline; fortunately for Burt, his wife has her own affair with someone else and wants out of the marriage. She reassures him that as a divorced man he will probably see more of the children than he used to, because that's what divorced fathers always do. So much for that set of Squaresville scruples. While Lancaster is trying to keep his airport open in a snowstorm, negotiating the divorce with his wife, dealing with an old lady stowaway and with the angry residents of an adjacent residential neighborhood who (in the middle of a blizzard) become incensed about the noise of jets over their homes, Van Heflin, the kook, carries his bomb onto Dean Martin's 707 with the intent of blowing himself and the plane to oblivion over the Atlantic. (There is one brief shot of a Norman Rockwell family in the adjacent neighborhood saying grace at the dinner table; grace is interrupted by the blast of a plane, falling dishes, etc., but you know that familial peace—that grace itself—must defer to technology.) The central confrontation of the film has nothing to do with morals: divorces, pregnancies, human encounters are easily manipulated, rationalized or mechanized. The showdown is between the gadgets themselves: Will Dean Martin's plane survive the explosion of Van Heflin's bomb? Can the machinery on the ground—the radar, the landing systems, the communications networks, the electronic circuits—mitigate the work of a madman (who, in fact, is one of the few human beings in the picture)? You bet they can. With the exception of a single hysterical passenger—always bitching about the service, always getting in the way—who nearly ruins the collective attempt to Pull Technology Through, the characters follow the path of reason, which is to help the machine live. On the way a few "ordinary" people—cliché nuns, a snotty-brained kid, an old lady—have to be patronized. (Can one still imagine playing a nun swilling her 1.6 ounces of airplane booze for laughs? That's Squaresville.) But what the hell—those people are okay, they're just a little obsolete.

The possibilities for indulging fantasies are endless. Disneyland and Playboyland fuse. Imagine me controlling all that power, flipping channels, dialing frequencies, revving up those engines. Imagine me in that world of superplastic, pushbutton offices and instant communication. Imagine me, under cover of flashing lights and radarscopes, walking out on the doughty old wife and taking up with the young stew. Maybe that used to be *bad*, but technology is bigger than all of us: technology is the emergency and the salvation through which the escape is made. The all-American answer to Cotton Mather and Dr. Strangelove rolled into one. Fail-safe works; plasticity will out; it will more than compensate for the price in Squaresville (a little noise, some busted windows, a divorce or two)—will, indeed, if properly managed, allow Squaresville to coexist.

II

Middle America, so called, has become a suburban masquerade. The plastic people disguise themselves as squares and try to strike a new bargain: If conscience will let us be, if you old moralists will leave us alone—to drink, to covet our neighbors' wives, to engage in our private vulgarities—we will pay lip service to "traditional" Americanism, will, indeed, embrace it so deeply that we ourselves will not be able to distinguish it from real conviction or from the growing fear that we are not certain just where conviction was irretrievably lost from our lives. Our mechanical figures will look like your idols; our rhetoric will sound like your textbooks; emptiness will strut like amplitude. We will make corporate subsidies sound like free enterprise, we will make credit look like thrift, we will try our best to make the church of the suburbs resemble Christianity. "That God loves you is the greatest truth ever enunciated," said Mr. Peale. "God doesn't want anyone to be hungry and oppressed. He just puts his big arms around everybody and hugs them up against Himself." Everything is available on the cheap.

No one can be certain how much is "genuine," how much contrived; nor does it matter, since the purpose—even of a genuine commitment—is to use "culture" to sink into a saccharine commonplace, to lose yourself not in a frenzy of drugs and hard rock but in a lullaby of muted strings, an elegy of padded sounds and unctuous respectability. It is the culture of the mortician—pardon, the funeral director. At its worst it is not cynical or manipulative; it is not kissing babies or twisting belief to suit the situation; it is not politicizing Mantovani or the breakfast prayer meeting in the White House; at its worst it is *real* emptiness, which is to say that it becomes untempered involvement with plasticity itself. When Nixon said—in the 1970 campaign—"I happen to believe that there are no second-class citizens in America," he was not articulating a barefaced political lie; he was, rather, stating one of the great pieties of his culture, was speaking synthetic truth, echoing Mr. Peale and Mr. DeWitt Wallace of *Reader's Digest*, and manufacturing out of plastic (like Disney's Lincoln, like Hefner's playmate) a benign and controllable—and therefore dead—reality. Plasticity is not a gadget to enlarge sensitivity, but to cast out experience. It is, at its worst, escape from all identity, the wish to be no one. We will make the beds of our synthetic love and bury our heads beneath the covers.

Again it is necessary to consider performance. In the counterculture the parts are labeled "individuality," "self-expression" and "independence" even if they come out on many occasions to be more conformist (and maudlin) than the billboards had advertised or the actors had intended. In the plastic culture, on the other hand, one does not perform to be noticed but to be obscure—not only among other people but to oneself. The historic American WASP was always something of a stoic; he took his lumps without complaining and kept his cool even under the greatest pressure. The plastic WASP, trying to imitate his heritage, turns the role into that of the "Good Sport," a part that demands the replacement of most suspicions of real feeling with their least offensive counterparts and of most genuine human acts with their closest agreeable substitutes. It is as if natural resources were too scarce or too risky for use, as if self-exposure were too dangerous, and as if passion—as in a mental hospital—were the cause of disorder. The plastic imitates the square. The living doll:

Who [wrote Judith Viorst in *The New York Times Magazine*] is this woman who denies that she shivers or sweats, that she fights with her husband or weeps with disappointment? Who is this woman who appears to have experienced nothing but elation at the sight of an ironing board? Who is this woman who has yet to be caught with a smudge or a wrinkle, whose stockings don't run, whose hair never blows in the breeze? Who is this woman who is invariably served up to the public in a hail of single-minded adjectives like "warm," "sweet," "thoughtful," "modest," "unselfish," "uncompetitive," "calm," "well organized," "sincere," "natural," "strong," "brave," "courteous," "loving," and "loyal"?

Who is this woman? She is the Girl Scout, the happy house-wife, the self-effacing better half dedicated to her husband's career and happiness, performing her little charities, being ever and always the good sport, taking shit. In this particular case she is Pat Nixon, but it is a version of Pat Nixon that is served up to satisfy categories: the "homemaker" vision of the pitchmen of detergents and appliances; the official ideals and constraints of the sorority; the model of the "good mother." We can only speculate about the existence of some "real" Pat Nixon; if she exists she must of necessity be a pathetic figure, a sort of superstew who married the airline's biggest customer, traded everything she had to make him still bigger, and now struggles hard to remember the moments—way back, way back—when things might have taken a different turn. The only time I saw her in person she was sitting alone on the Vice-Presidential campaign train in the fall of 1952, a sort of forgotten object in the back room, while Dick was gladhanding the Republicans of Fitchburg, Massachusetts. People who have seen her since, performing in what should be better days, describe her pretty much in the same way: walking with Dick's hand on her arm until they are out of sight of the White House guests, then being automatically turned loose, without a word, to proceed alone; being greeted by her husband with the formality accorded a foreign diplomat, and reminding him, with a touch, of who she is; being so accustomed to mechanical applause for someone else that she joins a television audience in applauding one of her own statements and, on realizing the mistake, hiding her face in her hands in shame.

"I never had it easy," she told Gloria Steinem in that bitter interview. "I never had time to think about things like who I wanted to be or whom I admired, or to have ideas. I never had time to dream about being anyone else. I had to work." Work denies self? Presumably a person who never had time for ideas or to dream "about being anyone else" never had time to consider her (or his) identity and regards the matters of belief and self-realization as luxuries that must be deferred. As a child of the thirties she did have to work, and often to struggle, and we might charitably conclude, therefore, that the Pat Nixons of this world paid an especially fearful price for their escape from the depression. But that depression is over and the gratifications that might at one time have had to be deferred have long since been realized in the avalanche of goodies to which we treated ourselves in the last twenty-five years. Perhaps some people carry their scars forever, but it is just as accurate to say that the Pat Nixons have had as much time and as many of the world's blessings (or what they would regard as blessings) as anyone in history, that choices were made, and that to represent oneself in terms of an unemployed miner (which Pat Nixon's father once was) or a domestic servant out of the black ghetto is to deny everything that has happened since 1945 and to disregard all the things that made one what he or she has become. If one were honest one might even ask whether it was "work" that did it and whether—to be somewhat more searching—that "it" was worth the price. Is it conceivable, perhaps even probable, that it was not "work" which required one to exile ideas and dreams, but the cultural role to which one aspired? Is it even more probable that it was precisely because "work" was not crucial that social and political conformity became so important? If the work were essential would conformity be required? If the job to be done had genuine value, if the worker had unquestioned skill, would they not of themselves generate—in any person of sensitivity— ideas and dreams, and curiosity about the ideas and dreams of others? (The world hardly lacks for humble examples: the Jewish socialists in the garment-industry sweatshops of New York; the Wobblies; the Italian anarchists; the Quaker pacifists; the "adventurers"—religious, economic, political—who settled this country.) What has happened is that the meaning of work has been turned around. Look at the adjectives on the list: "warm," "sweet," "modest," "unselfish" . . . Are those the ingredients of work or the imagined consequences? Are these the attributes one would seek in a lawyer, an entrepreneur or even a good secretary? Granted that the culture expects its women to be the demure, self-effacing, self-denying objects of male ambitions, it is still a peculiar list: nothing there about principles, convictions, tastes or manners (except, perhaps, "courteous"); no indication of what the lady is supposed to be "sincere" about and every indication that neither she nor her husband has ever been sincere about anything that they believed couldn't carry a public-opinion poll; no evidence that she has ever been loving of anything that had not previously been certified as officially worthy of love. What all these words suggest is that the object of work is to blend, to disappear, to keep your hems safely at the knee, to have your daughter choose a wedding dress with puffed sleeves and pleated yoke appropriate for the more conservative grade-school graduations and communions; to "campaign" for Republican candidates without saying anything—to do it, literally, without opening your mouth. The objective of work is plastic perfection, to collect "virtues" like merit badges and thereby create a padded cell of your attributes. Again discounting sex discrimination: one is "brave" but not daring; "strong" but not strong-minded; "sincere" but not candid; "loving" but not affectionate; "thoughtful" but not sensitive. One does not show pain or passion or sweat; one does not confess to moral or sartorial wrinkles; one does not disagree with one's husband or demonstrate that one might be a distinctive person of any sort. To amass such virtues obviously demands considerable discipline—it is, I would think, about the dirtiest work in all creation and entitles anyone to more bitterness than Pat Nixon revealed to Gloria Steinem—but it involves little risk. The whole point of moral plasticity is that you never have to lay anything on the line. Whenever Nixon says "Let me be perfectly clear" you know that he is on the verge of a platitude or a lie or some pathological form of evasive action which combines the two. It is like Captain Queeg saying "I kid you not."

The official descriptions of the Nixons and the little Eisenhowers, David and Julie, are made of the same stuff as Disney's mermaids and Hefner's playmates: cosmetic, hermetic, lifeless. When an irreverent garment-industry journalist reported that Julie Nixon's trousseau included see-through pajamas, the White House found it necessary to issue immediate and emphatic denials. No such thing for Julie, because it might suggest—might it not?—that she did indeed have a body and that her breasts might have real nipples. And when the Reverend Dr. Peale united the couple in holy matrimony there were endless stories about wedding gifts, shopping trips and housekeeping arrangements, but no sign of passion or religion: marriage is consumption. The most prominent symbol inside the church was the American flag; the only token of affection was a kiss that David, under pressure from the reporters, planted on Julie's cheek. The family that unctions together functions together.

Perhaps they are not *really* like this, but this is the way they wish to be seen; this is the way they try to synthesize a "tasteful" Middle American consensus. Mr. Nixon, someone said, "has pitted the Apostle Paul, strawberry shortcake and fried chicken, American jazz, and the Saturday afternoon baseball game against nudity, pot, the underground press, and the weekend riot." But even these things are accomplished without verve or style: the blemishes are compulsively erased, the spots taken out, the offending odors eliminated. No jackets are ever removed, no shoes kicked off, no muscles relaxed. Always on guard, always at work. The Air-wick is everywhere. Each social performance—the inaugural balls, the wedding, the entertainments at the White House—has been worked to lifeless perfection. It was not simply that social Washington began to collapse after the new Administration came to town in 1969 (everyone, it was said, now entertains at home), that there were no good parties, no contemporary music, no stylish entertainment, or that the comics (Skelton and Hope) and the musicians (Duke Ellington) who came to the White House, however talented, represented another age but—more important—that no revelations of taste or interest were permitted (or perhaps even felt) if they could not be placed squarely in "Middle America."

And yet the old "Middle America" is elusive; its values often tend to be contentious and abrasive, not soothing. Norman Vincent Peale isn't very big in the Bible Belt, and even Billy Graham is suspect among the fundamentalists of Arkansas and Oklahoma. So the symbols have to be manufactured: appearances at "safe" universities, Honor America Day, football. Although there are still candidates representing "Middle American" culture, they have less and less to do with the realities of American life, with its new music, its new humor, its new literature. At the same time, the old candidates are often unsatisfactory for the plastic culture of the suburbs which Nixon must represent. To be new and seemingly square, therefore, the thing has to be fabricated. When Nixon wanted to identify himself with big-time college football in the fall of 1969, his people concocted a plaque for the winner of the "national championship" (between Texas and Arkansas) which the President could award in a locker-room ceremony. But there is no such thing as a national champion (which even the most casual television fan knows); since all ratings and standings are debatable—and are endlessly debated—no previous President of the United States ever had the temerity to decide, without being asked, which team should be selected or whether, indeed, any team should be so recognized. If Nixon and his people had understood a little more about American sports they would have known that they should keep hands off; that here was a ritual to get people away from everything that politicians, including the President of the United States, symbolized. Football was still square, however commercial it had become; a man did something well or he did it poorly with no hidden motives or obfuscating rhetoric; a good block or a good tackle didn't lie; they produced immediate results, not equivocation, and if, on occasion, accidents or luck affected the balance, football was still a contest in which the honesty of good performance made the difference. It was everything that politics was not. The Nixies should have known all that, but the plastic is attracted to the square—and sometimes to "high" culture—with a nearly irresistible force, and so the President came to the locker room to award his plaque. It was not a serious political mistake but it was indicative of the attempt to generate a synthetic cultural consensus and throw yourself into its soothing ooze. Of all the places

Nixon could have been, this was one of the least appropriate. Standing there among the sweating, triumphant jocks, jacket buttoned, saying his spiel, he was at best an anticlimax. But he also looked like a phony, a man trying to turn a real victory into a plastic title.

III

In his essay "Masscult & Midcult" Dwight Macdonald talks about that "collective monstrosity, 'the masses,' 'the public,' " which is taken as "a human norm by the technicians of Masscult."

They at once degrade the public by treating it as an object, to be handled with the lack of ceremony of medical students dissecting a corpse, and at the same time flatter it and pander to its taste and ideas by taking them as the criterion of reality (in the case of the questionnaire-sociologists) or of art (in the case of the Lords of Masscult). When one hears a questionnaire-sociologist talk about "setting up" an investigation, one realized that he regards people as mere congeries of conditional reflexes, his concern being which reflex will be stimulated by which question. At the same time, of necessity, he sees the statistical majority as the great Reality, the secret life he is trying to unriddle. Like a Lord of Masscult, he is—professionally—without values, willing to take seriously any idiocy if it is held by many people . . .

The Masses are not people, they are not the Man in the Street or The Average Man, they are not even that figment of liberal condescension, The Common Man. The masses are, rather, man as non-man, that is, man in a special relationship to other men that makes it impossible for him to function as man. . . .

Macdonald defines masscult as the systematic manufacture by technicians of objects for mass cultural consumption; there is no pretense of artistic integrity, no test except that of the market: "everything becomes a commodity, to be mined for \$\$\$, used for something it is not, from Davy Crockett to Picasso." Midcult, the "bastard child" of masscult, dresses its equally market-oriented product in a fig leaf of cultural pretension. "It is a corruption of High Culture which has the enormous advantage over Masscult that while also in fact 'totally subject to the spectator,' in Malraux's phrase, it is able to pass itself off as the real thing." Midcult is *Horizon* magazine, the Book-of-the-Month Club, Thornton Wilder's *Our Town* and Archibald MacLeish's *J.B.* Midcult exploits the discoveries of the avant-garde, but it cheapens and panders to its audience; "it specializes in soft impeachments. Its cakes are forever eaten, forever intact." Midcult is kitsch for snots.

In 1960, when "Masscult & Midcult" was published, Macdonald suggested that midcult might well be on the way to becoming a permanent norm; that people who had been raised on it would lose all ability to make critical judgments of their own, would be incapable of demanding anything more honest and would cheerfully accept a "debased permanent standard," sinking into "the agreeable ooze of the Midcult swamp." Macdonald made it quite clear that he was not contemptuous of "the masses" but of the pitchmen and manufacturers of culture who regarded people in such terms; what he advocated was recognition of the idea that there is not "One Big Audience but rather a number of smaller, more specialized audiences that may still be commercially profitable . . . The mass audience is divisible, we have discovered—and the more divided it is, the better . . ."

In the years since the piece was written, some of the things that Macdonald advocated have come to pass. The audience is more divided, a few of the dinosaurs of the mass market are dying or already extinct—among them several of Macdonald's favorite *bêtes noires*—and masscult, which always managed to disregard aesthetic difficulties, is being sorely tried by unexpected political and social problems. *Life* has been rumored to be in deep trouble; *The Saturday Evening Post* is gone—and now resurrected as a quarterly (which makes it a sort of minority publication); the mass manufacturing of films has, at least for the moment, given way to independent, non-Hollywood producers; and the vitality of print seems to lie not in giant "general" publications but in special-interest magazines. (Television, needless to say, goes on, and the power of the mass media to co-opt the avant-garde remains undiminished. Even the most prosaic TV commercial is now played to a rock beat or adorned by a folk guitar.) More significant than the box score, however, is the fact that the whole topography has been altered, that the distinctions between high, mass- and midcult have radically shifted (or simply vanished) and that the vectors of cultural influence and style have changed direction. High cult, which, as Macdonald noted, never enjoyed a blessed existence in America, has become unfashionable; midcult is looking not to the top for its cues but to the bottom; masscult is losing its mass. At the same time, and for the same reasons, the old distinctions between masscult and midcult have been replaced, temporarily at least, by distinctions between hip, square and plastic: the highest form of social grace is not to patronize the opera but to raise funds for the defense of the Panthers; the grooviest trip isn't to Paris but to an Easthampton estate where the jet set is entertaining Cesar Chavez; the real social register isn't the late Mrs. Edward C. Barry's little black book, but the list of signers on the political advertisement in the *New York Times*. The instant establishment. High art, of course, has always borrowed or stolen material from folk art, especially in music, and cultural slumming is hardly new. But most of those journeys used to involve a vast amount of condescension; they were like trips through country auctions—a little amusement, a few low-priced items to grace the sophisticated scene, a little quaintness to enhance cosmopolitan self-esteem. In the last few years, however, the rubes got the drop on the slickers and put them on the defensive. Call a man a square and he immediately tries to prove not that he's high, but that he's hip. "What? You Haven't Smoked Pot Even Once?" Digging John Cage may be an answer, but familiarity with the Grateful Dead and Janis Joplin is more successful. The great national entertainers are the young and the black; the sale of classical records, once a major share of the long-playing market, has shrunk to something under ten percent, and the fashion in books dealing with social problems has shifted from the scholar's analysis and the journalist's "objective" report to the personal document: Mailer *feeling it* at the Pentagon; Claude Brown in the ghetto; Jonathan Kozol in a Boston classroom; Tom Hayden in court; Bobby Seale organizing the Panthers. The *Village Voice*, now the most fashionable of papers, is wedded to first-person journalism. Every man can have a Valuable Experience. Objectivity sucks. We can all write poetry, make films, weave cloth and fashion jewelry. The "authority" is the man who has felt it; the expert is a liar; high culture is art created by experts.

Because midcult no longer looks to the top but to the cultural and political dissidents at the bottom (*Easy Rider*; *Midnight Cowboy*; *The Greening of America*; rock; black revolt; etc.) and because masscult is flirting with television representations of poverty lawyers, ghetto doctors, black lovers and all the rest, neither will any longer serve as an adequate base for social or cultural cohesion. The old masscult could be sustained only as long as the consciousness of underclass struggle and upward mobility was sufficiently large and widespread to be respectable, while the majority was believed, in popular mythology, to be making it, and while only a minority was supposed to be affluent. In totalitarian societies it can be fostered officially as part of the collective national effort. In democratic societies it is sustained by the mythology of the common man moving up. But as more and more people join the ranks of the "affluent" or try to act as if they have joined, as the consciousness of consumption replaces the consciousness of production, midcult should—and sometimes does —take over: indulge yourself, ask for the "finer" things, for once in a lifetime . . . If you are affluent (or middle-class) you are supposed to give up the scandal sheet and buy a sedate Republican paper; you are supposed to forsake the saloon for the bridge party; are supposed to buy encyclopedias for the children, *Saturday Review* for the coffee table and the Book of the Month to be with it. People who haven't made it become hitchhikers on the cultural vehicles designed for those who think they have; if those are not satisfactory they can try to develop their own resources (or return, perhaps, to ethnic traditions) or they can seethe in quiet anger. As a consequence the old mass market becomes a cultural orphan: The giant magazine doesn't pay, because it is too expensive to produce and circulate, and because its readers no longer fit the "demographics" of affluence which the advertisers want. The last desperate act of a dying magazine dinosaur is deliberately to cut its own readership to achieve a more "select" audience.

But midcult has become treacherous; it is not sufficiently concerned with the "fine" things, and too much involved with the scuffy sides of life, too bemused with "problems." *Holiday* magazine manages its vicarious trips without race problems, poverty or the other unpleasantries of domestic life just as *The National Geographic* has managed to avoid the ugly facets of foreign politics: South Africa without apartheid, Portugal without Salazar, the world without dictators, exploitation and repression. But how many "unspoiled" places are left? How many clear lakes, how many clean pictures, how many happy books?

Even the tube is no longer secure: too many longhaired kids, too many freaks, too much talk about drugs and sex. In one of the stranger contemporary developments, Hollywood and television have been collaborating to bowdlerize recent feature films to make them acceptable for TV audiences—not only by cutting scenes, but by filming new ones; midcult trying to reshape itself into masscult. But the bind remains: There is no persuasive unsynthetic "American" image, no cohesive set of values, no certainty of aspirations or national effort. Not enough *good* things. We are not making America; we are not fighting the Great Depression; we are not Americanizing immigrants; we are not providing entertainment for the struggling industrial proletariat; we are not beating the Nazis and the Japs. Equally important, there is no longer a consistent image of high culture or the good life; everything carries more than a hint of qualification. Cars poison the air; detergents poison the water; cigarettes poison your lungs. At the same time, as Macdonald noted, the avant-garde of high culture has run out of juice: "We have become skilled at consuming high culture when it has been stamped PRIME QUALITY by the proper authorities, but we lack the kind of sophisticated audience that supported the achievements of the classic avant-garde, an audience that can appreciate and discriminate on its own."

We all turn sentimental. Richard Nixon digs *Chisum* because he likes movies in which the good guys win. And where you can tell who the good guys are. But he isn't alone. The groovy people call it camp: old movies and old comic strips and middle-aged *stuff* like Aubrey Beardsley drawings and Tiffany lamps. They like John Wayne too, some of them, even though they know that given half a chance he'd stomp 'em. But John Wayne isn't the enemy, isn't even part of the scene any more. Like Bogart and Edward G. Robinson and Victor Mature, like all those movies on the late show, or in the festivals at the Brattle and the Elgin and the New Yorker, Duke Wayne is a museum piece. "Camp is generous," says Susan Sontag, our leading explicator of the camp scene. "It wants to enjoy. It only seems like malice, cynicism." Put on your camp colored glasses, and the masscult of yesteryear becomes today's entertainment.

Very democratic. Very antisnoot. But there is a trick: Beyond the generosity, the democracy, the fun, camp makes it possible to avoid the difficult distinction between commitment and distance, lets you move in and out of the joke at will, and permits you to say "It's good *because* it's awful," which, in Sontag's estimation, is "the ultimate camp statement." Now they can't find you: are you sentimental, are you patronizing, are you *serious?* Who can tell? Yet one thing is certain: things were funnier in the old days. Maybe it was kitschy, maybe it was gross, but it was *amusing*. And it wasn't plastic. What the connoisseur appreciates in camp is its ingenuousness: "The Art Nouveau craftsman who makes a lamp with a snake coiled around it is not kidding, nor is he trying to be charming. He is saying, in all earnestness: *Voilà!* the Orient!" Camp, in other words, is a sophisticate's answer to plastic: it is ambivalently contemptuous of mass taste, but it demands no more of a commitment to standards—in aesthetics or in social belief—than the plastic. And it can be infinitely sentimental without having to take the rap.

And so the hip and the counterculture replace high culture as a source of fashion (and often resemble it in their contempt for "commercial" art and conventional life), while the plastic supplants masscult as a force of cohesion. The manufacturer of plastic may pay homage to Squaresville or advertise with-it-ness as the occasion demands, but what he really offers is the security of the cheap gadget and the easy trip. It is not a way to achieve value (or values) but an escape from them; not even a means of conspicuous consumption, but a way of remaining obscure. And while masscult played to a belief in real work for real goods and reassured those who hadn't made it that there were millions of other people just like them, that God must love the common people, and that there was nobility in their common-man virtues, plasticult thrives on shortcuts and synthetics: Making it becomes easy, and the common-man virtues are rendered relatively unimportant. God "just puts his big arms around everybody and hugs them up against Himself." Like Mommy. Everything is simple: divorce, illegitimacy, positive thinking, good orgasms, big cars, hermetic environments. In masscult you had to work before some *deus ex machina* delivered the boss's beautiful daughter. Now you just have to Push the Button.

IV

We have heard a great deal about contemporary alienation—perhaps too much: speculations, theories, reflections, laments. But if alienation means anything it is that the new mythic "American," that composite of advertising and television and statistics, of sociology and political rhetoric, of country clubs and corporations, is an unsatisfactory model not only for those who are officially "alienated" but for nearly everyone in America. Perhaps technology itself has outrun the human capacity to create myths and sources of identity; perhaps we are all suffering future shock. It is much more likely, however, that after the historic Americanism of the WASP ran out of steam there was little but technology to replace it. We know that we are all Americans but no longer understand why or how; we know we are supposed to be an affluent country, but we cannot comprehend why we feel so poor. We are held together by synthetics, fabrications and "systems." Consumption is our new puritanism, conformity our most pervasive mode of grace. And yet the more we achieve, the more we fulfill, the more detached we become from ourselves, the more we must learn to distrust our own frustrations, our own humanity, our own instincts. This is what we teach children in school, what we learn on television, and what we are taught in a million subtle ways every day of our lives. Most of us are not entirely plastic, are not synthetic people, but it is precisely that unsynthetic part that we learn to suspect. People who have found their communities of dissent or alienation can seek support—however unsatisfactory—among their peers; the rest have very little.

The traditional conception of the "mainstream" in America, the historic version of the WASP, gave people a place to go. Its essence was hopeful even if the hope was rarely fulfilled in practice. The new mainstream, the contemporary rendering of the plastic American, offers only the present and the past. We are supposed to have arrived wherever it was we used to be going. We have made it. But, says the secret heart, it doesn't *feel* right, doesn't feel at all, doesn't smell, doesn't taste, doesn't satisfy. All around are the casualties, not of failure, but of success; all around are the accumulating horrors of triumph; all around is the guilt, not of the old Puritan who distrusted all things that did not smack of piety and hard work, but of the new Puritan who suspects he is not enjoying enough. "You only go around once in life," says the beer that made Milwaukee famous. "Grab all the gusto you can get." The old American was supposed to deny himself a great deal for the sake of achieving what he wanted: someday, someday, he would enjoy; the plastic American, who is supposed to have it all, must still deny himself in an effort to preserve what he thinks he has. All the same, it doesn't taste as good as it was supposed to.

The historic WASP is giving way to the plastic American. Here is a man whose virtues are tested not in adversity but in social acceptability, who does not achieve his comforts but is born with a full complement already at his disposal, and for whom the greatest vice is any virtue carried to extremes. He is not necessarily an ethnic WASP (although certainly not an "ethnic" of any other sort), but he models himself—or is modeled by others—on the things that he imagines WASPs are nowadays supposed to be: a composite man who does not choose among personality characteristics and styles, but will try instead to blend them all. Hard-working but not pushy; aware but not "intellectual"; courageous but not reckless; thoughtful but not sensitive; generous but not open. For him the greatest fear is to be inconvenient, and it is this, rather than ambition, that drives him. Benjamin De Mott has an inventory:

"I am more interested in a man's behavior than in his inner life." Check. "In shaping character, externals are more important than inner tendencies." Check. "I sometimes have trouble figuring out the behavior of people who are emotionally unstable." Check. "Math is one of my best subjects." Check. "I think I'm practical and efficient when there's something that has to be done." Check. "I don't have the temperament for the 'romantic' point of view." Check. "I have few emotional problems." Check. "A first principle with me is that it's a man's duty to adjust himself to his environment." Check. "I am a fairly conventional person." Check. "My relations with other people are usually uncomplicated." Check. . . .

Not a bad fellow, not the kind to make a fuss, and often the first to settle things when a fuss is made. Always together. *Al-*

222

ways in place. If the natural world is an overtly hostile place, it is also one that can be controlled, sealed out or flown over; he can cross it on a single menu, sleeping in rooms with identical décor, signing the same credit slips billed to the same address and talking to people with similar attitudes (or non-attitudes). He carries his environment with him; what he demands most of all is predictability: no surprises in restaurants, airlines or people. If he is a military person he can go for months, perhaps forever, in a foreign country without resort to local currency: the PX in Karlsruhe is just like the PX in California or Saigon, same goods, same money, same system. And when the environment fails him he goes underground. At his ultimate he is a character out of "Mission Impossible," an infallible technician solving problems without any expression of belief, any sign of commitment—except to the "job"—and without the slightest likelihood that he will ever betray his real identity. A perpetual secret agent who understands the behavior of the enemy, anticipates him, and knows no limitations of technology.

He is, of course, not a "real" man. As a model he is less than a man; a mechanical man, the first hero in history who is not a demigod but a semihuman. And although you can't find him out there, there is a little of him in most of us. At the same time, the model is pervasive enough—is, indeed, the only model of "Americanism" in contemporary life—to make it frightening. We have other heroes, other figures for emulation, but all of them are oriented toward particular groups or particular moments in time: Panthers, Yippies, Spanish Americans, women. None of them will serve, at least not yet, as an integrating figure for the majority of Americans. The issue I am arguing here is not the old complaint about "the technocracy"—men against machines—but the subtly pervasive religion of technology, the idolatry of buttons, and the incompletely articulated (yet powerful) belief in an Americanism where technology is not a cultural artifact but the essence of identity, where we know who we are only by what we possess, and where the imagination is so limited that the buttons of which we dream produce nothing but more buttons. This is the "mainstream" that we are offered; not a mainstream where the kitsch is mitigated by the substantial strength of traditional culture and belief, where religion, for example, means something beyond Sunday church, where identity is forged through relations and places in small communities, where skills and jobs are related to the immediacy of a product or a necessary service, and where social and political arrangements are determined in large part by those who must live with them. Our mainstream is more like a common market than a common culture. To some extent we are all in it; to a growing extent we are all alienated, because it forces us to deny the things which we feel, which we desire and which we are. To be fully human is to look increasingly un-American. In the culture of plastic, the soul is an enemy of the state.

The question now is whether the image of the plastic American is sufficiently powerful to overwhelm (either by itself or with assistance from a repressive government) the cultural diversity, the hidden frustrations, the pockets of tradition and the growing fear of technological disaster which confront it. The old arbiters of American culture and the remnants of the liberal establishment—some of them—are looking to the young with fear and hope and no end of bemusement. The greening of America, it's called: We can't restore hope to this mess, but maybe the kids can. Maybe. But suppose they can't either; suppose that the kids and the blacks and everyone else among the dissidents can be beaten into silence, or into drugs or into jail. What if we could drive everybody to the good life that we currently advertise; what if everyone joined the mainstream? Perhaps then the culture of plastic will start to look really good: no anxieties, no outer disturbances, no crime in the streets, no race problems, just the lingering (but manageable) anxieties of the gut. (And if the secret heart still signals its annoyance, the hell with it. It can't be trusted anyway; the soul is an anarchist. Turn up the Mantovani a little; turn up the air conditioning; shut the doors.) You don't have to know that it's plastic; don't have to be told it's synthetic; don't even have to be intimidated by some version of Big Brother. All you have to know is that this is Americanism; that this is our achievement, and that there is no other.

5

GETTING IT
TOGETHER SEPARATELY

I

The fatal flaw of American intellectual liberalism in the twentieth century was its undeviating tendency to divide the world into cannibals and missionaries. It assumed that any man, if he could only be taught to understand his own best interests, if he could only be civilized, would want to become like the person who was looking at him and contemplating his salvation. It also assumed that the blessings of a good life depended on a unique set of possessions and achievements, and that those, in turn, derived from a particular collection of skills and attitudes: literacy, good work habits, punctuality, sobriety and all the rest. Since the liberal was a man of good will, he set out to teach those virtues to the criminals of his age: immigrants, Negroes, children and, more recently, the peasants of Latin America, Africa and Asia. The messianic spirit was upon him, was so thoroughly a part of his own "Americanism" that even now, when he has learned to talk about "giving people options" to choose between styles of life, it rarely occurs to him that they might in the end prefer something other than what he imagines for them, or that they could resent his efforts to help them out. He cannot understand why starving Hindus won't slaughter their cows, or why black girls in Harlem, even when offered contraceptives and abortions, decide to have babies anyway. He cannot understand why, just at the moment when the nation seems to have the resources for the ultimate program in liberal social engineering, no program seems to work, and why the clients for whom all his efforts were designed refuse to cooperate. Even if he is a Jew or a middle-class Negro, the liberal is so used to thinking about "Americanism" in WASP terms that he can imagine few other ideals and has difficulty remembering the things that sustained him (or his father) in the days before he made it. He may understand, may even celebrate, his own culture (as religion, as literature, as tradition), but he rarely suspects that there might be an Americanism that isn't White Anglo-Saxon Protestant or a liberalism that isn't soaked in Puritanical ambitions. Nathan Glazer explains his conversion from "mild radical" to "mild conservative" by explaining that "we are entering a world in which various forms of new social control will become necessary," a world in which

human demands, demands that most of us consider good and proper, and that the radicals support most enthusiastically, cannot be satisfied without highly developed organizations and some limits on human freedom.

This is a position that is easy to misunderstand, and radicals—and not they alone—regularly misunderstand it. The democratic and egalitarian revolution means that people do not accept traditional limits on their standards of living, on their desire for material goods, on their demand for political participation and for control of their own lives. Most of us generally see all this as leading ultimately to a better society, a society in which every person receives varied and nutritious food, good housing, adequate clothing, proper medical care, access to higher education, opportunities for travel and for wider experience and for playing more active political and social roles. If we are to be truly equal, such goods and services cannot be denied to anyone; if we are democratic, people will insist on a higher and higher level of governmental responsibility to provide these goods and services; if our systems of communication are such that everyone is aware of the level of goods and services that prevail in some places, and the deficiencies that still obtain in others, then a democratic people, in an egalitarian society, will know what to demand.

To meet such demands inevitably means greater social control. It means heavy taxation, to pay the cost; it means setting limits on the building of houses and on the growth of towns to maintain some measure of amenity as population and production expand; it means stricter regulation not only of industry in its disposal of waste but of ordinary people who may wish to burn refuse or discard litter ("Alice's Restaurant" deals with larger issues than Arlo Guthrie perhaps knows, and the heroes may well turn out to be the officer and the judge). In the end it may mean the control of such intimate human functions as the right to bring children into the world. The expansion of human freedom in some directions, one can demonstrate, must ultimately mean the limitation of human freedom in others. Young people, wishing to divest themselves of a corrupt civilization, take to what they conceive to be the wilderness, to live with freedom and without restraint. But if they litter the wilderness, pollute the streams, and abandon cars in the forest, their freedom to seek what they consider the good life will have to be restrained so that some aspect of the good life can be retained for others. . . .

There is something depressingly familiar about all this. We have heard it before: greater social control, regulation of industry, a higher level of governmental responsibility. The man of reason who regarded himself as a "mild radical" (opposing bureaucratic rigidity, the Cold War, Vietnam, etc.) refurbishes the liberal wisdom of the thirties to dress down the kids. We will add environmental control and other blessings to ICC, FCC, SEC, AEC and similar industry-dominated regulatory agencies. We will make it possible for all men to join the mainstream of the good life: varied and nutritious food, good housing, adequate clothing, proper medical care. We know what they want; we will get it for them. We will do their thing. The New Deal liberal was the doorman of the WASP ethic.

But what if . . . What if—as Ivan Illich wrote in *Celebration of Awareness*—"the poor refuse to dream on command"? What if people want something more, or something other, than "varied and nutritious food, good housing, adequate clothing" and all the rest? What if they don't like the menu that the planners serve up? What if they don't want to take the jobs? What if they have babies in defiance of the population quotas? What if they don't like the colleges (not because they are part of the war machine, but simply because they are full of dull, pompous and patronizing people called professors)? What if some people, and perhaps many, refuse either to serve or to be served? What if they decide not to patronize the great American supermarket? What if some of them, rather than wishing to play "more active political or social roles," just want to be left alone? What if—horror of horrors —no program can fulfill even the requirements that Glazer regards as universal? The American liberal has become so persuaded that the "better society" is nothing other than universal admission for all men to the world of plastic that he now seems ready to support forced conscription of unwilling recruits to achieve it. If children or parents are allowed to run their own schools the graduates will be ill-prepared to cope or to compete; if they are left alone—unregulated and uncontrolled—they will litter, contaminate, pollute and destroy; if they are not marched through universities the "complexities of the technological society" will gobble them up. Inevitably the liberal realist regards "the better society" as a technocratic jungle, to be tamed not by the biophilic instincts of its inhabitants, but rather by the manipulation of "experts." Was it young people wishing to "divest themselves of a corrupt civilization" who polluted the wilderness, or was it civilization itself? Is it radicals who systematically harass demonstrators, dissenters, longhairs, freaks, blacks, Mexicans, and Puerto Ricans? Is it students who perpetuate the mindless system of certification, grades, tests, degrees and requirements of the American educational system? This is not to deny that some people, young and old, are ambivalent, romantic, ineffective, violent, ignorant or vulgar, but "radicals" have no corner on any of them. Every travesty of romanticism can be matched by a travesty of "reason," and every excess of know-nothingism on the left can be duplicated on the right and in the liberal center. The tragedy of the moment is not the excesses of extremists but the fact that reason itself is in bad repute and that so many people, in and out of universities, prefer to patronize the young for their unreasonableness rather than defend reason itself. "To dismantle the structures of modern society will mean a radical reduction in the general standard of living," Glazer says. "Rather than weakening these structures we must alas strengthen them." If ever there was an unreasonable statement, that is one. Which structures is he talking about? The Pentagon? The General Motors Corporation? The FBI, the CIA, the American Medical Association? Is it reasonable to say, without qualification, that the university has a "right to distance itself from the world, to remain free or foolish or irrelevant or outrageous no matter how great the horrors of the world outside"? What is the meaning of "free inquiry" in an age when the academy itself has too often become a willing weapon of war, when very few "objective" statements are politically neutral, and when the men who dominate the campuses unquestioningly define the "better society" in the terms of an aging liberalism and a dubious life style which celebrates consumption above all things? If some of the "radicals" become excessive in their contempt for all structures, should the "man of reason" begin his refutation by defending them all and by assuming that the disaffection of the world and the nation can be cured through "goods and services"? If the "West" has learned any lesson in the last generation it is that three fourths of the world's population holds a strong suspicion of our particular brand of salvation, and that even in America a growing number of people who are already supposed to enjoy the blessings of the "better society" are alienated, dissatisfied and angry.

We have witnessed the initial shock in many Americans dedicated to the war against poverty [wrote Illich], when they observed and studied Latin America and realized for the first time that there is a link between minority marginality at home and mass margination overseas. Their emotional reaction is usually more acute than the intellectual insight that produces it. We have seen more than one man lose his balance as he suddenly lost the faith that for him had previously supported the balance, the faith that says: "The American way is the solution for all." For any good man, whether he is a social worker in Watts or a missioner on his way to Bolivia, it means pain and panic to realize that he is seen by 90 percent of mankind as the exploiting outsider who shores up his privilege by promoting a delusive belief in the ideals of democracy, equal opportunity, and free enterprise among people who haven't a remote possibility of profiting from them. . . .

The war on poverty aims at the integration of the so-called underprivileged minorities of the United States into the mainstream of the American way of life; the Alliance for Progress aims at the integration of the so-called underdeveloped countries of Latin America into the community of industrialized nations. Both programs failed. The poor refused to dream on command. The order to dream and the money they got only made them rambunctious. Huge funds were appropriated to start the United States minorities and the Latin American majorities on the way of integration into a United States–style middle class; the world of college attendance, universal consumer credit, the world of household appliances and insurance, the world of church and movie attendance. An army of generous volunteers swarmed through New York ghettoes and Latin American jungle canyons, pushing the persuasion that makes America tick.

The frustrated social worker and the former Peace Corps volunteer are now among the few who explain to mainline America that the poor are right in rejecting forced conversion to the American gospel. Only seven years after the majority missionary enterprise of the Alliance was launched, riot squads at home, military governments in Latin America, and the army in Vietnam keep asking for more funds. But now it can be seen that the money is needed not for the uplift of the poor, but to protect the frail beachhead into the middle class that has been gained by the few converts who have benefited here or there by the American way of life.

. . . This rejection goes hand in hand with a growing loss of faith in his own tenets on the part of the salesman of United States social consensus. Disaffection, helplessness, and the response of anger at the United States have undermined the thrust of the formerly guileless enthusiast of the American way and American methods.

The American liberal paid lip service to pluralism, but he generally assumed that diversity was only a transitional stage for people who wanted to go somewhere else; he acknowledged the validity of the WASP ideal as the integrating mechanism in America and cheerfully accepted the task of assisting all Americans in going where he assumed they wanted to go. If they had doubts, he took it upon himself to persuade them: he organized campaigns against dropping out of school, collected data on the cash value of a college education, urged black children—and Indians and Mexicans—to become "a credit to your race" (which meant they should become WASPs), sent social workers to make certain the welfare money was spent on things he regarded as important, and worked diligently to create the appearance—if not the substance—of institutional responsiveness to minority interests. In his view conservatives were bad people who wanted to make it hard to bring the underprivileged into the mainstream; liberals were good people who were trying to make it easy. But neither seriously questioned the qualities and life styles that Americanization and integration required, and neither—with some reservations among genuine conservatives (the Amish, or the Hassidic Jews)—ever doubted that entry into that mainstream was worth the sacrifices in group identity and personal life which it required. In the end, the really hardheaded liberals came to regard the whole process as a technical problem; intellectuals, they decided, were no longer divided over ideologies—everyone believed in the welfare state, personal freedom, and so on —only about tactics.

For at least a generation, a large portion of the liberal case for an open society and human fulfillment has rested on the schools, the place where cannibals are converted into missionaries. The schools were to be the instruments of social mobility and integration, and in some cases they were and still are. But in the past decade many students—and others—have punctured the mystique of schooling and discovered the brutal inconsistencies of the current version of the open society. The rhetoric of technological complexity (Sputnik, computers, lasers) has replaced the creation of WASPs and the WASP ethic as the motivating instrument of public education in America. But in presenting the existing technology as a constant, a given, and in asking all people to adapt, the schools dehumanize in the name of preparation and modernity. Technology thus becomes a club to impose conformity and order, and not an instrument of liberation from drudgery and disease. In learning a skill we are also taught to distrust ourselves, to judge ourselves in terms of a place in the system, rather than generate confidence in the possibilities of expanding awareness and sensitivity. What the schools teach most of all, said Illich, is the importance of schooling. They legitimize success and failure, encourage people to accept the system's assessments of their merits, and create the idea that what isn't learned in school is without value. In the cosmology of schooling, technology is a deity that can be tricked or manipulated, always at considerable personal expense, but it cannot be mastered. The statement that "this is a complex society" is an order to think small and feel little. It teaches everyone that the system is bigger than the individual, that the system is transcendent and the individual dependent. At the same time it also puts the burden of social success on the schools. Where the schools fail, where they reject and destroy, so does society. Students do not rebel only because the educational system is the most convenient and vulnerable institution to attack; they rebel because the school has been advertised—especially by those liberals who are always issuing the invitations to join the system—as the institution that keeps the system open. But the school discriminates, it tends to be invidious, and it encourages every child to succeed at the expense of another child's embarrassment. All of these things have been pointed out time and again by people like Edgar Friedenberg, Paul Goodman and John Holt. They have pointed out that the schools do not "fail" because they are aberrations from the social structure, but because they are part of it.

And yet it rarely occurred to many liberals, and has not occurred to most of them even now, to assess the human costs of the "better society" or to investigate the possibility that there might be a way to decent housing, nutritious food and adequate clothing that does not extract such a fearful price in personal identity—does not subject people to the rat race, does not require them to demean themselves, or be demeaned, in order to succeed—or that the "better society" might in itself be as concerned with intangibles as it is with goods and services. It is obvious by now that many people in America (and not just the children of the suburban middle class) are alienated because those goods and services by themselves do not provide a satisfactory life and will not replace the loss of belief in the WASP values of the past. To be middle-class by itself is not enough; it may, in fact, represent the most enervating, the most anxious of all situations, because it regards itself as so "reasonable," so devoid of mythology and ritual that its members remain in perpetual states of insecurity. To be middle-class in America—and to be *only* middle-class—has always involved the subtle but pervasive belief that if one isn't rising, then one must be going down; and yet, for most Americans, there is nothing else to rise to, no place to go, either as a nation (as "Americans") or as individuals. More pay, perhaps, a better car, longer vacations, but very little in greater glory, little in substantial satisfaction, little that isn't transitory and perishable. Easy come, easy go. The middle class has lost confidence in itself because the old Americanism, the America of the WASP, with which it was associated has lost its mythic power; historically it was vitalized through its links with stronger stuff—with causes, traditions, myths, with the flag, the unlimited blessings of technology, the supposed preeminence of the American way of life, and with the things that energize creativity and that furnish its conventions. Much of that is going, and some is already gone. The missionary still tries to make converts, but his faith is shaken. Technology has become a ritual and a religion, but for a growing number of people it is patently dehumanizing and empty. We love our things, but they do not love us.

Most self-styled radicals in America are onetime liberals who freaked out. They share the cannibal-missionary outlook, but they have turned it upside down and joined the cannibals (who, as often as not, don't want them around). Rather than trying to bring the dispossessed into the mainstream—in whose existence they firmly believe—they are trying to keep them the hell out. They are rigidly anti-WASP, but they are even more fanatically antiliberal because they regard the liberals—often with ample justification—as the great WASP-makers in America. The liberal is the secret agent of the establishment, the CIA fink, the social-science planner of anti-insurgency warfare for Southeast Asia, the apologist for the system, the man who will make it easy (or appears to make it easy) for everyone to join up. The radical believes in pluralism for everyone but WASPs; at the same time he already has a complete and unambiguous vision of what the cannibals are really like, or what they would be like if, through his efforts, they could become completely themselves. Since he is unable to separate the acquisition of technical skills and the possession of physical comforts from WASP life, he cannot offer even the minimal possessions that most of the cannibals desire: he likes black people but cannot imagine that a middle-class black could be anything but a WASP under the skin; he is sympathetic to striking postal workers and wants to help them organize their resistance to the insensitive system but cannot fathom—indeed, resents—their bourgeois aspirations. Of all people in America, the self-appointed radical still believes most deeply in the noble savage—as Negro, as Indian, as Chicano, as Vietnamese peasant—and in his more self-indulgent moments he fancies that he is or might become one himself. Julius Lester's declaration that "Che is Alive—on East 103rd Street" is sheer romantic fantasy, not only in fact but in spirit.

And yet there is a possibility for genuine radicalism in America—aggressive, contentious, often threatening—and that lies in the recognition that the liberal failed in his de-facto disregard for pluralism and his excessive emphasis on economic security at the expense of all other things. He was often prepared to champion the downtrodden but only rarely able or willing to teach them to champion themselves on their own terms; he was frequently a defender of civil rights and civil liberties because he wanted people to have faith in the system, not because he wanted them to have faith in themselves. Even though he called himself a Jeffersonian he believed more in institutions than in people, was more a nationalist than a pluralist, more a preacher than a teacher. For each problem he tried to create a new agency, a new program, a new department, and for each instance of disaffection, antisocial conduct, alienation or dissent he offered new instrumentalities of adjustment, compensation and edification: new courses in schools and colleges, mental-health clinics, social workers, welfare agencies, Job Corps centers and all the rest. Some of these things were and are imperative, and some function adequately. But until recently few if any were premised on the idea that freedom also meant the opportunity not to join, or to join on your terms, and that it meant, above all things, not having to give up all the things that were of most value. Saul Alinsky's professional radicalism has always recognized that the people to be organized were not necessarily WASPs (and did not necessarily want to become WASPs) even though they wanted more income, better housing and a larger slice of political power. It attempted, with some modifications, to teach people the same things that the ward politicians taught urban immigrants seventy years ago. Its primary lesson was in organizing. The appeal of the Muslims is shot through with bourgeois aspirations—and with old-fashioned puritanical moralism—but it is still emphatically ethnic in its commitment to black pride, black identity and black history. The success of Cesar Chavez is the success of a Mexican-American Catholic who taught the grape pickers that they are worth more, as workers and as human beings, than the system had ordained. None of them is trying to make converts, and none of them assumes that when you buy a refrigerator you necessarily have to buy your WASP identity with it: You can learn from the man, but you don't have to *be* the man. The genuinely radical faith is in fulfillment and prosperity without the melting pot.

II

We are now left with several possibilities, only one of them remotely cheerful. The failure of the liberal crusades of the sixties—integration, the New Frontier, the Great Society, the politics of joy—combined with the threat of depression puts the rediscovery of unresolved economic problems back in first place on the liberal priority list. The liberals, relieved, will once again be able to run against Herbert Hoover and to revert to the conventional economic rhetoric that they know best. While the Nixon Republicans pursue the hardhat vote, the sons of the New Deal will try to woo the same man in the guise of the American worker, promising stable employment and prices and offering, once again, programs and policies that twenty years ago had been regarded as permanently established and universally accepted. The 1972 campaign may well come out of a political museum full of relics from 1932 and 1936; our politics will then become as camp as our entertainment.

Or worse. For the first time in a generation, both sides may agree that this is no time for deviance or dissent, no moment to fool with our uncertain sources of loyalty and consensus, no time to indulge such luxuries as alienation, personal fulfillment, freedom of expression or radical politics. There are signs already that the liberals and the Right will be tempted to

238

strike a bargain that trades economic "planning" for higher employment and stable incomes against political controls on personal and cultural deviation. The liberals will permit the reactionaries to pursue cultural deviants as long as the reactionaries permit the liberals their historic role—helping all those who wish, or can be persuaded, to join (or remain in) the mainstream. The Left will bring the carrot and the Right will bring the stick. The radicals, who destroyed their credibility with violent rhetoric, bad manners, and an excessive disdain for middle-class aspirations, will go underground; if the depression becomes sufficiently severe there is likely to be all manner of violence—sabotage, bombings, riots—but the so-called New Left (black, white, young and old) will take the major share of the blame. People who do not want to join or who want to do it their own way will be pursued as enemies of the state, or as impediments to social planning, and those who never shared even the illusive affluence of the fifties and sixties will be told to wait while we secure or restore to the "mainstream" the dubious blessings that the mainstream was supposed to have enjoyed all these years. We will try to put the country back together on the basis of a national economic emergency, but in the legitimate attempt to impose economic controls on the major forces of the technology we will, in the name of rationalizing the system, eliminate the most promising sources of diversity, initiative and change. There will be no money for publicly supported schools outside the established bureaucratic systems, no resources for experiments not controlled by central planners, no opportunity to organize community health services undominated by public-health bureaucracies or agents of the welfare system. At the same time there will be no end of funds to rescue billion-dollar corporations: mismanaged railroads which have invested their capital in real estate instead of rolling stock; aerospace industries grown fat and dependent on defense contracts; automotive manufacturers and "free-enterprise" contractors who profit from a perennial expansion of the "national transportation" system (highways). All familiar stuff, but to be amplified in a depression or national "emergency" and to be glorified against all challenges in the name of recovery. The cry will be for jobs, not for work that has meaning; for security, not fulfillment; for positive thinking, not imaginative criticism. Neither the kids nor the black militants will take kindly to this new cause, but if they are not to go underground, either as revolutionaries or as drug-culture dropouts, there may be no other choice.

And yet without them, without the powerful sense that the old ethic and the old values have seen their day, even a souped-up version of New Deal politics is futile. Although it is fashionable these days to say that the kids of the counterculture can survive only as long as the economy produces enough fat and waste to enable unproductive people (i.e., freaks and hippies) to live like parasites on the surplus, many freaks live without the fat that the rest of the society takes for granted and learn to survive with marginal resources, subsistence farming, handicrafts and other "obsolescent" economic measures. For some of them panhandling has become a way of life; if they have the education or the family resources to bail out—and some undoubtedly will—they also have the ability to sustain styles of life which are sufficiently unrespectable to threaten or destroy more conventional individuals; there are people in the East Village, Harlem, Hough, Hashbury, Boulder, Cambridge, and on communes in a hundred different places who have been living in a depression economy for years. What they believe may be romantic, but they do understand something that most straight people do not: that the problems of the economy are intimately connected to the problems of the culture; that social engineering, whether for consensus or prosperity, has limited possibilities unless all the assumptions change; that the affluence of plastic is also the affluence of destruction and despair; and that the historic conditions which made the American WASP the preeminent citizen of the highest of civilizations no longer exist. They know that a depression is not a "technical" economic problem, even if it can be temporarily mitigated by some fiscal tricks in Washington, and that, in any case, it is only a casual symptom of deeper and more pervasive ailments in the society. What they feel in their gut is the futility of deferral, that life does not get better in some programmed future but only through the exercise of freedom in the present, that conditions do not change if people are perennially taught that the price of a decent life is the repression of those qualities that make it worth living. If life on the planet is finite—and there are millions of kids who believe that we will either bomb or pollute ourselves into oblivion—then the great moments of experience, the sharing of affection, and the human gestures of expression and generosity are imperative now, and not after the next program of social reconstruction, the next step in Vietnamization or the next university degree. There is no simple language to explain this critique of conventional liberalism. It is not enough to say that as long as we spend $80 billion annually on the military we will continue to be pressed by inflation and will have to disregard the requisites of better housing, medical care and all the rest. It is not sufficient to say that the priorities of war and peace are reversed; and it is not sufficient to say that we do not yet know how to plan for a stable and secure economy. The issue is, rather, in human deferral—deferring to conditions, to experts, to time. We are taught to gratify ourselves in the possession of goods but not in the exercise of freedom, are taught, indeed, that the goods can be achieved only at the expense of freedom. We are buying ourselves off.

But without the WASP image and ethic as integrating and disciplining forces in American society there will be a strong temptation to substitute the discipline of "technology"—to control and repress men in the name of controlling machines. The promised reward will be plastic, but the cost of a ticket will be higher with each passing day: more noise, pollution, congestion, crime and depersonalization; more experts and fewer citizens; more national institutions and agencies and less decentralization. We will be afraid of Big Brother, but even more afraid of the possibility that he does not exist, that no one is in charge, that things are in the saddle. Events, systems, accidents, machines will increasingly be regarded as constants, as "nature," and we will slowly become a plastic-encrusted *Lumpenproletariat* seeking a leader, a figure, a fantasy, anything to which we can relate and which we can call our own. Whether or not we will actually have Big Brother is immaterial; what is important is that we will, in the name of values long vanished, impose on ourselves the most rigid forms of regimentation, worshiping technology on the one hand and demanding, on the other, that it must be controlled. As a consequence we will succeed only in controlling men, not machines or systems. Given existing values and practices, the real inflation is not in dollars but in the human costs of the shabby goods and amenities of "affluence." The old liberalism of the thirties can unite the contentious elements of American society only by destroying the freedom, diversity and humanity that it is presumably committed to respect.

The most promising alternative to this destructive cycle is to institutionalize wherever possible the social and cultural pluralism that we are now beginning to rediscover, and which people like Glazer are so tempted to repress. A tyranny of experts and planners isn't much improvement over a tyranny of gauleiters and commissars. I am not talking about changing people's values, am not recommending any form of what the kids call mind fucking (and for which there is no precise phrase in the official language). We have tried too much of those things in the past—often, unfortunately, with success. I am talking rather about recognizing values and attitudes that already exist and permitting them to function unmolested. There are scores of obvious examples: legalizing practices which are not demonstrably dangerous to public health or safety (marijuana, abortion, homosexuality, gambling, pornography); decentralizing schools, police forces, health services, neighborhood planning and renewal; protecting and encouraging ethnic and social diversity in neighborhoods, regions and tribal lands; subsidizing local-initiative public-service enterprises in law, medicine, education, art, journalism, and recreation; reforming and enforcing the tax laws to eliminate all depletion allowances, encourage the formation of small, employee-controlled businesses, revitalize small cooperatives, and tax all large incomes at full value no matter what the source; revising credentialing practices to accord with required skills and performance, and not with years of schooling or courses completed; encouraging, through subsidies and other policy measures, the revitalization of apprenticeships and other forms of in-service training; providing access on all commercial television channels to independent community organizations of broadcasters who are not affiliated with those channels or the networks; allocating all forms of public educational support directly to parents and students, and not to school boards, university trustees or academic executives. The intent of all these measures is to try to re-create some meaningful forms of citizenship and community, to restore the legitimacy of institutions, and to dampen, as much as possible, the bribery that exchanges personal freedom and responsibility for the great plastic payoff. Obviously this will require planning and government control—limiting the power of corporations and complexes, providing public services which cannot be operated on a local basis (transportation, for example) and restricting pollution and resource exploitation. What is new about such planning (and, in some respects, as old as the Republic) is the context in which it must be conducted and the objectives for which it is designed. As long as we could assume that America was and would forever be a nation of WASPs, WASP in thought, manners, culture, ideas and aspirations, it did not matter if we confused the objectives and tactics of planning: once we overcame the cantankerous particularism of certain geographic regions (and especially the South) we were all going to be the same anyway. One man was like another, wanted the same things and thought in the same way. The WASP ethic was well designed for the task of making it, for the exploitation of nature and for enlisting certain recruits in the tasks of the nation. If some people were left out or disregarded—well, there was always the future, always another opportunity, another frontier, another program. What the normal processes of making it failed to accommodate, the liberal, who followed behind, would sweep into the mainstream. *E pluribus unum*. But now, when it is no longer possible without repression, and no longer desirable, the objectives of planning, the rhetoric used to defend it and the tactics employed to carry it out all require reexamination. Planning for pluralism and individual freedom is not the same as planning for growth and achievement. Fostering economic development and resource exploitation is not the same as managing a society for purposes that must, of necessity, include a great deal more than material payoffs. Given the new circumstances of the nation, the considerations of ecology and the limitations of growth, the obvious failures of social and economic integration, and the desperate need to revive the legitimacy of institutions and to provide all people with personal and cultural resources which they can trust and call their own, no single set of standards, no unique set of values is likely to serve. We have to keep the Irish cops and the hippie freaks from cutting each other up; have to protect ethnic pride and resources, preserving not only neighborhoods but regions of the mind; have to support community leadership and institutions in Harlem, Little Italy, Greenwich Village and Sunflower County; have to entertain the possibility of honest and dignified citizenship on the part of people who don't want to make it big or don't want to make it at all; have to recognize that marijuana will not necessarily lead to the fall of the Republic, and perhaps not even to the end of ambition; have to understand that social stability is not necessarily based on the enforcement of a single set of beliefs, and that the most exciting and creative developments of the last five years have largely been the work of ethnic, social and cultural minorities. The real objective of social policy is not to make men identical but to enable them to remain different and distinct.

The conventional response to such suggestions is either (among liberals) to raise the issue of racial discrimination and segregation or (among knee-jerk reactionaries) to talk about "federalism." Isn't pluralism something like "freedom of choice"—a cover for racially segregated schools or discrimination in employment? Can the black sharecroppers of Mississippi maintain decent schools without the pressure of the federal government? Can we eradicate hunger or disease in backward areas without outside interference? So far there is little evidence that what has been accomplished through integration might not have been achieved more easily by making it possible for any student or parent to secede from the public schools and, with an equivalent amount of tax money, to run his own educational system or buy learning as an individual. Local control has always meant, at best, majority rule, not individual choice. Nor is there any evidence that there is a better way to eliminate poverty than by simply giving people money —a guaranteed minimum income, family allowances, or whatever—but not on the paltry humiliating basis on which we have done it so far. We can—if we want—enforce nondiscrimination (or at least define it) in employment, in medicine and in housing, but what is nondiscrimination in education, personal friendships or cultural identity? If an institution has public support, then clearly it should be open to all—meaning, wherever possible, open to people who do not necessarily want to adopt the cultural styles of the majority or of those who run it. But in the thousands of cases (universities, schools, museums, even hospitals) where that is not possible they should be able to take the equivalent dollars and start their own. The whole notion of federalism is a hoax because it shifts the arbitrary impositions of national bureaucrats to state bureaucrats (who are generally more corrupt and stupid) without necessarily offering more choice. State lines correspond to little more than accidents of geography; the most vicious oligarchies, moreover, are often local. We cannot define freedom or civil liberties geographically; the required definitions are more organic, more cultural, more intrinsic. To say New York State or New York City or Manhattan is not enough; perhaps one can say Upper West Side or East Harlem, but one might also have to define ages, ethnic groups, income, sex and cultural style. The definition is nearly impossible except in terms of function, nor is it necessary if the functions are recognized and encouraged. The issue is not the "new federalism" of Nixon or how fast the South integrates its schools: the issue is the choices people have, the ability of the system to respond, and, at least in part, how the various constituencies are addressed by their own leaders. The issue is community, and communities vary in size, interest and composition. To say it again: the real objective of social policy is not to make men identical but to enable them to remain different and distinct.

One of the more hopeful consequences of the cultural prison break of the late sixties was the rediscovery of diversity and dissent as a genuine, and not merely a fossilized, tradition in American life. We slowly began to rewrite our history, to find (again) the forgotten pluralism of our past, to reexamine the failures of the melting pot, and to understand the "present-mindedness"—meaning the cultural and social bias—endemic in all social science, no matter how much it asserted its own objectivity. In the new revisionist history, and in the work of "radical" historians, the losers are also Americans; the miners who were shot down by militia troopers in the great Colorado strike of 1903, the Indians who fought Custer, the slaves of the plantation, the Thoreauvians, the millenarians and the Utopians are not just freaks or "victims of progress." We started making a little more room in history and therefore more room in the present, allowing black men (for example) an identity that is neither WASP nor African but American, and rediscovering resources in ourselves that antedate the "Americanism" of the single image. It is still difficult for most people to believe that the Panthers, despite all the romantic rhetoric, the disclaimers and the invective, are about three parts Jefferson to every part Marx, or that the political radicalism of students, blacks, Chicanos, pacifists and almost anything else you can name is founded not on some "alien ideology" but on the promises of the Declaration of Independence and the Constitution, but it is less difficult to believe than it would have been a decade ago. The cultural material comes from everywhere and nowhere, but the politics derive primarily from the thirteen colonies and the Revolution. Tom Paine, Sam Adams, the Haymarket anarchists, the Wobblies, the Committees of Correspondence, the abolitionist editors and the labor organizers who worked without benefit of the Wagner Act were also Americans.

For two generations the professors and the planners tried to disavow the populists, to depict them as the enemy, or to pay them patronizing respect as the unreasonable forerunners of subsequent "responsible" reforms. Thus Franklin Roosevelt came out as the man who fulfilled the unruly, impolite demands of Tom Watson, Huey Long, Big Bill Haywood, the farmers of Wisconsin and the socialists of California; but Roosevelt, we like to say, did it nicely, *pragmatically*—didn't break anybody's glasses. And thus Andrew Jackson became not a cantankerous individualist, a backwoodsman or a frontier warrior, but a neolithic labor reformer representing urban workingmen, an FDR-in-anticipation. We robbed every protest of its contentiousness, its potential for violence, its anger, and turned it, in the historical memory, into another request for some changes please. If it seemed too discourteous, a little too earthy, a little excessive in its Anglo-Saxon innuendos, the liberal historians busied themselves in exposing its racism or its anti-Semitism rather than trying to understand its passion; they insisted on depicting the system as a decorous mechanism which perennially confirmed itself through its capacity to accommodate polite people.

As long as we were committed to the WASP model, any other version of history would have been improbable. If America were represented as excessively pluralistic, factional or divided there would be no hope of consensus or union, and so contentiousness and dissension were played down as aberrations of the moment, and minorities relegated to limbo or patronized in passing. Ultimately the historians succeeded in emasculating the WASP almost as thoroughly as everyone else: he too had to be cleaned up for polite company, was not permitted too many biases, was not allowed to use four-letter words, and was not allowed to protest too stridently without being banished from the mainstream of acceptable historical company. Liberal intellectuals, said Richard Hofstadter, "periodically exaggerate the measure of agreement that exists between movements of popular reform and the considered principles of political liberalism. They remake the image of popular rebellion closer to their heart's desire. They choose to ignore not only the elements of illiberalism that frequently seem to be an indissoluble part of popular movements but also the very complexity of the historical process itself." What Hofstadter did not say (and what he probably did not consider) is that the "liberal intellectual" carried his allegiance to what he imagined was the mainstream of history like a badge of honor and therefore ignored not only "illiberalism" in popular movements but most other forms of extreme dissent, including whatever "liberalism" appeared too radical for his gut or too strident for his taste. He had good reason to be suspicious of moral fanaticism during and after World War II— true believers of whatever sort could well be dangerous men— but his conclusions tended almost invariably to lead him to a vision of history shaped in his own image of the good society. It rarely occurred to him to consider the possibility that in America—as in other countries—the bad guys often won, not only in politics but in the adulation of the historians who wrote about them, and that mediation and compromise were not necessarily unqualified virtues.

The revisionist scholarship produced by Howard Zinn, Staughton Lynd and the black historians (among others) has begun to rescue obscure movements and individuals from their historical limbo and, in the process, to redefine and reassert traditions of dissent and deviance as central factors in American experience. If every slave wasn't seething with the spirit of insurrection, it is also true that most field hands weren't happy darkies singing spirituals as they chopped cotton on the plantation; if many original "old stock" Americans made it big in trade or industry, they often did it by exploiting not only immigrants from Eastern Europe but their own WASP cousins in Appalachia, the rural South and New England who never made it at all; and if WASPs ran the country almost, it seemed, by right of birth, there were also WASPs who, more than a century ago, were persuaded that this was a sick society on the road to destruction. One of the consequences of revisionism, not only in historical scholarship but in the contemporary view of the country, is that the rediscovery of dissent and pluralism may help restore the WASP's own place in America, may free him of the obligation to be the universal all-purpose American, and may enable him to understand why he, like most people, seems out of place, a man without a usable tradition, even a man without a country. More important, it may help to reestablish such a tradition, to find him a "new" set of ancestors, and to recover for him a style that had nearly been sacrificed to the cause of technological and social accommodation. In the world of the social planners almost everyone tends to become a nigger.

The possibilities of contemporary ethnic and cultural movements lie, more than anything else, in their search for place, the place of individuals, of groups, of styles. To the extent that any of them is forced to accommodate in the name of order or unity or "technology," its position is compromised. Obviously such compromise is necessary—it is necessary in any society—but we have become excessively committed to enforcing compromises where there is little justification, and where the only act required to mitigate the offense (of bad manners, speech, loud music or whatever) is to leave the room: we are fighting about the kinds of political buttons students are allowed to wear in school, about the right of people to burn the American flag, about the length of their hair and the style of their clothes. We have made the brassiere into a political issue, have turned poverty into "cultural deprivation" and have regarded stable ethnic neighborhoods as impediments to progress. Order is the great watchword of the day, but the greatest violation of order in America is the systemic injunction, whether spoken by cops, planners or teachers, to move along, to find a new block, a new neighborhood, a new thing to play with. We are all in danger of becoming refugees in a world of systems controlled by no one.

The only alternative to the modern forms of "rationalization" and displacement (or to life underground for more and more people) is to construct, wherever possible, bastions of personal and cultural resistance, and to recognize that when it comes to such systems we share not only a majority interest in their control but, even more significantly, an interest in maintaining our separate places as minorities. If we need planning, we also need anti-planning, to create reservations for freedom. The average welfare worker in Detroit represents only a minor advance over the Southern sheriff: both are there to keep people in their place (which means a place chosen for them by someone else); neither is interested in helping them create a place of their own. Both are planners.

The political experience of the past two years indicates that there is still some populist energy left in America, even if we often fail to recognize it or insist on emphasizing its flaws rather than its possibilities. Most polite liberals contemplating figures like George Wallace or Lester Maddox are almost compulsively driven to the wrong lessons. It does not occur to them that alongside Wallace's racism there is a populist streak, an egalitarian appeal to cussedness and irreverence and an understanding of a simple language that is rarely spoken nowadays in official America. (If it does occur to them, they don't like it, because Wallace is a vulgar fellow; to the *New York Times* and the Democrats of latter-day Humphreyism, Wallace's vulgarity is more offensive than Nixon's obscenity.) But Wallace and Bobby Kennedy often appealed to the same impulses; neither was as unctuous and pious as the "mainstream" candidates. Wallace has been running against banks and utilities, foundations and government planners, bosses and pointy-headed intellectuals; if he plays to racism he also plays to people who are impatient with the pieties and equivocation of established rhetoric: many of his young supporters were blue-collar workers who felt no loyalty to the old Democratic Party or to the labor leaders who supposedly represented them. Clearly Wallace expressed their racial resentments, but just as clearly he spoke to their sense of displacement, to an alienation that no planner (other than a fascist) can satisfy. What his success—and his failure—seem to indicate is that irreverence still lives in America and that it may still be possible to rally diverse constituencies against the impersonal, the systemic, perhaps even the plastic. Johnny Cash for President? Bella Abzug? Muhammad Ali? If there is any possibility for an effective coalition among anti-establishment groups—kids, black people, hardhats, Italians, Poles—it will be in a populist cause directed *against* depersonalizing corporations and institutions and not necessarily in behalf of an all-absorbing whole. It will, in short, be urban ethnic politics on a national scale. Coalition politics and not consensus politics. The rallying cry: "Don't take no shit from nobody." It is a slogan everybody will understand.

The essential attraction of industrial America, beyond its

substantial wealth of natural resources, was in making it possible to be a Pole without Russians, a Russian without the secret police, a Jew without pogroms, an Irishman without the British, a Sicilian without a padrone, and a black (tentatively) without apartheid. Although we prided ourselves on our political freedom, civil liberties and constitutional rights, we never believed fully in our own professions and therefore invented a melting pot to transform men into the sort of citizens who would not jeopardize the system by placing excessive demands on its tolerance. They were supposed to go in as ethnics and come out as WASPs. We have made a lot of WASPs but overlooked the cultural possibilities for other forms of Americanism and now find ourselves with the choice between enforcing allegiance to an increasingly unattractive mainstream and trying to establish the pluralism that might have been and might still be. The possibilities exist, but they are frail and gravely jeopardized not only by reactionaries but by liberals. Although we have largely failed in imposing our cultural hegemony on the underdeveloped world (despite Coca-Cola, transistors and the "cheap" automobile) we are still trying, with fatal consequences, to impose it on ourselves. The country seems to be coming apart because it *is* coming apart, because the Americanism of the moment cannot hold us together without violence. At the same time, however, it would be unfortunate, perhaps even fatal, if the mediating functions created by WASPs (and often still dominated by WASPs) were to be further eroded. Even if the courts and the conventional political processes do not work well—and often they do not—it is still unlikely that, given the present state of the country, we will be able to invent acceptable improvements. The judicial process in the past two decades has done far more to protect individual and cultural integrity than the social agencies designed to deal with "modern" problems; the most persistent institutional defenders of the poor, of students, of Chicanos and of civil liberties in general are not school-teachers, welfare agents, planners or bureaucrats, but lawyers and the chosen advocates of the victims.

It is inconceivable that this country can ever be integrated on ethnic terms, that we will ever become a black America or an Irish America. But neither will it ever again be possible to imagine the United States as completely white or middle-aged or anything else. If the minorities no longer accept the main-stream—if, indeed, there is still a mainstream worth the name —they are even further from accepting each other as models of what one ought to be or become. Someone or something will have to mediate, to keep people from tearing each other apart. Where WASP institutions have failed was in their in-ability to accommodate or recognize the nation's pluralism, or in their excessive attention—out of guilt or pressure—to one minority culture at the expense of others. For the first time, therefore, mediation will have to do more than pay lip service to minorities and to our pluralism of styles, cultures and be-liefs, and will have to recognize that the WASP way of mak-ing it is not the only choice and—as we understand more about the minorities of the past—may never have been the only route to Americanism. If some immigrant children were acculturated in school, there were many others who learned the ways of the nation from ward politicians, straw bosses or union organizers, or from those relatives who, through con-nections, found them a job in a sweatshop, on a farm or in civil service. In the two years since his debacle in the New York City school strike and his confrontations with other organized groups, John Lindsay has begun to understand the problem of minorities, to point out that "New York was supposed to be a melting pot, but it never melted, and that's a good thing," and to seek ways, however crude, of speaking to that pluralism, of speaking to and on behalf of the young, of mediating, encouraging, recognizing, rather than trying to teach people manners. In his willingness to testify for the defense in the trial of the Chicago Seven (denied by Judge Hoffman) Ramsey Clark demonstrated a similar belief in the mediating capacity of judicial institutions and in the importance of making those institutions work for social and cultural minorities who do not share the convictions of the mainstream. And in his advocacy of the rights of students and in his willingness to concede that a Black Panther cannot get a fair trial in America, Kingman Brewster, the president of Yale, became a powerful and effective mediator between students and those on the outside who were prepared to beat them into line. Brewster the WASP, Clark the WASP, Lindsay the WASP.

For nearly a decade a string of commissions on violence, urban problems and campus unrest have struggled with the problem of American pluralism but were unable to see beyond their assumptions to the logical conclusion. America is not on the verge of becoming two separate societies, one rich and white, the other poor and black. It is becoming, in all its dreams and anxieties, a nation of outsiders for whom no single style or ethic remains possible. All sorts of pressures will be applied to force the country together—through the economy, the media, the common necessity to reestablish control over our lives and our technology, and through the police. But there is a growing necessity to preserve and enlarge the place apart, to reestablish the legitimacy of the things a man can call his own; not the goods of plastic, not the future of anonymity, but the privileges of being intrinsic, the integrity of place, the ability to love and to create in the present, the gratifications of immediate expression and engagement, and the ability to live where one feels most at home.